ALL COLOUR COLLECTION

365

QUICK
& EASY
DISHES

EBURY

ALL COLOUR COLLECTION

365

QUICK & EASY DISHES

EBURY PRESS LONDON

First published by Ebury Press
an imprint of The Random Century Group
Random Century House
20 Vauxhall Bridge Road
London SWIV 2SA

A catalogue record for this book is available from the British Library

ISBN 0-09-175368-6

Photography by Sue Atkinson, Jan Baldwin, Martin Brigdale,
Laurie Evans, Ken Field, Melvin Grey, John Heseltine, Tim Hill,
James Jackson, David Johnson, Paul Kemp, Don Last,
James Murphy, Peter Myers, Alan Newnham, Grant Symon,
Rosemary Weller, Andrew Whittuck, Paul Williams

Typeset by Clive Dorman
Printed and bound in Italy by New Interlitho S.p.a., Milan

COOK'S NOTES

- Both metric and imperial measures are given in the recipes in this book. Follow one set of measures only as they are not interchangeable.
- All spoon measures are level unless otherwise stated.
- All ovens should be preheated to the specified temperature.
- Microwave cooking instructions are given for some of the recipes in this book. When using these, please note that HIGH refers to 100% full power output of a 600-700 watt cooker; MEDIUM refers to 60% of full power; LOW refers to 35% of full power.

  If your microwave power output is lower than 600 watts, it may be necessary to allow longer than recommended. In any event you should always check food before the end of the cooking time, to ensure that it does not overcook.

CONTENTS

SOUPS & STARTERS

This tempting selection of speedy soups and starters includes ideas for all occasions from simple suppers to smart dinner parties. Many of the recipes are substantial enough to serve as light snack meals in themselves, accompanied by plenty of crusty bread or crispbreads.

AVOCADO SOUP

SERVES 4

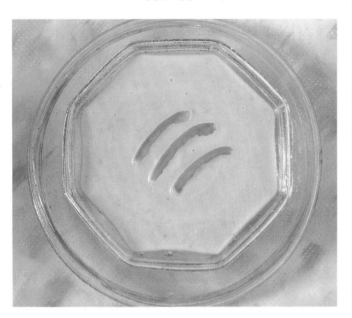

1 avocado	5 ml (1 tsp) golden syrup
450 ml (¾ pint) chicken stock	pinch of cayenne pepper
30 ml (2 tbsp) lemon juice	salt and pepper
200 ml (7 fl oz) milk	2 ripe tomatoes, to garnish

1 Halve the avocado, discard the stone and peel and roughly chop the flesh.

2 Put the avocado into a blender or food processor with the chicken stock, lemon juice, milk, golden syrup and cayenne and blend until smooth. Season to taste with salt and pepper. Pour into a bowl, cover and chill in the refrigerator for no longer than 2 hours. (The soup will begin to discolour if you leave it for longer.)

3 Meanwhile, plunge the tomatoes into boiling water for 10 seconds, remove from the water and peel off the skin. Halve the tomatoes, remove the seeds, then cut each half into thin slivers.

4 Taste and adjust the seasoning of the soup. Garnish with the tomato slivers just before serving.

TOMATO SOUP WITH BASIL

SERVES 6

50 g (2 oz) butter or margarine	900 ml (1½ pints) chicken stock
2 onions, thinly sliced	30 ml (2 tbsp) tomato purée
900 g (2 lb) tomatoes	7.5 ml (1½ tsp) chopped fresh basil or 2.5 ml (½ tsp) dried
45 ml (3 tbsp) plain flour	basil leaves and single cream, to garnish

1 Melt the butter in a saucepan, add the onions and fry gently until golden brown.

2 Meanwhile, halve the tomatoes and scoop out the seeds into a sieve placed over a bowl. Press to extract all the tomato pulp and juice; discard the seeds.

3 Remove the pan from the heat. Stir in the flour and cook gently for 1 minute, stirring. Remove from the heat and gradually stir in the stock. Bring to the boil slowly and continue to cook, stirring, until thickened.

4 Stir in the tomato purée, herbs and the tomatoes with reserved juice and seasoning. Cover the pan and simmer gently for about 30 minutes.

5 Leave the soup to cool slightly, then sieve or purée in a blender or food processor. Strain into a clean pan and reheat gently. Garnish with basil and cream.

FRENCH BEAN SOUP

SERVES 4-6

30 ml (2 tbsp) vegetable oil	900 ml (1½ pints) chicken stock)
125 g (4 oz) onion, finely chopped	150 ml (¼ pint) milk
450 g (1 lb) frozen whole French beans	45 ml (3 tbsp) natural yogurt (optional)
30 ml (2 tbsp) flour	salt and pepper
15 ml (1 tbsp) chopped parsley	snipped grilled bacon or garlic croûtons, to garnish

1 Heat the oil in a large saucepan and stir in the onion. Cook for 3-4 minutes until soft but not coloured. Mix in the beans, flour, parsley and stock. Bring to the boil, cover and simmer for 10-12 minutes, stirring occasionally or until the beans are quite tender.
2 Allow the soup to cool slightly, then purée in a blender or food processor. Return to the rinsed-out saucepan, add the milk and reheat gently.
3 Stir in the yogurt and adjust seasoning before serving. Garnish with snipped grilled bacon or croûtons.

COOK'S TIP

Instead of frying bread croûtons, make them from toasted slices of bread. Rub with a cut garlic clove and cut into dice.

CHEESY VEGETABLE SOUP

SERVES 3-4

30 ml (2 tbsp) vegetable oil	600 ml (1 pint) chicken stock
50 g (2 oz) onion, finely chopped	150 ml (¼ pint) milk
225 g (8 oz) old potatoes	large pinch of cayenne pepper (optional)
125 g (4 oz) courgette	salt and pepper
125 g (4 oz) frozen sweetcorn kernels, thawed	150 g (5 oz) mature Cheddar cheese
30 ml (2 tbsp) flour	

1 Heat the oil in a large pan. Add the onion and soften over a low heat while preparing the remaining vegetables. Peel and roughly dice the potatoes. Thinly slice the courgette into half-moons.
2 Add the potatoes and courgette to the saucepan with the sweetcorn and sauté until coated in oil. Stir in the flour and cook gently, stirring, for 1-2 minutes before adding the stock with the milk, cayenne pepper and other seasoning to taste.
3 Bring to the boil, cover and simmer gently for 10-12 minutes or until the vegetables are tender. Stir in the grated cheese and adjust the seasoning before serving.

CHICK PEA AND WATERCRESS SOUP

SERVES 4

50 g (2 oz) butter	1.7 litres (3 pints) vegetable stock
225 g (8 oz) onion, roughly chopped	salt and pepper
1 clove garlic, crushed	1 bunch watercress
50 g (2 oz) red lentils	400 g (14 oz) can chick peas, drained
50 g (2 oz) long-grain white rice	

1 Melt the butter in a large saucepan, add the onion and garlic and cook until beginning to soften but not colour.
2 Rinse the lentils and rice, then stir into the pan. Add the stock and seasoning and bring to the boil. Cover and simmer for about 15 minutes or until the lentils and rice are just tender.
3 Meanwhile, rinse and roughly chop the watercress; rinse and drain the chick peas. Add both to the pan and simmer for a further 5 minutes. Adjust the seasoning before serving.

MEDITERRANEAN SUMMER SOUP

SERVES 4

2 very large Marmande or Beefsteak tomatoes	4 garlic cloves
1 medium Spanish onion	60 ml (4 tbsp) wine vinegar
1 green pepper, cored and seeded	30 ml (2 tbsp) olive oil
450 g (1 lb) can potatoes, drained	2.5 ml (½ tsp) paprika
	salt and pepper
	few ice cubes and mint sprigs, to serve

1 Chop all the vegetables and the garlic roughly and then put half of them in a blender or food processor with the vinegar and about 150 ml (¼ pint) water. Work to a smooth purée.
2 Sieve the purée to remove the tomato skins, working it into a large soup tureen or bowl.
3 Repeat the puréeing and sieving with the remaining vegetables and another 150 ml (¼ pint) water. Add to the purée in the tureen or bowl.
4 Add 750 ml (1¼ pints) water to the soup with the oil, paprika and seasoning to taste. Stir well to mix, cover and chill in the refrigerator for at least 1 hour before serving.
5 To serve, taste and adjust the seasoning, then stir in the ice cubes. Float mint sprigs on top.

SERVING SUGGESTION

Serve as a starter for a summer luncheon or barbecue party, with bowls of garnish such as tiny bread croûtons (fried or toasted), diced red and green pepper, diced cucumber and finely chopped hard-boiled eggs.

ZUPPA ALLA PAVESE

SERVES 4

1.2 litres (2 pints) well-flavoured homemade chicken or beef stock	4 eggs
	salt and pepper
4 thick slices white bread	60 ml (4 tbsp) grated Parmesan cheese
75 g (3 oz) butter	

1 Bring the stock to the boil in a large saucepan and keep at simmering point while preparing the remaining ingredients for the soup.
2 Cut the crusts off the slices of bread, then cut each slice into 2 or 3 pieces.
3 Melt the butter in a frying pan, add the bread and fry over moderate heat until crisp and golden on both sides.
4 Place the fried bread in 4 warmed soup bowls. Crack the eggs, one at a time, into a saucer. Slide each egg into the simmering stock and poach lightly. Lift the eggs out with a slotted spoon and place one in each bowl.
5 Pour over the stock, sprinkle 15 ml (1 tbsp) grated Parmesan into each bowl, and serve immediately, while piping hot.

SERVING SUGGESTION

This tasty, nutritious soup is good served with grissini (Italian bread sticks) as a first course for an evening meal. Alternatively, serve Zuppa alla Pavese on its own for a quick lunch or supper dish, with hot rolls or crusty French bread, plus extra grated Parmesan cheese.

COURGETTE AND BLUE CHEESE SOUP

SERVES 8

25 g (1 oz) butter	350 g (12 oz) blue cheese, eg Gorgonzola, Stilton, dolcelatte, rind removed
30 ml (2 tbsp) olive oil	
2 small onions, roughly chopped	salt and pepper
1.4 kg (3 lb) courgettes, thinly sliced	150 ml (¼ pint) whipping cream, lightly whipped
1.75 litres (3 pints) vegetable stock	chopped herbs, to garnish

1 Melt the butter with the oil in a large heavy saucepan. Add the onions and cook gently, stirring frequently for about 5 minutes, until soft but not coloured. Add the courgettes and stir well.
2 Cover the pan tightly and cook gently for 10 minutes, shaking the pan occasionally.
3 Pour in the stock and bring to the boil, stirring. Lower the heat, crumble in the cheese, then add salt and pepper to taste. Half cover with the lid and simmer for 20 minutes until the courgettes are tender.
4 Cool the soup slightly, then purée in batches in a blender or food processor until very smooth. Either reheat and serve hot, or let cool and chill before serving.
5 To serve, stir well and adjust seasoning. Pour into bowls, swirl in the cream, feather with a skewer and sprinkle with herbs.

ANTIPASTO MISTO

SERVES 6

TUNA STUFFED EGGS

SERVES 4-6

1 head radicchio or 1 small lettuce	3 tomatoes, sliced
175 g (6 oz) mozzarella cheese	160 g (5½ oz) can mussels in oil (optional)
12 thin slices Italian salami	280 g (10 oz) jar artichoke hearts in oil (optional)
6 thin slices mortadella sausage	280 g (10 oz) jar sweet and sour peppers (optional)
6 thin slices Parma ham	black olives and anchovies, to garnish
3 hard-boiled eggs, quartered	

1   Separate the radicchio or lettuce leaves.
2   Using a sharp knife, carefully cut the mozzarella cheese into thin slices.
3   Ease any skin or rind off the salami and the mortadella sausage with your fingers.
4   Place a bed of radicchio or lettuce on a large serving platter. Arrange the slices of salami, mortadella, Parma ham and mozzarella, hard-boiled eggs, tomatoes, mussels, artichoke hearts and peppers on top. Garnish with black olives and anchovies.
5   Cover and refrigerate for at least 2 hours. Leave at cool room temperature for about 20 minutes before serving, with breadsticks.

COOK'S TIP

The word 'antipasto' means 'before the meal', and it can be anything from one or two slices of salami to a huge selection of cold meats, fish, eggs, vegetables and salads. For everyday meals, most Italian families have the simplest of antipasto, say a slice or two of cold meat and hard-boiled eggs with some olives and fresh bread – just enough to whet the appetite before the pasta course.

6 hard-boiled eggs, shelled	squeeze of lemon juice
50 g (2 oz) canned tuna fish in oil, drained	shredded radicchio or curly endive, to serve
100 ml (4 fl oz) mayonnaise	black olives, stoned, to garnish
salt and pepper	

1   Halve the hard-boiled eggs lengthways and scoop out the yolks with a teaspoon.
2   Sieve or mash the tuna fish and add it to the mayonnaise with the hard-boiled egg yolks, mixing well. Add seasoning, with lemon juice to taste.
3   To serve, fill the cavities of the hard-boiled eggs by piping or spooning in the mayonnaise mixture. Arrange radicchio or endive on individual plates, then place the stuffed eggs on top. Garnish with slivers of black olive.

SERVING SUGGESTION

These stuffed eggs are substantial enough to be served on their own, but they would also make an attractive addition to an antipasto misto. Tuna fish is a popular starter in Italy, but you can vary this according to taste. Mashed prawns, shrimps or mussels could be substituted for the tuna.

WATERCRESS, POTATO AND BACON SALAD

SERVES 4

450 g (1 lb) very small new potatoes	45 ml (3 tbsp) vegetable oil
salt and pepper	15 ml (1 tbsp) white wine vinegar
8 rashers streaky bacon, rinded and chopped	1 bunch watercress, trimmed and roughly chopped

1 Cook the potatoes in boiling salted water for 10-15 minutes, until tender.
2 Meanwhile, fry the bacon in its own fat for 5 minutes, until crisp. Add the oil and vinegar to the bacon fat and bring to the boil, stirring in any sediment from the bottom of the pan. Season with pepper.
3 Drain the cooked potatoes and put in a serving dish. Pour over the bacon and dressing while they are still warm and toss together. Toss in the watercress and serve warm.

COOK'S TIP

Tender little new potatoes are bathed in a vinaigrette dressing while still warm to sop up the maximum flavour. Peppery watercress from the Hampshire beds and crispy bits of bacon add more colour and texture to this interesting and attractive salad.

SALAD TIEDE AUX LARDONS

SERVES 4

135 ml (9 tbsp) olive oil	4 thick slices white bread, crusts removed
30 ml (2 tbsp) wine vinegar	30 ml (2 tbsp) single or double cream
2 garlic cloves, crushed	
5 ml (1 tsp) French mustard	1 small head curly endive, leaves separated
salt and pepper	
8 streaky bacon rashers, rinded	

1 Put 90 ml (6 tbsp) of the oil in a salad bowl with the wine vinegar, garlic, mustard and salt and pepper to taste. Whisk with a fork until thick.
2 Cut the bacon and bread into small dice. Heat the remaining oil in a frying pan, add the bacon and bread and fry over brisk heat until crisp and golden brown on all sides. Remove with a slotted spoon and drain on absorbent kitchen paper.
3 Stir the cream into the dressing, then add the endive and warm bacon and croûtons. Toss quickly to combine and serve immediately.

CELERIAC REMOULADE

SERVES 6

1 large head celeriac	30 ml (2 tbsp) French mustard
30 ml (2 tbsp) lemon juice	salt and pepper
300 ml (½ pint) mayonnaise	1 lettuce or curly endive
30 ml (2 tbsp) snipped chives	chopped parsley, to garnish

1 Peel and coarsely grate the celeriac. Toss immediately in the lemon juice to prevent discolouration.
2 Add the mayonnaise, chives and mustard with seasoning to taste and mix well together.
3 Line individual dishes or plates with lettuce, then pile the celeriac mixture in the centre. Sprinkle with chopped parsley and serve immediately.

COOK'S TIP

Celeriac tastes much like celery, but is a knobbly vegetable that looks like a rough turnip and can vary from about the size of a large apple to as big as a coconut.

MEXICAN AVOCADO DIP

SERVES 4

30 ml (2 tbsp) vegetable oil	2 ripe avocados
1 small onion, finely chopped	juice of ½ lemon
2 garlic cloves, crushed	150 ml (5 fl oz) soured cream
2.5 ml (½ tsp) chilli powder	salt and pepper
4 tomatoes, skinned and chopped	tomato slices, to garnish

1 Heat the oil in a small pan, add the onion, garlic and chilli powder and fry gently, stirring, until the onion is soft. Add the tomatoes and fry for a further 5 minutes, breaking them up with a wooden spoon.
2 Put the tomato mixture into a blender or food processor and blend until smooth. Turn into a bowl and leave to cool.
3 Halve and stone the avocados, then peel three halves. Add to the tomato mixture with the lemon juice and mash to a purée. Blend in half the soured cream, then taste and add salt and pepper and more chilli powder, if liked.
4 Transfer the dip to a shallow serving bowl. Peel and slice the remaining avocado half. Arrange avocado slices on top of the dip, alternating with tomato slices.
5 To serve, spoon the remaining cream into the centre and sprinkle with a little chilli powder. Serve immediately.

AVOCADO WITH CRAB

SERVES 4

30 ml (2 tbsp) vegetable oil	finely grated rind and juice of ½ lemon
1 small onion, finely chopped	salt and pepper
10 ml (2 tsp) garam masala	225 g (8 oz) white crab meat
150 ml (¼ pint) thick mayonnaise	2 ripe avocados
10 ml (2 tsp) tomato purée	lemon twists and paprika, to garnish

1 To make the filling, heat the oil in a small pan, add the onion and garam masala and fry gently, stirring constantly, for 5 minutes until the onion is soft. Turn into a bowl and leave until cold.
2 Add the mayonnaise to the cold onion with the tomato purée, lemon rind and juice. Add seasoning to taste.
3 Flake the crab meat and fold gently into the mayonnaise, taking care not to break up the pieces of crab.
4 Cut the avocados in half lengthways and then prise the halves apart by twisting them in opposite directions.
5 Remove the stones from the avocados by gently easing them out with the fingers.
6 Place an avocado half on each serving dish or plate, then pile the filling into each half. Garnish with lemon twists and a sprinkling of paprika. Serve immediately.

AVOCADO WITH PARMA HAM

SERVES 6

50 g (2 oz) Parma ham	salt and pepper
90 ml (6 tbsp) vegetable oil	3 spring onions, finely chopped
45 ml (3 tbsp) lemon juice	3 ripe avocados
5 ml (1 tsp) Dijon mustard	

1 With lightly oiled kitchen scissors, cut the ham into fine shreds. Whisk the oil, lemon juice, mustard and seasoning together.
2 Stir in the spring onions and the ham. Cut the avocados in half and twist to remove the stones; put each half on a plate. If necessary, cut a thin slice off the base of each one so that it stands level on the serving plate.
3 Spoon the ham mixture into the avocados. Serve at once with hot French bread, if wished.

COOK'S TIP

A ripe avocado always 'gives' slightly when pressed gently at the pointed end. A hard, under-ripe fruit will ripen in 1-2 days at room temperature if stored in a fruit bowl with ripe fruit or in about a week in the refrigerator. Ripe avocados can be stored successfully for 3-4 days on the lower shelf of the refrigerator.

BRANDIED CHICKEN LIVER PATE

SERVES 4-6

100 g (4 oz) unsalted butter	2.5 ml (½ tsp) dried mixed herbs
225 g (8 oz) chicken livers	salt and pepper
30 ml (2 tbsp) brandy	bay leaves, to garnish
1 garlic clove	

1 Melt half the butter in a heavy frying pan, add the livers and cook them over moderate heat for 5 minutes, stirring so that they cook evenly. The livers should be brown on the outside, and pink but set in the centre.
2 Pour the contents of the frying pan straight into a blender or food processor.
3 Pour the brandy into the pan and bring quickly to the boil, stirring well to incorporate any sediment left on the bottom of the pan. Allow to bubble for 1 minute.
4 Add the brandy and juices to the livers with the garlic and dried herbs and blend until smooth. Blend in the remaining butter and salt and pepper to taste.
5 Pour the pâté into one terrine, or four to six individual ramekin dishes. Place the bay leaves on top and refrigerate for 3-4 hours before serving.
6 If the pâté is to be kept for several days before serving, pour enough cooled, melted butter over the top to form a complete seal. The pâté will then keep for at least 1 week in the refrigerator.

VARIATION

A delicious way of varying this rich and flavoursome dish is by substituting 50 g (2 oz) of the chicken livers with the same weight of sliced mushrooms. Choose cap or field mushrooms for a more distinctive flavour, and fry them together with the chicken livers in the pan. Instead of using dried mixed herbs, use the same quantity of dried thyme, or 5 ml (1 tsp) chopped fresh thyme.

LEMON AND ALMOND LIVER PATE

SERVES 6-8

450 g (1 lb) turkey or chicken livers	30 ml (2 tbsp) double cream
225 g (8 oz) butter, softened	5 ml (1 tsp) grated nutmeg
2 medium onions, sliced	30 ml (2 t'sp) brandy
10 ml (2 tsp) French mustard	175 g (6 oz) ground almonds
15 ml (1 tbsp) lemon juice	salt and pepper
finely grated rind of 1 lemon	parsley sprigs, to garnish

1 Trim the livers. Melt 50 g (2 oz) butter in a frying pan and fry the onions gently for 5 minutes until soft. Add the livers to the pan and cook gently for a further 5 minutes.
2 Purée the contents of the pan in a blender or food processor. Then leave for 10 minutes to cool slightly.
3 Beat in 50 g (2 oz) butter and the rest of the ingredients, except the remaining butter. Season well, then spoon into six to eight individual ramekin dishes.
4 Melt the remaining butter and pour over the tops of the pâtés. Chill before serving, garnished with parsley.

COOK'S TIP

The unusual addition of almonds adds an exotic touch to this liver pâté. Although almonds are available ready ground, you can also buy them in and out of their shells, blanched, flaked, shredded and diced. You can make your own ground almonds by simply putting any of these prepared, shelled almonds into a coffee grinder and switching the motor on and off a couple of times, when they will be reduced to a fine powder ready for use.

POTTED PRAWN PATE

SERVES 8

175 g (6 oz) peeled prawns	20 ml (4 tsp) chopped parsley
75 g (3 oz) butter, softened	salt and pepper
10 ml (2 tsp) lemon juice	cooked whole prawns and lemon slices, to garnish

1 Finely chop the prawns. Beat into 50 g (2 oz) butter with the lemon juice, parsley and seasoning.

2 Spoon into a serving dish and level the surface. Melt the remaining butter and pour over the prawn mixture. Refrigerate for 1 hour. Garnish with prawns and lemon slices. Serve with French bread.

VARIATION

Replace the parsley with freshly chopped tarragon leaves.

NUTTY CAMEMBERT PATE

SERVES 4-6

175 g (6 oz) soft ripe Camembert cheese	salt and pepper
225 g (8 oz) full-fat soft cheese	75 g (3 oz) finely chopped blanched almonds
2.5 ml (½ tsp) paprika	paprika, to garnish

1 Cut the rind off the Camembert, then work the cheese through a sieve into a bowl, or mix in a food processor until smooth.

2 Add the soft cheese, paprika and seasoning to taste. Beat vigorously with a wooden spoon to combine the ingredients well together.

3 Spoon the pâté into a greased and base-lined 300 ml (½ pint) dish or mould. Press down well and smooth the surface with the back of the spoon. Cover the dish and freeze for 1 hour.

4 Loosen the pâté from the dish by running a palette knife between the two. Turn the pâté out upside down on to a serving plate and peel off the lining paper. Chill before serving.

5 Sprinkle the nuts over the pâté, then press evenly over the top and around the sides with the palette knife. Sprinkle with paprika. Serve chilled with wholemeal toast, crispbreads or crackers.

FRIED BRIE WITH CRANBERRY SAUCE

SERVES 6

	FOR THE CRANBERRY SAUCE
30 ml (2 tbsp) flour	175 g (6 oz) cranberries, fresh or frozen
750 g (1½ lb) brie, cut into 6 wedges	75 ml (3 fl oz) water
1 egg, lightly beaten	75 g (3 oz) sugar
75 g (3 oz) fresh breadcrumbs vegetable oil, for deep frying	

1 First make the cranberry sauce. Place the cranberries and water in a saucepan and bring to the boil. Cover and simmer for 5 minutes. Remove from the heat and stir in the sugar. Return the pan to the heat and simmer for 5 minutes. Pour into a serving bowl and keep hot.
2 Sift the flour on to a plate and coat the cheese on all sides. Dip into the beaten egg, then coat with the breadcrumbs. Heat the oil in a deep-fat fryer to 180°C (350°F). Deep-fry the brie for 1½-2 minutes, or until the breadcrumbs are golden. Drain well on absorbent kitchen paper.
3 Serve hot, accompanied by the cranberry sauce.

COOK'S TIP

The brie for this recipe should not be over-ripe. Serve as a starter or light luncheon dish, with a crisp green salad.

CAMEMBERT WITH REDCURRANT JELLY

SERVES 4

150 g (5 oz) Camembert cheese	about 60 ml (4 tbsp) vegetable oil
1 egg, beaten	30 ml (2 tbsp) redcurrant jelly
50 g (2 oz) fresh wholemeal breadcrumbs	shredded lettuce, to serve
	redcurrants, to garnish

1 Cut the cheese into 4 slices. Brush with beaten egg and coat in the breadcrumbs.
2 Heat some oil in a large frying pan and fry the cheese slices for 10 seconds on each side until golden. Drain on absorbent kitchen paper. Fry in batches if necessary.
3 Put the redcurrant jelly and 15 ml (1 tbsp) water in a saucepan and heat gently until the jelly melts.
4 Place each slice of cheese on a bed of shredded lettuce and pour over the redcurrant sauce. Garnish with the redcurrants and serve at once.

STILTON PEARS

SERVES 4

2 large dessert pears, ripe but firm	15 ml (1 tbsp) mayonnaise
30 ml (2 tbsp) lemon juice	pinch of mustard powder
50 g (2 oz) curd cheese	pinch of sugar
75 g (3 oz) Stilton cheese, crumbled	5 ml (1 tsp) poppy seeds
30 ml (2 tbsp) vegetable oil	salt and pepper

1 Using an apple corer, remove the cores from the pears. Sprinkle the cavities with 15 ml (1 tbsp) of the lemon juice.
2 Cream together the two cheeses. Press as much cheese mixture as possible into the cavities, then cover and chill until ready to serve.
3 Just before serving, whisk the oil, mayonnaise, remaining lemon juice, mustard, sugar, poppy seeds, salt and pepper together. Spoon on to 4 individual plates. Cut each pear in half lengthways then slice, fan out and arrange, cut side down, in the dressing. Serve at once.

COOK'S TIP

Cheese and pears are a delightful combination, and dessert pears make a refreshing change from avocados in this starter. Comice are a good choice, as they are mouth wateringly juicy when fully ripe. Make sure they are still firm though because, as with all pears, they have to be eaten at just the right moment.

COUNTRY MUSHROOMS

SERVES 4

25 g (1 oz) butter or margarine	10 ml (2 tsp) chopped fresh tarragon or 2.5 ml (½ tsp) dried
450 g (1 lb) button mushrooms	45 ml (3 tbsp) soured cream or smetana
15 ml (1 tbsp) plain flour	radicchio and lettuce, to serve
150 ml (¼ pint) milk	tarragon leaves, to garnish
10 ml (2 tsp) wholegrain mustard	

1 Melt the butter or margarine in a medium saucepan, add the mushrooms and fry for 2 minutes.
2 Stir in the flour, then gradually stir in the milk. Heat, stirring continuously until the sauce thickens, boils and is smooth. Simmer for 1-2 minutes.
3 Stir in the mustard, tarragon and soured cream or smetana.
4 Serve hot on a nest of radicchio and lettuce leaves, garnished with tarragon.

COOK'S TIP

Choose button mushrooms for their delicate flavour. There's no need to wash or peel them - a wipe with a damp cloth is all that's needed. Tarragon is very distinctive and marries well with mushrooms. Soured cream or smetana gives a hint of piquancy.

CROSTINI

225 g (8 oz) chicken livers	10 ml (2 tsp) tomato purée
30 ml (2 tbsp) olive oil	10 ml (2 tsp) chopped sage or parsley
1 small onion, finely chopped	salt and pepper
1 garlic clove, crushed	about 60 ml (4 tbsp) dry white wine
2 celery sticks, finely chopped	sage leaves, to garnish

1 Trim the chicken livers and cut into small bite-sized pieces.

2 Heat the oil in a frying pan, add the chicken livers and fry over brisk heat until just changing in colour, stirring constantly. Remove with a slotted spoon and set aside.

3 Add the onion, garlic and celery to the pan and fry gently for 7-10 minutes until softened.

4 Stir in the tomato purée, sage and salt and pepper. Return the chicken livers to the pan and add enough wine to moisten. Cook gently for about 5 minutes, stirring frequently, until just tender.

5 Pile on to hot toasted French bread to serve and garnish with sage.

ONION BHAJIAS

150 g (5 oz) gram or besan flour	5 ml (1 tsp) chilli powder
5 ml (1 tsp) bicarbonate of soda	4 green cardamoms
10 ml (2 tsp) salt	30 ml (2 tbsp) chopped mint or coriander (optional)
10 ml (2 tsp) coriander seeds, crushed	2 large onions, chopped
2.5 ml (½ tsp) garam masala	salt and pepper
5 ml (1 tsp) turmeric	vegetable oil, for deep-frying
	lemon or lime wedges, to garnish

1 Sift the flour, bicarbonate of soda and salt into a bowl. Add the crushed coriander seeds, garam masala, turmeric and chilli powder and mix well.

2 Open the cardamom pods and take out the seeds. Discard the husks and crush the seeds lightly. Add these to the flour mixture together with the mint or coriander, if using, onions, salt and pepper to taste and 30 ml (2 tbsp) water. Mix together thoroughly to a fairly stiff paste.

3 Heat the oil in a deep-fat fryer to 180°C (350°F). Using 2 wet dessertspoons, drop 6 spoonfuls of the mixture into the hot oil and deep-fry the fritters for 3-4 minutes or until darkish brown in colour.

4 Remove from the oil with a slotted spoon and transfer to absorbent kitchen paper to drain. Repeat with the remaining mixture.

5 Serve piping hot, with lemon or lime wedges.

COOK'S TIP

There is often confusion between pakoras and bhajias. In North India they are known as pakoras and served as a teatime snack, in South and West India they are known as bhajias and served as part of a vegetarian main meal.

STUFFED BAKED MUSHROOMS

SERVES 4

8 large flat mushrooms	50 g (2 oz) Gouda cheese, grated
25 g (1 oz) butter	salt and pepper
125 g (4 oz) onion, finely chopped	15 ml (1 tbsp) lemon juice
1 clove garlic, crushed	50 g (2 oz) Parmesan cheese, freshly grated
50 g (2 oz) cup mushrooms, roughly chopped	4 large slices wholemeal bread
30 ml (2 tbsp) chopped parsley	paprika and parsley sprigs, to garnish
400 g (14 oz) can chick peas, drained and roughly chopped	

1 Remove the stalks from the flat mushrooms. Set aside the mushroom caps; roughly chop the stalks.

2 Melt the butter in a large sauté pan. Add the onions and garlic and cook until beginning to soften. Stir in all the chopped mushrooms and cook over a high heat, stirring continuously, until well reduced and all excess liquid has evaporated. Mix in the parsley, chick peas and Gouda. Adjust the seasoning.

3 Lightly oil a shallow ovenproof dish. Arrange the flat mushroom caps in the dish, in a single layer, and spoon in the stuffing. Drizzle over the lemon juice; sprinkle with the grated Parmesan cheese.

4 Bake in the oven at 200°C (400°F) mark 6 for about 10 minutes or until golden brown and bubbling. Meanwhile, toast the bread on both sides.

5 Place the stuffed mushrooms on the toast. Dust with paprika and garnish with parsley to serve.

SERVING SUGGESTION

This substantial starter can also be served as a light lunch or supper, with a crisp salad.

PASTA WITH CREAMY MUSHROOM SAUCE

SERVES 4

275 g (10 oz) pasta shapes, eg shells	350 g (12 oz) mushrooms, finely chopped
salt and pepper	150 ml (¼ pint) single cream
5 ml (1 tsp) olive or vegetable oil	150 ml (¼ pint) soured cream
75 g (3 oz) butter	75 ml (5 tbsp) finely chopped parsley
2 garlic cloves, crushed	

1 Cook the pasta shapes in a large saucepan of boiling salted water, to which the oil has been added, for about 15 minutes, until tender.

2 Meanwhile, melt 50 g (2 oz) of the butter in a separate pan, add the garlic and mushrooms and fry gently for about 7 minutes, stirring frequently, until the juices run from the mushrooms.

3 Add the creams and salt and pepper to taste and heat through without boiling. Stir gently to mix the ingredients together.

4 Drain the pasta shells thoroughly. Melt the remaining butter in the pan in which the pasta was cooked, then return the drained pasta to the pan and toss to coat in the melted butter.

5 Stir 60 ml (4 tbsp) parsley into the mushroom sauce and taste and adjust seasoning. Pile the pasta into 4 warmed serving dishes and pour the sauce over the top. Sprinkle with remaining parsley. Serve immediately.

COOK'S TIP

Pasta shells, called *conchiglie* in Italian, are available in white, green, pink and wholemeal varieties. With pale-coloured sauces such as this one, it is best to choose a coloured pasta, to provide a good contrast.

MELON WITH PORT

SERVES 4

2 small Charentais, Cantaloupe or Ogen melons	180 ml (12 tbsp) port
	mint sprigs, to garnish

1 Halve the melons horizontally, trimming the bases so they will stand firmly. Scoop out the seeds with a teaspoon and discard.
2 Pour 45 ml (3 tbsp) port into each half. Cover and chill in the refrigerator for at least 1 hour.
3 Serve garnished with sprigs of mint.

COOK'S TIP

Melons are available all year round. They have perfumed, sweet juicy flesh; usually the more fragrant the melon, the sweeter and juicer its flesh. Charentais is a small round melon with green skin and fragrant orange flesh. The cantaloupe melon has a green to yellow skin and fragrant orange-yellow flesh. The Ogen melon is a variety of Cantaloupe.

TARRAGON STUFFED TOMATOES

SERVES 4

4 large firm tomatoes	30 ml (2 tbsp) chopped tarragon
salt and pepper	90 ml (6 tbsp) sunflower or corn oil
100 g (4 oz) full-fat soft cheese	30 ml (2 tbsp) tarragon wine vinegar
30 ml (2 tbsp) thick mayonnaise	1.25 ml (¼ tsp) mustard powder
1 bunch spring onions, trimmed and very finely chopped	pinch of sugar
	tarragon sprigs, to garnish

1 Cut a slice off the top of each tomato and set aside.
2 Using a sharp-edged teaspoon, carefully scoop out the pulp and seeds from the insides of the tomatoes. Then sprinkle the insides lightly with salt and stand upside down to drain.
3 Meanwhile, mix the cheese with the mayonnaise, spring onions, half the tarragon and salt and pepper to taste. Spoon the cheese mixture into the tomato cases and replace the reserved slices at an angle.
4 Put the oil and vinegar in a bowl with the remaining tarragon, the mustard, sugar and salt and pepper to taste. Whisk with a fork until thick, then pour slowly over the tomatoes. Chill in the refrigerator for 30 minutes.
5 Serve garnished with tarragon sprigs.

PRAWN AND SMOKED SALMON AVOCADOS

SERVES 4

60 ml (4 tbsp) mayonnaise	100 g (4 oz) smoked salmon
60 ml (4 tbsp) soured cream or natural yogurt	100 g (4 oz) cooked peeled prawns, defrosted and thoroughly dried if frozen
30 ml (2 tbsp) snipped chives	2 ripe avocados
10 ml (2 tsp) lemon juice	lemon slices and 4 cooked whole prawns (optional), to garnish
few drops of Tabasco sauce	
salt and pepper	

1 To make the dressing, put the mayonnaise in a bowl with the soured cream or yogurt, chives, lemon juice and Tabasco sauce to taste. Add plenty of salt and pepper, then whisk vigorously with a fork to combine all the ingredients together.
2 Cut the smoked salmon into bite-sized pieces. Chop the prawns roughly. Add to the dressing and fold gently to mix.
3 Just before serving, halve and stone the avocados. Scoop out the flesh and chop.
4 Fold the avocado into the fish mixture and spoon into the avocado shells. Garnish with lemon slices and serve immediately.

SERVING SUGGESTION

Serve this luxurious starter for a special dinner party, with thinly sliced brown bread and butter.

PRAWN AND GRUYERE COCOTTES

SERVES 4

15 g (½ oz) butter	350 g (12 oz) cooked peeled prawns, defrosted and thoroughly dried if frozen
15 ml (1 tbsp) olive or vegetable oil	150 ml (¼ pint) soured cream
1 small onion, finely chopped	1 egg, beaten
4 rashers back bacon, rinded and chopped	salt and pepper
	100 g (4 oz) gruyère cheese, grated

1 Melt the butter with the oil in a heavy-based saucepan, add the onion and fry gently for 5 minutes until soft but not coloured.
2 Add the bacon and fry until turning colour, stirring frequently. Add the prawns, increase the heat and stir-fry for 5 minutes.
3 Transfer the mixture to the bowl, add the soured cream and egg and salt and pepper to taste. Mix well.
4 Divide the mixture equally between 4 cocottes or ramekins. Sprinkle with gruyère. Bake in the oven at 190°C (375°F) mark 5 for 15 minutes until golden and bubbling. Serve hot.

SERVING SUGGESTION

Serve with crusty rolls and chilled dry white wine for a special dinner party. Follow with a meaty main course, such as steak au poivre or veal in Marsala.

DEEP-FRIED WHITEBAIT

SERVES 4

450 g (1 lb) whitebait	vegetable oil, for deep frying
90 ml (6 tbsp) plain flour	15 ml (1 tbsp) chopped parsley
salt and pepper	lemon slices, to garnish

1 Rinse the whitebait thoroughly in a colander, drain well and dry on absorbent kitchen paper. Toss in the flour seasoned with salt and pepper.
2 Heat the oil in a deep-fat fryer to 180°C (350°F). Deep fry the whitebait, in 4 batches, allowing 2-3 minutes for each batch until crisp. Drain on absorbent kitchen paper. Keep warm, uncovered, in the oven at 200°C (400°F) mark 6 until all the fish are cooked.
3 Sprinkle with salt and parsley and garnish with lemon slices. Serve hot, with triangles of thinly sliced brown bread and butter.

COOK'S TIP

Whitebait are available frozen in 450 g (1 lb) bags at most supermarkets and freezer centres. They must always be thawed before coating and deep-frying, otherwise the tiny fish stick together and are difficult to serve. Drain them thoroughly after thawing and pat dry with absorbent kitchen paper.

SCANDINAVIAN ROLLMOP SALAD

SERVES 4

8 rollmops	150 ml (¼ pint) soured cream
1 small onion, skinned	freshly ground pepper
30 ml (2 tbsp) capers, chopped	30 ml (2 tbsp) snipped chives

1 Slice the rollmops and the onion into thin rings.
2 Arrange the slices of rollmops and onion in a circle around the edge of a shallow serving dish.
3 Mix the capers, soured cream and black pepper. Spoon into the centre of the dish and sprinkle with chives. Chill.

COOK'S TIP

Rollmops are boned herrings, rolled with chopped onions, gherkins and capers, marinated in spiced vinegar. They are sold in jars.

BUTTERFLY PRAWNS

SERVES 4

900 g (2 lb) medium raw prawns, or 12 raw 'jumbo' Mediterranean prawns, in the shell	15 ml (1 tbsp) ground coriander
50 g (2 oz) butter	30 ml (2 tbsp) ground cumin
6 garlic cloves, crushed	2.5 ml (½ tsp) ground cardamom
juice of 4 limes or 2 lemons	15 ml (1 tbsp) turmeric
2.5 cm (1 inch) piece fresh root ginger, peeled and chopped	15 ml (1 tbsp) paprika
	2.5 ml (½ tsp) chilli powder
	5 ml (1 tsp) salt
	lime wedges, to garnish

1 Remove the prawn shells, leaving the tail shell intact.
2 Split the prawn along the inner curve, stopping at the tail shell to expose the dark vein.
3 Spread the prawn wide open, remove the dark vein and rinse under cold running water. Dry well on absorbent kitchen paper.
4 Melt the butter in a saucepan, then set aside. Put the garlic in a bowl, add the lime or lemon juice, ginger, spices and salt. Mix well, then stir in the melted butter.
5 Coat the prawns with this mixture, cover and marinate in the refrigerator for 3-4 hours.
6 Place the prawns in a grill pan and cook under a preheated hot grill for 2 minutes on each side. Serve immediately, with the juices spooned over, garnished with lemon wedges.

SKEWERED PRAWNS WITH GARLIC BUTTER

SERVES 4

16 raw Pacific prawns or Dublin Bay prawn tails, thawed	30 ml (2 tbsp) lemon juice
12 bay leaves	salt and pepper
75 g (3 oz) butter	30 ml (2 tbsp) chopped parsley
3 large garlic cloves, crushed	lemon or lime wedges, to serve
15 ml (1 tbsp) chopped fresh oregano or 5 ml (1 tsp) dried	

1 If using Pacific prawns, remove the legs and with a sharp knife, make a slit down the centre of the back and remove the intestinal vein. Wash well. If using Dublin Bay prawn tails, make a slit though the shell on either side of the underside. Wash well.
2 Thread the prawns and bay leaves onto 4 skewers and place in a single layer on a well oiled grill pan.
3 Melt the butter in a saucepan, add the garlic and fry gently until golden. Remove from the heat and stir in the oregano, lemon juice and salt and pepper to taste.
4 Pour the garlic butter over the prawns, turning them to coat well. Grill for 5-8 minutes until the prawns turn pink. Arrange on a warmed serving platter, pour over the pan juices and sprinkle with chopped parsley. Serve hot, with lemon wedges.

COOK'S TIP

For this recipe it is absolutely essential to buy giant prawns which are only usually available at good supermarket fish counters and fishmongers. Pacific prawns are caught in the warm Pacific and Indian oceans, where they grow to a huge size, sometimes weighing as much as 50 g (2 oz) each. Large Dublin Bay prawns are simply scampi by another name. They come from the Atlantic, but are called 'Dublin Bay' because they were originally fished there. If your fishmonger sells 'jumbo' or 'Mediterranean' prawns, these are also suitable for this recipe.

MELON
AND PRAWN SALAD

SERVES 8

1 small honeydew melon	225 g (8 oz) cucumber, diced
30 ml (2 tbsp) tomato juice	15 ml (1 tbsp) chopped tarragon
30 ml (2 tbsp) cider vinegar	salt and pepper
30 ml (2 tbsp) clear honey	tarragon sprigs and cooked whole king prawns, to garnish
1 egg yolk	
450 g (1 lb) cooked peeled prawns	

1 Cut the melon in half and scrape out the pips from the centre with a teaspoon.

2 Scoop out the melon flesh with a melon baller. Divide the melon balls equally between 8 individual serving dishes.

3 To make the tomato dressing, put the tomato juice, vinegar, honey and egg yolk in a blender or food processor and blend together until evenly mixed.

4 Toss the prawns, cucumber and tarragon in the tomato dressing. Add salt and pepper to taste. Spoon on top of the melon balls and chill in the refrigerator until required.

5 Garnish with sprigs of tarragon and whole prawns before serving.

SPICY
SPARERIBS

SERVES 4

1.8 kg (4 lb) pork spareribs	30 ml (2 tbsp) clear honey
1 onion, sliced	10 ml (2 tsp) salt
350 ml (12 fl oz) tomato juice	5 ml (1 tsp) paprika
45 ml (3 tbsp) cider vinegar	3.75 (¾ tsp) chilli powder

1 Separate the spareribs into sections of 2 or 3 ribs. Place in a shallow dish. Mix all the remaining ingredients together and pour over the ribs. Cover and leave in the refrigerator until ready to cook.

2 Place the spareribs on a preheated grill rack. Brush with the marinade. Grill for 20 minutes, brushing with the marinade and turning occasionally. Heat the marinade in a saucepan for 1-2 minutes to make a sauce.

3 Serve the spareribs with the sauce.

COOK'S TIP

If you have time, leave the spareribs to marinate for about 2 hours before grilling.

LUNCHES, SNACKS & SALADS

When there isn't time to prepare a full meal, tasty snacks and light meals which you can throw together in minutes are essential. Storecupboard standbys form the basis of many of the recipes in this section. A tempting selection of substantial salads makes the most of fresh salad ingredients.

SPINACH PANCAKES

SERVES 4

75 g (3 oz) plain flour	25 g (1 oz) butter, plus extra for frying
pinch of salt	grated rind of lemon
1 egg, size 6	1 bay leaf
450 ml (¾ pint) milk	100 g (4 oz) smoked haddock, skinned and cubed
50 g (2 oz) spinach, trimmed and finely chopped	100 g (4 oz) cod, skinned and cubed

1 Sift 50 g (2 oz) of the flour and the salt into a bowl. Break in the egg. Gradually add 150 ml (¼ pint) milk, beating to form a smooth batter. Stir in the spinach.
2 Heat a little butter in a 20 cm (8 inch) frying pan. When hot, pour in 45 ml (3 tbsp) batter, tilting the pan to cover the base. Cook until the pancake moves freely, turn and cook until golden. Repeat to make 4 pancakes.
3 Put the remaining butter, flour and milk in a saucepan. Heat, whisking continuously, until the sauce thickens, boils and is smooth. Stir in the lemon rind, bay leaf and fish. Cook for 6 minutes.
4 Divide the mixture equally between the pancakes, then roll up. Serve hot with a green salad.

PIPERADE

SERVES 4

3 large ripe tomatoes	salt and pepper
30 ml (2 tbsp) olive or vegetable oil	50 g (2 oz) butter or margarine, softened
1 red pepper, seeded and chopped	4 slices of crusty bread
1 small onion, chopped	3 eggs, beaten
2 garlic cloves, crushed	chopped parsley, to garnish

1 To skin the tomatoes, plunge into boiling water for 10 seconds, then slip off the skins. Remove the pips and chop the tomato flesh roughly.
2 Heat 15 ml (1 tbsp) of the olive oil in a frying pan, add the tomatoes, red pepper, onion, half of the garlic and salt and pepper to taste and fry gently for about 15 minutes, until the vegetables are soft and pulpy.
3 Meanwhile, cream together the butter and the remaining garlic, spread on both sides of the bread and grill or fry until golden brown. Keep warm.
4 Add the remaining oil and the eggs to the vegetables in the pan and stir gently until the eggs begin to scramble. Serve at once with the hot toast, garnished with plenty of chopped parsley.

NOODLES IN WALNUT SAUCE

SERVES 4

100 g (4 oz) walnut pieces	275 g (10 oz) green tagliatelle
75 g (3 oz) butter, softened	5 ml (1 tsp) vegetable oil
1 small garlic clove, roughly chopped	salt and pepper
30 ml (2 tbsp) flour	100 g (4 oz) Cheddar cheese, grated
300 ml (½ pint) milk	freshly grated nutmeg

1 In a blender or food processor, mix together the walnuts, 50 g (2 oz) of the butter and the garlic. Turn into a bowl.
2 Put the remaining 25 g (1 oz) of butter in the blender or food processor. Add the flour and milk and work until evenly mixed.
3 Turn the sauce mixture into a saucepan and bring slowly to the boil, stirring. Simmer for 2-3 minutes.
4 Meanwhile, cook the tagliatelle in plenty of boiling salted water, with the oil added to prevent the pasta from sticking together, until *al dente* (tender, but firm to the bite).
5 Drain the pasta thoroughly, then return to the pan. Add the nut butter and heat through gently, stirring all the time.
6 Divide the pasta mixture equally between 4 large, individual gratin dishes. Add seasoning to the white sauce, then use to coat the pasta.
7 Scatter the grated cheese on top, sprinkle with the nutmeg, then grill for 5-10 minutes until brown and bubbling. Serve immediately.

TAGLIATELLE WITH GORGONZOLA SAUCE

SERVES 4

25 g (1 oz) butter	30 ml (2 tbsp) dry white wine
175 g (6 oz) Gorgonzola cheese	15 ml (1 tbsp) chopped sage
150 ml (¼ pint) whipping cream	salt and pepper
	350 g (12 oz) dried tagliatelle or other long thin pasta

1 To make the sauce, melt the butter in a heavy-based saucepan. Crumble in the Gorgonzola cheese, then stir over gentle heat for 2-3 minutes until melted. Pour in the cream and wine, whisking vigorously. Stir in the sage, season and cook, stirring, until the sauce thickens. Remove the pan from the heat.
2 Cook the tagliatelle in a large a pan of boiling salted water for 8-10 minutes until *al dente* (tender, but firm to the bite). Drain thoroughly.
3 Gently reheat the Gorgonzola sauce, whisking vigorously all the time. Taste and adjust seasoning.
4 Divide the tagliatelle between warmed serving bowls. Top each portion with sauce and serve immediately.

TAGLIATELLE WITH SUN-DRIED TOMATO

SERVES 4

125 g (4 oz) sun-dried tomatoes, drained and finely chopped	1 clove garlic, crushed
	400 g (14 oz) can chopped tomatoes
25 ml (1 fl oz) oil (preferably from sun-dried tomato jar)	100 ml (4 fl oz) dry white wine
25 g (1 oz) butter or margarine	salt and pepper
75 g (3 oz) onion, chopped	450-600 g (1-1¼ lb) fresh or dried tagliatelle
75 g (3 oz) celery, chopped	slivers of Parmesan and crème fraîche, to serve
75 g (3 oz) carrot, chopped	

1 Heat the oil and butter in a large saucepan. Add the onion, celery, carrot and garlic and cook, stirring, for 8-10 minutes or until beginning to soften.

2 Stir in the canned tomatoes, sun-dried tomatoes, wine and seasoning. Simmer, covered, for about 30 minutes, stirring occasionally.

3 Transfer about half the sauce to a food processor or blender and work until quite smooth. Stir into the remaining sauce.

4 Cook the tagliatelle in a large saucepan of fast boiling water for about 3 minutes for fresh pasta, 10 minutes for dried, until just tender. Drain well.

5 Serve the tagliatelle topped with the sauce, Parmesan and a spoonful of crème fraîche.

SPRING VEGETABLE PASTA

SERVES 4

125 g (4 oz) fresh asparagus or French beans	30 ml (2 tbsp) olive oil
225 g (8 oz) leeks, thinly sliced diagonally	1 medium onion, finely chopped
salt and pepper	125 g (4 oz) baby carrots
175 g (6 oz) creamy chèvre or full-fat soft cheese with garlic and herbs	225 g (8 oz) brown cap mushrooms, thinly sliced
	125 g (4 oz) petit pois
150 g (5 oz) mascarpone cheese or 150 ml (5 fl oz) extra-thick double cream	100 ml (4 fl oz) dry white wine
350-400 g (12-14 oz) dried penne (pasta quills) or rigatoni	350 g (12 oz) crème fraîche
	60 ml (4 tbsp) chopped herbs, eg parsley, thyme, sage
50 g (2 oz) butter or margarine	mascarpone, to serve (optional)

1 Cut the asparagus into 5 cm (2 inch) lengths. Briefly blanch the asparagus or beans, and leeks in boiling salted water for 3-4 minutes. Drain thoroughly.

2 Mix together the chèvre and mascarpone; set aside.

3 Cook the pasta in fast boiling salted water for about 10 minutes until just tender. Drain well.

4 Meanwhile, in a large sauté pan, heat together the butter and oil. Stir in the onion and cook stirring, for 3-4 minutes. Add the carrots and mushrooms and continue to cook for 2-3 minutes, or until beginning to soften.

5 Stir in the other vegetables, with the wine, crème fraîche and herbs. Simmer very gently until thickened to a good coating consistency. Remove the pan from the heat and gently stir in the cheese mixture until thoroughly mixed. Season to taste.

6 Divide the hot pasta between individual serving plates. Spoon the sauce over the pasta and top each portion with a spoonful of mascarpone, if desired. Serve immediately.

SPAGHETTI ALLA CARBONARA

SERVES 4

30 ml (2 tbsp) olive oil	60 ml (4 tbsp) dry white wine (optional)
1 onion, finely chopped	3 eggs
1 garlic clove crushed	60 ml (4 tbsp) freshly grated Parmesan cheese
400 g (14 oz) spaghetti or other long thin pasta	30 ml (2 tbsp) single cream
6 rashers pancetta or unsmoked streaky bacon, rinded and cut into thin strips	30 ml (2 tbsp) chopped parsley
	salt and pepper

1 Heat the oil in a pan, add the onion and fry gently for 5 minutes until soft but not coloured. Add the garlic and cook for a further 1 minute.

2 Cook the spaghetti in a large pan of boiling salted water for 8-10 minutes or until just tender.

3 Meanwhile, add the bacon to the onion and fry for 2 minutes over high heat. Add the wine, if using, and boil until evaporated.

4 In a bowl, lightly beat the eggs with the Parmesan, cream, chopped parsley and salt and pepper to taste.

5 Drain the spaghetti, return to the pan with the bacon and onion mixture. Mix well over moderate heat for 1 minute.

6 Remove from the heat and pour in the egg mixture, mixing well; the heat from the spaghetti will cook the egg. Turn into a warmed serving dish and serve immediately.

PASTA SHELLS WITH CHEESE AND WALNUTS

SERVES 4

275 g (10 oz) large pasta shells (conchiglie) or other pasta shapes	225 g (8 oz) mascarpone or other full-fat soft cheese
salt and pepper	30 ml (2 tbsp) freshly grated Parmesan cheese
25 g (1 oz) butter	75 g (3 oz) walnuts, roughly chopped

1 Cook the pasta shells in a large pan of boiling salted water for 20 minutes or until just tender. Drain well.

2 In the same pan, melt the butter, add the cheese and stir for about 2-3 minutes until heated through. Do not boil.

3 Add the Parmesan and walnuts, stir, then add the pasta. Mix well until evenly coated with sauce. Season to taste. Serve immediately.

VARIATION

Replace the walnuts with pine nuts and add 15 ml (1 tbsp) chopped basil to the sauce just before serving.

BROCCOLI AND HAM TAGLIATELLE

SERVES 4

225 g (8 oz) dried green or white tagliatelle	125 g (4 oz) yellow pepper, seeded and chopped
salt and pepper	25 g (1 oz) plain white flour
50 g (2 oz) butter or margarine	600 ml (1 pint) milk
125 g (4 oz) onion, sliced	225 g (8 oz) ham, chopped
225 g (8 oz) small broccoli florets	2.5 ml (½ tsp) grated nutmeg
	125 g (4 oz) Cheddar cheese, grated

1   Cook the pasta in boiling salted water until just tender; drain.

2   Meanwhile, melt the butter in a large saucepan, add the onion, broccoli and pepper and fry lightly until beginning to soften.

3   Add the flour and cook for 1 minute, stirring. Remove the pan from the heat and stir in the milk, ham, nutmeg and seasoning. Return to the heat and bring to the boil, stirring. Cook for 1-2 minutes, stirring. Adjust the seasoning.

4   Stir the sauce through the cooked pasta and turn into a shallow, flameproof dish. Scatter the Cheddar cheese over the top and grill until golden and bubbling. Serve with a green salad.

COOK'S TIP

For a delicious vegetarian alternative, omit the ham and use any vegetables that can be cooked quickly, such as mangetout, mushrooms or leeks. Other dried pasta shapes can be used for this dish – pasta shells work particularly well.

PEPPERONI PAN PIZZA

SERVES 4

125 g (4 oz) self-raising wholemeal flour	400 g (14 oz) can chopped tomatoes
125 g (4 oz) self-raising white flour	50 g (2 oz) mushrooms, sliced
salt and pepper	3 thin salami snack sticks (pepperoni), about 75 g (3 oz), sliced
5 ml (1 tsp) baking powder	6 pitted black olives, halved
5 ml (1 tsp) mustard powder	15 ml (1 tbsp) chopped fresh thyme or 5 ml (1 tsp) dried
40 g (1½ oz) butter or margarine	225 g (8 oz) Cheddar cheese, grated
about 150 ml (¼ pint) milk	
olive oil, for cooking	
30 ml (2 tbsp) tomato purée	

1   Mix together the flours, a pinch of salt, the baking powder and mustard in a bowl. Rub in the fat, then mix in enough milk to make a soft dough.

2   Knead the dough lightly on a lightly floured surface. Roll out to a round to fit a large oiled frying pan, about 21.5 cm (8½ inches) in diameter.

3   Cook the dough in the pan gently for 3-5 minutes until the base is golden. Turn out on to a baking sheet, then slide back into the pan uncooked side down.

4   Spread the tomato purée and chopped tomatoes on top of the dough, then cover with the mushrooms, salami, olives and thyme. Sprinkle with the cheese, season well and drizzle with oil.

5   Continue to cook until the underside of the pizza is golden, then place under a moderate grill for about 5 minutes to brown the topping. Serve immediately.

COOK'S TIP

Use any other toppings you have in your storecupboard, such as tuna or anchovies.

COCOTTE EGGS

SERVES 4

25 g (1 oz) butter	10 ml (2 tsp) chopped tarragon
1 small onion, finely chopped	salt and pepper
4 rashers lean back bacon, rinded and finely chopped	4 eggs, size 2
100 g (4 oz) button mushrooms, finely chopped	120 ml (8 tbsp) double cream
10 ml (2 tsp) tomato purée	chopped tarragon, to garnish

1 Melt the butter in a small saucepan, add the onion and fry gently until soft. Add the bacon and fry until beginning to change colour, then add the mushrooms and tomato purée. Continue frying for 2-3 minutes until the juices run, stirring constantly.

2 Remove from the heat and stir in the tarragon and seasoning to taste. Divide the mixture equally between 4 cocottes, ramekins or individual soufflé dishes. Make a slight indentation in the centre of each one.

3 Break an egg into each dish, on top of the mushroom and bacon mixture, then slowly pour 30 ml (2 tbsp) cream over each one. Sprinkle with salt and pepper to taste.

4 Place the cocottes on a baking tray and bake in the oven at 180°C (350°F) mark 4 for 10-12 minutes until the eggs are set. Serve immediately, garnished with tarragon.

VARIATION

Replace the mushrooms with 4 medium tomatoes, skinned and chopped, and substitute the tarragon with basil.

FRITTATA

SERVES 4

6 eggs	15 ml (1 tbsp) olive oil
30 ml (2 tbsp) freshly grated Parmesan cheese	100 g (4 oz) mortadella sausage, cut into thin strips
salt and pepper	100 g (4 oz) mozzarella cheese, cut into thin slices
25 g (1 oz) butter	

1 Beat the eggs together in a bowl. Add the freshly grated Parmesan cheese and salt and pepper to taste.

2 Melt the butter with the oil in a large heavy-based frying pan and, when hot, add the eggs. Cook gently for about 5-8 minutes until the mixture is half set underneath and the top of the omelette is still runny.

3 Scatter the mortadella and mozzarella over the omelette, then cook for 5 minutes until eggs are set.

4 Place the pan under a hot grill for 2-3 minutes until the top of the omelette is set. Serve hot, cut into wedges.

VARIATIONS

Omit the Mortadella and Mozzarella, then add one of the following variations.

ONION FRITTATA

Heat 30 ml (2 tbsp) olive oil in a frying pan, slowly cook 3 finely sliced large onions over low heat until soft and golden. Add to the beaten eggs and cook as above.

SALAMI FRITTATA

Scatter 100 g (4 oz) diced salami over the omelette at step 3.

CHEESE FRITTATA

Add 100 g (4 oz) freshly grated Parmesan cheese to the beaten egg mixture and cook as above.

MIXED VEGETABLE AND EGG SUPPER

SERVES 4

30 ml (2 tbsp) olive oil	10 ml (2 tsp) chopped fresh rosemary or 2.5 ml (½ tsp) dried
350 g (12 oz) courgettes, sliced	
1 medium green pepper, roughly chopped	400 g (14 oz) can chopped tomatoes
125 g (4 oz) onion, sliced	4 eggs
1 clove garlic, crushed	50 g (2 oz) Cheddar or gruyère cheese, grated
salt and pepper	

1   Heat the oil in a large flameproof sauté pan. Add the courgettes, pepper and onion and cook until beginning to soften and brown, stirring occasionally.
2   Stir in the garlic, seasoning, rosemary and tomatoes. Simmer, uncovered, until the vegetables are tender and the liquid is well reduced.
3   Make four slight hollows in the vegetable mixture and carefully break an egg into each. Season the eggs with salt and plenty of pepper and top with the grated cheese.
4   Cook under a preheated grill for about 10 minutes, depending on how well cooked you like your eggs.

COOK'S TIP

Use individual flameproof dishes for this recipe if you have them, or protect the pan handle with foil if necessary.

SPINACH AND FETA PUFFS

SERVES 4

25 g (1 oz) butter	pepper
50 g (2 oz) onion, finely chopped	two 20 cm (8 inch) ready-rolled squares puff pastry, thawed
125 g (4 oz) ready prepared fresh spinach, or 75 g (3 oz) frozen leaf spinach, thawed	50-75 g (2-3 oz) feta cheese, sliced
freshly grated nutmeg	beaten egg or milk, to glaze

1   Melt the butter in a medium saucepan and sauté the onion for 2 minutes or until softened. Add the spinach with plenty of nutmeg. Cook for 3-4 minutes; or 2 minutes if using frozen spinach; stirring until the spinach is soft and the juices have evaporated. Season with pepper and cool slightly.
2   Cut each pastry square in half diagonally. Divide the spinach mixture between each triangle. Top with feta cheese. Dampen the edges of the pastry, fold over and seal well. Brush with beaten egg or milk to glaze.
3   Place on a baking sheet and cook in the oven at 200°C (400°F) mark 6 for about 15 minutes or until cooked through and golden brown. Serve immediately, with a mixed salad.

COOK'S TIP

Don't use too much filling or it will ooze out on cooking.

FETA CHEESE PUFFS WITH BASIL

MAKES 8

225 g (8 oz) feta cheese, grated	pepper
150 ml (5 fl oz) natural yogurt	397 g (14 oz) packet frozen puff pastry, thawed
30 ml (2 tbsp) chopped fresh basil or 5 ml (1 tsp) dried	beaten egg, to glaze
	basil leaves, to garnish

1 Mix the grated cheese with the yogurt, chopped basil and pepper to taste. (Don't add salt as the cheese adds sufficient.)

2 Roll out the pastry thinly on a lightly floured surface and cut out sixteen 10 cm (4½ inch) rounds. Fold and re-roll the pastry as necessary.

3 Place half the rounds on two dampened baking sheets. Spoon some of the cheese mixture into the centre of each one.

4 Brush the pastry edges with beaten egg. Cover with the remaining rounds, knocking up and pressing the pastry edges together to seal. Make a small slit in the top of each pastry puff.

5 Brush with beaten egg. Bake in the oven at 220°C (425°F) mark 7 for about 15 minutes or until well browned and crisp. Serve warm, garnished with basil.

COOK'S TIP

Feta is a Greek cheese made from goat's or ewe's milk. Vacuum packs, which tend to be rather salty, are available at some large supermarkets, but the best feta (sold loose in brine) is found in Greek and Middle Eastern stores.

RED FLANNEL HASH

SERVES 4

450 g (1 lb) potatoes, scrubbed	5 ml (1 tsp) garlic salt
salt and pepper	225 g (8 oz) cooked beetroot, diced
225 g (8 oz) salt beef or corned beef, chopped	30 ml (2 tbsp) chopped parsley
1 medium onion, finely chopped	50 g (2 oz) butter or margarine

1 Cook the potatoes in their skins in lightly salted boiling water for about 20 minutes or until tender.

2 Drain the potatoes, leave until cool enough to handle, then peel off the skins with your fingers. Dice the flesh.

3 Put the diced potatoes in a large bowl, add the beef, onion, garlic salt, beetroot and parsley and toss to combine. Add pepper to taste.

4 Heat the butter or margarine in a heavy-based frying pan until very hot. Add the hash mixture and spread evenly with a fish slice or spatula.

5 Lower the heat to moderate and cook the hash, uncovered, for 10-15 minutes. Break up and turn frequently with the slice or spatula, so that the hash becomes evenly browned. Serve hot, cut into wedges.

VARIATION

Serve each portion of hash topped with a poached or fried egg.

RATATOUILLE
WITH TUNA

SERVES 4

200 g (7 oz) can tuna fish in brine, drained	3 cloves garlic, crushed
390 g (13.7 oz) can ready-made ratatouille	125 g (4 oz) frozen green beans
30 ml (2 tbsp) dry sherry	175 g (6 oz) tomatoes, chopped
60 ml (4 tbsp) chopped parsley	1 small baguette
	30 ml (2 tbsp) olive oil

1   Roughly flake the tuna and place in a saucepan with the ratatouille, sherry, parsley, 1 clove garlic and the green beans. Cover and simmer for 3-4 minutes or until the beans are tender. Stir in the tomatoes. Bring to the boil and simmer for 2-3 minutes or until piping hot.
2   Meanwhile, cut the bread into 1 cm (½ inch) slices. Place on a baking sheet and toast one side. Turn the slices over, drizzle with the olive oil mixed with the remaining garlic, then toast lightly.
3   Top the ratatouille mixture with the slices of garlic bread. Serve with a crisp salad.

SPEEDY
CHICKEN RISOTTO

SERVES 4

350 g (12 oz) boneless chicken thighs, skinned and sliced into strips	750 ml (1¼ pints) chicken stock
175 g (6 oz) onion, chopped	1.25 ml (¼ tsp) turmeric
3 tomatoes, chopped	5 ml (1 tsp) paprika
175 g (6 oz) button mushrooms, quartered or halved if necessary	salt and pepper
	175 g (6 oz) cooked peeled prawns
1 clove garlic, crushed	75 g (3 oz) frozen peas
350 g (12 oz) long-grain white rice	45 ml (3 tbsp) chopped parsley
	lemon slices and whole cooked prawns, to garnish

1   Place the chicken in a large saucepan with the onion, tomatoes, mushrooms, garlic and rice. Stir in the stock, spices and seasoning.
2   Bring to the boil, cover and simmer gently for 15-20 minutes or until the chicken is tender, stirring occasionally.
3   Add the prawns and peas and continue to cook, stirring occasionally, for about 5 minutes until the prawns and peas are heated through. Stir in the parsley and adjust the seasoning. Serve immediately, garnished with lemon slices and prawns.

COOK'S TIP

Cooking the rice with the other ingredients gives it a rich full flavour.

Leftovers such as cold chicken and ham can also be used in this dish. Simply stir in at stage 3 with the prawns etc.

CHICKEN EGGAH

SERVES 4-6

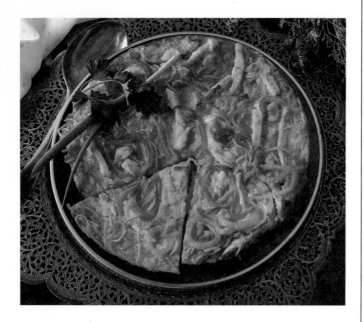

8 chicken thighs	6 eggs
600 ml (1 pint) chicken stock	50 g (2 oz) butter or margarine
10 ml (2 tsp) ground cumin	1 medium onion, sliced
1.25 ml (¼ tsp) chilli powder	1 garlic clove, crushed
salt and pepper	10 ml (2 tsp) paprika
100 g (4 oz) Chinese egg noodles	

1 Put the chicken thighs in a large saucepan, then add the chicken stock, cumin and chilli powder and season with salt and pepper to taste. Simmer for 30 minutes or until the chicken is tender.

2 Remove the chicken from the pan and set aside. Add 1.1 litres (2 pints) water to the pan and bring to the boil. Add the egg noodles and boil for about 5 minutes, or according to the packet instructions, until tender. Leave to drain thoroughly in a colander or sieve.

3 Remove the chicken flesh from the bones and discard the skin. Cut the meat into small strips.

4 Using kitchen scissors, cut the cooked, drained egg noodles into short lengths.

5 Beat the eggs lightly in a large bowl, then add the noodles and chicken and stir gently to mix. Melt the butter or margarine in a large heavy-based frying pan, add the onion, garlic and paprika and fry gently for about 5 minutes.

6 Pour in the egg mixture and stir lightly with a fork. Cook over a moderate heat for 15 minutes or until set and golden brown underneath.

7 Turn the eggah out on to a plate, then slide back into the pan so that the underside is uppermost. Cook for a further 15 minutes or until golden brown. Serve hot.

CHICKEN TACOS

SERVES 6

6 taco shells	4 tomatoes, skinned and chopped
25 g (1 oz) butter or margarine	salt and pepper
1 medium onion, chopped	½ lettuce, shredded
450 g (1 lb) cooked chicken meat, diced	100 g (4 oz) Cheddar cheese, grated
	Tabasco sauce, to taste

1 Put the taco shells in the oven at 150°C (300°F) mark 2 for 2-3 minutes to warm, or according to the packet instructions.

2 To make the filling, melt the butter or margarine in a frying pan, add the onion and fry for about 5 minutes or until soft but not coloured. Stir in the chicken and half the tomatoes, season to taste and heat through.

3 Spoon 15-30 ml (1-2 tbsp) filling into each shell. Add a little lettuce, the remaining tomatoes and the cheese with a few drops of Tabasco sauce. Serve immediately.

QUICK CHILLI TACOS

SERVES 4

450 g (1 lb) lean minced beef	15 ml (1 tbsp) tomato purée
125 g (4 oz) onion, chopped	2.5 ml (½ tsp) chilli powder
1 clove garlic, crushed	15 ml (1 tbsp) ground cumin
1 green pepper, seeded and chopped	salt and pepper
	8 taco shells
397 g (14 oz) can chopped tomatoes	125 g (4 oz) Cheddar cheese, grated
397 g (14 oz) can red kidney beans, drained and rinsed	soured cream, to serve

1 Place the minced beef, onion, garlic and green pepper in a large saucepan and heat gently, stirring until the mince is beginning to brown and the vegetables soften.
2 Add the tomatoes, kidney beans, tomato purée, spices and seasoning, with 300 ml (½ pint) water and stir well. Simmer for 20-25 minutes or until well reduced.
3 Just before serving, heat the taco shells in the oven at 150°C (300°F) mark 2 for 2-3 minutes, until crisp. Spoon a little of the spiced mince into each taco shell.
4 Serve topped with grated cheese and accompanied by soured cream. Serve with a crisp leafy salad.

COOK'S TIP

The mince mixture also makes a good filling for pancakes or a tasty sauce for pasta. Add fibre to the recipe by mixing kidney beans with the mince.

OATY BEEF BURGERS

SERVES 4

450 g (1 lb) lean minced beef	flour, for dusting
50 g (2 oz) rolled oats	vegetable oil, for brushing
5 ml (1 tsp) dried mixed herbs	TO SERVE
	warm burger buns
45 ml (3 tbsp) tomato chutney	carrot, orange and peanut salad
salt and pepper	onion rings
1 egg, beaten	

1 In a medium bowl, mix together the beef, oats, herbs, chutney and seasoning, adding sufficient beaten egg to bind the mixture.
2 With lightly floured hands, shape the mixture into 4 or 8 flat burgers.
3 Brush each one lightly with oil, and grill until golden and cooked through, about 4 minutes on each side, depending on the thickness of the burgers.
4 Serve in warm burger buns on a carrot, orange and peanut salad. Top with onion rings.

COOK'S TIP

Oats add valuable fibre to these tasty burgers. For a healthier salad, use unsalted or dry roasted peanuts rather than salted ones.

BEEFBURGERS

SERVES 4

450 g (1 lb) lean beef, eg chuck, shoulder or rump steak, minced	melted butter or vegetable oil, for grilling, or vegetable oil, for shallow frying
½ small onion, grated (optional)	4 large burger buns
salt and pepper	butter or margarine, for spreading
	lettuce and onion rings, to serve (optional)

1 Mix the minced beef well with the onion, if using, and plenty of salt and pepper.
2 Shape the mixture lightly into 4 round flat patties. Brush sparingly with melted butter or vegetable oil.
3 Grill the burgers for 8-10 minutes until cooked according to taste, turning once, or fry in a little oil in a frying pan, turning them once and allowing the same amount of time.
4 Meanwhile, split the buns in half and spread with a little butter. Put 1 beefburger inside each bun. Add a lettuce leaf and some onion rings, if liked, and serve immediately.

VARIATIONS

CHEESEBURGERS
Top each of the cooked beefburgers with a slice of Cheddar or gruyère cheese and cook under the grill for a further minute or until the cheese has melted.

CHILLIBURGERS
Add 15 ml (1 tbsp) chilli seasoning when mixing the minced beef and onion together.

PEPPERCORNBURGERS
Crush 15 ml (1 tbsp) green peppercorns and add when mixing the minced beef and onion together.

SESAME CHICKEN PITTAS

SERVES 4

30 ml (2 tbsp) sesame oil	225 g (8 oz) cooked chicken breast, sliced into thin strips
1 onion, sliced	100 g (4 oz) beansprouts
100 g (4 oz) broccoli, cut into tiny florets	15 ml (1 tbsp) dark soy sauce
1 red pepper, seeded and diced	30 ml (2 tbsp) toasted sesame seeds
	4 large pitta breads

1 Heat the oil in a large frying pan and stir-fry the onion for 2 minutes. Add the broccoli and pepper and cook for 3-4 minutes, stirring frequently.
2 Add the chicken strips to the pan, stir well, then add the beansprouts and soy sauce. Continue to cook for 2-3 minutes. Sprinkle over the sesame seeds and stir to combine. Remove from the heat, keeping the pan covered to keep warm.
3 Cut through a long side of each pitta bread and open the cavity to form a pocket. Place the pitta breads on a baking sheet. Bake in the oven at 200°C (400°F) mark 6 for 5-10 minutes to heat.
4 Using a slotted spoon, fill each pitta pocket with the chicken mixture.

VARIATION

Replace the chicken with lean roast beef or lamb.

SIZZLING STEAK SANDWICHES

SERVES 2

2 'flash-fry' steaks, about 75 g (3 oz) each	butter or margarine, for spreading
15 ml (1 tbsp) vegetable oil	30 ml (2 tbsp) mayonnaise
salt and pepper	about 4 small lettuce leaves, shredded
4 slices granary or wholemeal bread, from a large loaf	1 tomato, skinned and sliced
	10 ml (2 tsp) Dijon mustard

1 Brush the steaks on one side with half of the oil and sprinkle with pepper to taste. Grill under a hot grill for 3 minutes, then turn them over, brush with the remaining oil, sprinkle with more pepper and grill for a further 3 minutes, or until done to your liking.

2 Meanwhile, toast the bread on both sides, removing the crusts if wished. Spread one side of each slice with butter, then with the mayonnaise. Top 2 slices of toast with the shredded lettuce and sliced tomato and sprinkle with salt and pepper to taste.

3 Place the steaks on top of the salad and spread evenly with the mustard. Cover with the remaining 2 slices of toast.

4 Cut each sandwich in half with a serrated knife to make 2 triangles and place on individual plates. Serve immediately.

VARIATION

Replace the tomato with 3-4 sun-dried tomatoes, roughly chopped. Omit the mustard.

CLUB SANDWICHES

SERVES 2

6 rashers streaky bacon, rinded	few lettuce leaves
6 slices white bread, toasted	2 large slices cooked turkey
about 45 ml (3 tbsp) mayonnaise	salt and pepper
	1 large tomato, sliced

1 Fry the bacon in its own fat until crisp; drain on absorbent kitchen paper. Spread one side of each slice of toast with some of the mayonnaise.

2 Arrange half the lettuce on two slices of toast; top with turkey. Sprinkle with salt and pepper then add another slice of toast, mayonnaise side up.

3 Arrange the rest of the lettuce, the tomato slices, and the bacon on the two sandwiches. Top with the remaining toast slices, mayonnaise side down.

4 Cut the sandwiches diagonally into quarters and secure each one with a cocktail stick. Arrange, crust sides down, on two plates.

VARIATIONS

Vary the filling according to the ingredients you have to hand. Try replacing the tomato with avocado, or use slices of salt beef or roast beef instead of turkey.

DEEP-FRIED MOZZARELLA SANDWICHES

MAKES 10

175 g (6 oz) mozzarella cheese	2 eggs
10 large slices white bread, crusts removed	175 ml (6 fl oz) milk
	plain flour, for coating
salt and pepper	vegetable oil, for frying

1 Slice the cheese thinly and arrange on five slices of bread, leaving a narrow margin around the edges. Season with salt and pepper and cover with the remaining bread slices. Cut each sandwich in half diagonally or widthways.
2 Beat the eggs in a shallow bowl and add the milk. Season generously with salt and pepper. Spread the flour out on a flat plate.
3 Brush a little egg and milk mixture on the inside edges of the sandwiches and press together.
4 Quickly dip each sandwich into the egg mixture, then coat lightly with the flour. Dip again into the egg mixture, shaking off any excess.
5 Pour enough oil into a frying pan to come 1 cm (½ inch) up the sides of the pan and heat until it is hot.
6 Carefully place the sandwiches in the pan, in a single layer. (If your pan is not large enough you may have to use two pans or cook the sandwiches in batches.) Fry for about 3 minutes on each side until brown. Drain on absorbent kitchen paper and serve immediately.

CHESHIRE POTTED CHEESE

SERVES 4

about 225 g (8 oz) Cheshire cheese, grated	30 ml (2 tbsp) sweet sherry or Madeira
50 g (2 oz) butter, softened	melted butter, for sealing
1.25 ml (¼ tsp) ground mace or allspice	

1 Mix the cheese with the softened butter and spice. The exact amount of butter will depend to a certain extent on how dry or moist the cheese is. Beat thoroughly. Add the sherry and mix again.
2 When the cheese is well amalgamated with the other ingredients, put it into small pots or ramekin dishes, pressing it well down and smoothing the tops. Cover each with melted butter and store in a refrigerator. Remove from the refrigerator about 1 hour before serving. Serve spread on toast or bread with fruit and celery.

COOK'S TIP

This is an excellent way to use up odd pieces of cheese. They can be grated up together. As long as the butter seal is unbroken, this mixture keeps well in the refrigerator.

QUICK MUFFIN PIZZAS

SERVES 4

4 muffins	salt and pepper
butter or margarine, for spreading	125 g (4 oz) mozzarella cheese, thinly sliced
45 ml (3 tbsp) tomato ketchup	8 black olives, stoned and sliced
200 g (7 oz) can tuna fish, drained	

1 Split the muffins and toast lightly on both sides. Spread the inner sides with a little butter and tomato ketchup.
2 Break the tuna into medium-sized flakes and place on top of the muffins. Season with salt and plenty of pepper.
3 Cover the tuna with the mozzarella slices. Top with the olives. Grill until the cheese is melted and bubbling. Serve immediately.

DEVILLED MUSHROOM BAGUETTES

SERVES 4

about 75 g (3 oz) butter	dash of Worcestershire or Tabasco sauce
175 g (6 oz) onion, finely chopped	30 ml (2 tbsp) tomato ketchup
1 clove garlic, crushed	salt and pepper
350 g (12 oz) button mushrooms, sliced	1 long baguette
30 ml (2 tbsp) red wine vinegar	30 ml (2 tbsp) chopped parsley
5 ml (1 tsp) mustard powder	

1 Melt 50 g (2 oz) butter in a small saucepan. Add the onion and garlic and cook until beginning to soften.
2 Mix in the mushrooms and stir over a high heat for a further 3-4 minutes. Add the vinegar, mustard, Worcestershire sauce and ketchup with seasoning to taste. Simmer gently for 1-2 minutes.
3 Meanwhile, cut the baguette in half and then cut each piece in half lengthwise to give 4 long pieces. Toast under the grill, lightly butter and top with the hot mushroom mixture. Sprinkle with parsley to serve.

VARIATION

Add a little cream or mascarpone to the warm mushroom mixture.

AVOCADO, LEMON AND OMELETTE SALAD

SERVES 4-6

4 eggs	5 ml (1 tsp) coriander seeds
50 g (2 oz) Cheddar cheese, grated	90 ml (6 tbsp) olive or vegetable oil
salt and pepper	45 ml (3 tbsp) lemon juice
25 g (1 oz) butter or margarine	2 ripe avocados
5 ml (1 tsp) black peppercorns	parsley sprigs, to garnish

1 Put the eggs in a bowl with the cheese and 15 ml (1 tbsp) water. Season with salt and pepper to taste and whisk together.

2 Melt a quarter of the butter or margarine in an omelette pan or small non-stick frying pan. When foaming, pour in a quarter of the egg mixture. After a few seconds, push the set egg mixture into the centre of the pan and tilt the pan to allow the egg to run to the edges. Cook until just set.

3 Brown the omelette under a preheated hot grill. Turn out on to a plate. Repeat with the remaining egg mixture to make another three omelettes.

4 While the omelettes are still warm, roll them up loosely. Wrap in greaseproof paper and leave to cool.

5 Meanwhile, crush the peppercorns and coriander seeds coarsely with a pestle and mortar, or with the end of a rolling pin in a strong bowl.

6 Whisk together the oil, lemon juice and crushed spices and season to taste. Halve, stone and peel the avocados, then slice thickly into the dressing. Toss gently to coat.

7 Slice the rolled omelettes thinly. Arrange the omelette rings and avocado slices in individual serving plates. Spoon over the dressing and garnish with sprigs of parsley. Serve immediately.

CELERY, CHEESE AND APPLE SALAD

SERVES 4

FOR THE DRESSING	3 Granny Smith apples
150 ml (¼ pint) natural yogurt	lemon juice, for sprinkling
50 ml (2 fl oz) mayonnaise	175g (6 oz) celery, chopped
10 ml (2 tsp) lemon juice	175g (6 oz) cheese, Cheddar, double Gloucester or Leicester, diced
salt and pepper	1 small spring onion, finely chopped
5 ml (1 tsp) chopped parsley	celery leaves, to garnish

1 For the dressing, beat the yogurt until smooth then beat in the mayonnaise. Add the lemon juice, seasoning and parsley.

2 Core and slice the apples thinly, but do not peel. Sprinkle with lemon juice to prevent discolouration. Place two of the sliced apples in a bowl and add the celery, cheese and spring onion. Pour over the dressing and toss well. Arrange the remaining apple slices on a serving dish and place the salad in the centre. Garnish with celery leaves.

VARIATION

Prepare the salad as above, omitting the spring onion and substituting 50 g (2 oz) coarsely chopped walnut or toasted blanched almonds. Sprinkle the nuts over the top of the salad just before serving so they retain their crunchiness.

VEGETABLE SALAMAGUNDY

SERVES 8

50 g (2 oz) green lentils	1 yellow pepper, seeded and cut into strips
1 bay leaf	½ small head of celery, trimmed and sliced
salt and pepper	
225 g (8 oz) French beans, trimmed	50 g (2 oz) lamb's lettuce, trimmed
225 g (8 oz) mangetout, trimmed	1 small onion, thinly sliced
	2 Cox's apples, sliced
225 g (8 oz) beef tomatoes, sliced	few black olives
225 g (8 oz) cherry tomatoes	120 ml (4 fl oz) vinaigrette
	fresh herbs, to garnish

1 Cook the lentils in boiling salted water with the bay leaf, until just tender. Drain and leave to cool. Blanch the beans and mangetout in boiling salted water for 2 minutes. Drain, rinse under cold running water and drain.

2 Arrange all the ingredients on one or two large platters in a symmetrical pattern. Sprinkle with the dressing and garnish with the fresh herbs.

COOK'S TIP

Salamagundy is an old English supper dish which dates back to the eighteenth century. It originally contained a varied mixture of meats. Here we make the most of fresh colourful vegetables. Use others in season if you prefer. Add hard-boiled quail's eggs, or nuts, if liked.

MIXED BEAN SALAD

SERVES 4

450 g (1 lb) broad beans, shelled	15 ml (1 tbsp) mild wholegrain mustard
salt and pepper	15 ml (1 tbsp) lemon juice
225 g (8 oz) French beans, trimmed	397 g (14 oz) can red kidney beans, drained and rinsed
15 ml (1 tbsp) vegetable oil	125 g (4 oz) Charnwood or Applewood cheese, cubed
150 ml (5 fl oz) natural yogurt	chopped parsley, to garnish

1 Cook the broad beans in boiling salted water for 10 minutes. Add the French beans and continue to cook for 5-10 minutes, until both are tender.

2 Meanwhile, mix together the oil, yogurt, mustard, lemon juice and salt and pepper until well blended.

3 Drain the cooked beans and while still hot, combine with the drained kidney beans and dressing. Leave to cool.

4 Toss in the cubes of cheese and garnish with chopped parsley just before serving.

COOK'S TIP

Charnwood, or Applewood, cheese is a mature Cheddar variation, smoked and coated with paprika. Cubed, it adds colour and bite to this summertime salad, which mixes fresh French and broad beans with canned kidney beans.

GREEK SALAD

SERVES 4

½ large cucumber	100 g (4 oz) feta cheese, cut into cubes
salt and pepper	
450 g (1 lb) firm ripe tomatoes	60 ml (4 tbsp) olive oil
	15 ml (1 tbsp) lemon juice
1 medium red onion	good pinch of dried oregano
18 black olives	

1 Peel the cucumber and slice thinly. Put into a colander or sieve, sprinkle with a little salt and leave to stand for about 15 minutes.
2 Slice the tomatoes thinly. Slice the onion into thin rings. Rinse the cucumber under cold running water, drain and pat dry with absorbent kitchen paper.
3 Arrange the cucumber, tomatoes and onion in a serving dish. Scatter the olives and cubed cheese over the top.
4 In a bowl, whisk together the oil, lemon juice, oregano and salt and pepper to taste. Spoon the dressing over the salad. Serve with warm pitta bread.

CHEESE, BEANSPROUT AND PINEAPPLE SALAD

SERVES 4

225 g (8 oz) carrots, peeled	275 g (10 oz) beansprouts
225 g (8 oz) Edam cheese	10 ml (2 tsp) wine vinegar
227 g (8 oz) can pineapple slices in natural juice	salt and pepper

1 Cut the carrots into 2.5 cm (1 inch) matchstick thin strips. Coarsely grate the cheese.
2 Drain the pineapple, reserving the juice. Cut the pineapple into thin strips.
3 In a large bowl, mix together the beansprouts, carrot, cheese and pineapple.
4 To make the dressing, whisk the pineapple juice and vinegar together with seasoning to taste.
5 Just before serving, pour the dressing over the salad and toss well to mix.

VARIATION

Replace the cheese with the same quantity of tofu – cut into cubes. Tofu is available from the chilled cabinet of health food stores and large supermarkets.

BEAN, CHEESE
AND AVOCADO SALAD

SERVES 4

425 g (15 oz) can red kidney beans, drained	1 small onion, finely chopped
90 ml (6 tbsp) olive oil	2 celery sticks, finely chopped
finely grated rind and juice of 1 lemon	2 tomatoes, skinned and chopped
1.25 ml (¼ tsp) Tabasco sauce	1 ripe avocado
salt and pepper	celery leaves, to garnish
175 g (6 oz) Edam cheese, rinded and diced	

1 Rinse the kidney beans, drain well and put in a bowl. Add the oil, lemon rind and juice, Tabasco and seasoning. Toss well.
2 Add the cheese, onion, celery and tomatoes to the beans and toss again to mix the ingredients together. Cover and chill in the refrigerator until required.
3 When ready to serve, peel the avocado, cut in half and remove the stone. Chop the flesh into chunky pieces. Fold the avocado pieces gently into the bean salad and taste and adjust seasoning. Garnish with celery leaves and serve.

EGG, CHICORY
AND CELERY SALAD

SERVES 4-6

1 eating apple, cored and chopped	2.5 ml (½ tsp) prepared English mustard
1 head of celery, trimmed and sliced	2.5 ml (½ tsp) sugar
1 cooked beetroot, peeled and sliced	60 ml (4 tbsp) single cream
2 heads of chicory, sliced	10 ml (2 tsp) white wine vinegar
1 punnet of mustard and cress, trimmed	salt and pepper
	3 eggs, hard-boiled and cut into wedges

1 Lightly mix the apple, celery, beetroot and chicory together with the cress in a large salad bowl.
2 To make the dressing, whisk the mustard, sugar, cream and vinegar together. Season to taste. Pour over the salad and toss together so that everything is coated in the dressing. Add the eggs, then serve at once.

CRAB SALAD

SERVES 2

15 ml (1 tbsp) lemon juice	50 g (2 oz) pasta shells, cooked
15 ml (1 tbsp) mayonnaise	pepper
15 ml (1 tbsp) natural yogurt	TO SERVE
225 g (8 oz) cooked crab meat, thawed if frozen	shredded lettuce
½ cucumber, diced	lemon slices, to garnish
2 tomatoes, skinned and cubed	

1 Mix together the lemon juice, mayonnaise and yogurt. Combine the crab meat with the dressing.
2 Mix the remaining ingredients together and spoon on to serving plates. Top with shredded lettuce and arrange the crab salad in the centre. Garnish with cucumber and lemon slices.

COOK'S TIP

You can buy fresh or frozen cooked crab meat (if the latter, thaw thoroughly before use) in a mixture of dark and light meat. If buying freshly cooked crabs in their shells you'll need one large crab to produce about the weight specified. If you have them, garnish the dish with crab claws.

SALAD NICOISE

SERVES 4

175 g (6 oz) small new potatoes, scrubbed and halved	50 g (2 oz) black olives, stoned
salt and pepper	½ small cucumber, thinly sliced
90 ml (6 tbsp) olive oil	225 g (8 oz) cooked French beans
30 ml (2 tbsp) white wine vinegar	2 hard-boiled eggs, shelled and quartered
15 ml (1 tbsp) lemon juice	½ iceberg lettuce, cut into chunks
15 ml (1 tbsp) mild wholegrain mustard	30 ml (2 tbsp) chopped parsley
large pinch of sugar	8 anchovy fillets, drained and halved
198 g (7 oz) can tuna fish, drained	
225 g (8 oz) tomatoes, quartered	

1 Cook the potatoes in boiling salted water until tender. Meanwhile, make the dressing by whisking together the oil, vinegar, lemon juice, mustard and sugar. Season generously with salt and pepper.
2 Drain the potatoes and toss in the dressing. Leave to cool, stirring occasionally.
3 Flake the tuna into large chunks. Arrange in a bowl with the tomatoes, olives, cucumber, beans, eggs, lettuce and cold potatoes. Sprinkle with parsley and anchovies. Serve with French bread.

WARM SEAFOOD SALAD

SERVES 2

selection of salad leaves, eg radicchio, frisée (curly endive), lamb's lettuce	50 g (2 oz) streaky bacon, rinded and cut into strips
few chives, snipped	50 g (2 oz) peeled prawns
60 ml (4 tbsp) French dressing	200 g (7 oz) can artichoke bottoms, drained and thickly sliced
12 medium scallops	salt and pepper
25 g (1 oz) butter or margarine	chives, to garnish

1 Arrange the salad leaves on a serving platter or individual plates. Sprinkle over the chives and drizzle over the French dressing.

2 Remove and discard the white muscle from each scallop. Separate the corals and reserve. Cut the white flesh into thick slices.

3 Melt the butter in a sauté pan and fry the bacon for 2-3 minutes. Add the scallops and fry for a further 2-3 minutes, or until just cooked through.

4 Add the reserved corals, prawns and artichokes. Stir over the heat for 1 minute or until heated through. Adjust seasoning. Divide the seafood mixture between the serving plates. Garnish with chives and serve immediately, with warm crusty bread.

SMOKED HADDOCK AND BEAN SALAD

SERVES 4-6

450 g (1 lb) smoked haddock fillet	45 ml (3 tbsp) chopped parsley
a little milk and water	pepper
439 g (15 oz) can borlotti beans, drained	3 eggs, hard-boiled and quartered
150 ml (5 fl oz) soured cream	mixed salad leaves, to serve
5-10 ml (1-2 tsp) curry paste	herbs, to garnish
45-60 ml (3-4 tbsp) lemon juice	

1 Put the fish in a pan and add just enough milk and water to cover. Bring to the boil, then lower the heat, cover and gently poach for about 5 minutes, or until tender. Drain, discarding the skin, and divide the fish into large chunks. Add the borlotti beans.

2 Combine the soured cream, curry paste, lemon juice and parsley in a bowl. Season with pepper. Lightly fold into the haddock mixture.

3 Arrange on a bed of salad leaves, with the hard-boiled egg quarters. Garnish with herbs.

SMOKED MACKEREL AND PASTA SALAD

SERVES 4

225 g (8 oz) dried pasta shapes, eg shells or spirals	2 oranges
salt and pepper	45 ml (3 tbsp) vegetable oil
3 medium courgettes, about 275 g (10 oz) total weight, sliced	350 g (12 oz) smoked mackerel fillets, flaked
	snipped chives, to garnish

1 Cook the pasta in boiling salted water according to the manufacturer's instructions until just tender; drain.
2 Cook the courgettes in boiling salted water for 2-3 minutes until just tender; drain.
3 Meanwhile, finely grate the rind from the oranges and reserve. Using a serrated knife, peel and segment the oranges over a bowl to catch the juice, discarding all pith.
4 In a large bowl, whisk together the oil, orange rind and reserved juice. Season well and stir in the hot pasta; allow to cool.
5 Add the courgettes, orange segments and flaked mackerel to the pasta and toss well. Adjust the seasoning.
6 Cover and refrigerate until required. Garnish with snipped chives to serve.

VARIATIONS

You could also use canned salmon, tuna or sardines, or smoked trout in place of the mackerel - just keep the quantities the same.

WARM LAMB SALAD

SERVES 4

4 lamb leg steaks, each about 125 g (4 oz)	350 g (12 oz) leeks, trimmed and thinly sliced
150 ml (¼ pint) sunflower oil	350 g (12 oz) spring cabbage greens, trimmed and thinly sliced
60 ml (4 tbsp) fresh orange juice	75 g (3 oz) beansprouts
15 ml (1 tbsp) wholegrain mustard	50 g (2 oz) walnut pieces, toasted
salt and pepper	

1 Brush the lamb steaks with a little of the oil and grill under a moderately high heat for about 4 minutes on each side. Cut into thick slices.
2 To make the dressing, whisk together the remaining oil, orange juice, mustard and seasoning.
3 Heat the dressing in a large saucepan, then add the leeks and cabbage. Cook over a high heat for 3-4 minutes or until just tender, stirring frequently.
4 Add the beansprouts, toasted walnuts and lamb and continue to cook for 1 minute. Serve with crusty bread.

COOK'S TIP

If you have time, marinate the lamb steaks in the orange dressing overnight. This gives the dish an extra tangy flavour.

MAIN MEALS

Marvellous meals in minutes can be yours with this varied collection of delicious, nutritious main course dishes – featuring fish, poultry and cuts of meat which are quick and easy to prepare and cook. A tempting selection of vegetarian main meals includes spicy curries, tasty kebabs and quick vegetable bakes.

SEAFOOD KEBABS

SERVES 4

450 g (1 lb) monkfish or cod fillet	75 ml (3 fl oz) vinaigrette, flavoured with garlic
125 g (4 oz) cucumber	15 ml (1 tbsp) chopped fresh dill or 2.5 ml (½ tsp) dried dill
1 lemon or lime, thinly sliced	
50 g (2 oz) large cooked peeled prawns	salt and pepper
	salad leaves and dill sprigs, to garnish

1 Skin the fish if necessary, then cut into 2.5 cm (1 inch) cubes. Halve the cucumber lengthways and thickly slice.

2 Wrap a lemon or lime slice round each prawn. Thread onto four wooden skewers, alternating with the cubes of fish and cucumber. Place the kebabs in a flameproof dish.

3 Spoon the vinaigrette and chopped dill over the kebabs. Cook under a preheated grill for about 4-5 minutes on each side, basting occasionally.

4 Season with salt and pepper and serve immediately on a bed of crisp salad leaves. Garnish with a few dill sprigs and serve accompanied by crusty bread.

HADDOCK AND SOURED CREAM GRATIN

SERVES 2

350 g (12 oz) fresh or frozen haddock fillet, thawed	15 ml (1 tbsp) chopped chives
knob of butter	15 ml (1 tbsp) chopped parsley
2 medium firm tomatoes	25 g (1 oz) gruyère cheese
150 ml (5 fl oz) soured cream	salt and pepper

1 Skin the haddock if necessary and chop roughly. Choose a shallow flameproof serving dish just large enough to take the fish in a single layer. Put the knob of butter in the dish and place under a hot grill to melt.

2 Add the fish to the dish and turn in the butter. Grill for 10 minutes turning occasionally, until cooked.

3 Chop the tomatoes and mix with the soured cream, herbs, grated cheese and seasoning. Spoon over the fish and cook under the grill until bubbling. Serve immediately, with boiled new potatoes and spinach.

ROLLED PLAICE WITH APPLE

SERVES 4

225 g (8 oz) button mushrooms	30 ml (2 tbsp) chopped parsley
125 g (4 oz) eating apple	salt and pepper
25 g (1 oz) low-fat spread	4 plaice fillets , each about 125 g (4 oz), skinned
25 g (1 oz) fresh brown breadcrumbs	60 ml (4 tbsp) dry cider
5 ml (1 tsp) wholegrain mustard	apple slices, to garnish

1 Finely chop the mushrooms. Peel, core and chop the apple. Melt the low-fat spread in a small pan and sauté the mushrooms and apple for 2-3 minutes. Increase the heat and cook, stirring, for 1-2 minutes, until most of the excess liquid has evaporated.

2 Off the heat, stir in the fresh brown breadcrumbs, half the wholegrain mustard and the chopped parsley. Season with salt and pepper.

3 Divide the mixture among the plaice fillets and roll up. Secure with wooden cocktail sticks. Place seam side down in a small shallow flameproof dish.

4 Whisk together the remaining mustard and the cider. Spoon over the fish. Cook under a preheated hot grill for about 10 minutes, turning occasionally and brushing with the mustard mixture.

5 Serve immediately, garnished with apple slices. Accompany with steamed potatoes and a green salad or steamed broccoli.

MONKFISH AND HALIBUT WITH CORIANDER

SERVES 6

700 g (1½ lb) monkfish fillets	40 g (1½ oz) butter
450 g (1 lb) halibut cutlets	45 ml (3 tbsp) plain flour
150 ml (¼ pint) dry vermouth	30 ml (2 tbsp) chopped coriander
1 small onion, sliced	60 ml (4 tbsp) single cream
salt and pepper	coriander sprigs, to garnish
100 g (4 oz) small button mushrooms	

1 Cut the monkfish and halibut into large, fork-sized pieces, discarding skin and bone.

2 Place the fish in a medium saucepan, cover with cold water and bring slowly to the boil. Drain the fish in a colander and rinse off any scum.

3 Return the fish to the clean pan and pour over the vermouth and 300 ml (½ pint) water. Add the onion, season to taste and bring to the boil. Cover the pan, reduce the heat and simmer gently for 6 minutes. Add the mushrooms and cook for a further 2-4 minutes, or until the fish is just tender and beginning to flake.

4 Strain off the cooking liquor and reserve.

5 Melt the butter in a separate saucepan, stir in the flour and cook for 1-2 minutes. Gradually add the cooking liquor. Bring slowly to the boil, stirring all the time, and bubble for 2 minutes or until thickened and smooth.

6 Stir in the chopped coriander, cream, mushrooms, onion and fish and adjust the seasoning. Warm through gently, being careful not to break up the fish. Serve hot, garnished with sprigs of coriander.

MONKFISH WITH MUSTARD SEEDS

SERVES 6

45 ml (3 tbsp) black mustard seeds	1 medium onion, thinly sliced
30 ml (2 tbsp) plain white flour	300 ml (½ pint) natural yogurt
900 g (2 lb) monkish fillet, skinned	1 garlic clove, crushed
30 ml (2 tbsp) mustard oil or vegetable oil	15 ml (1 tbsp) lemon juice
	salt and pepper
	cooked whole prawns and coriander sprigs, to garnish

1 Finely grind 30 ml (2 tbsp) of the mustard seeds in a small electric mill or with a pestle and mortar. Mix them with the flour.
2 Cut the monkfish into 2.5 cm (1 inch) cubes and toss in the flour and ground mustard seeds.
3 Heat the oil in a large heavy-based frying pan and fry the onion for about 5 minutes until golden.
4 Add the remaining mustard seeds to the pan with the monkfish. Fry over moderate heat for 3-4 minutes, turning very gently once or twice.
5 Gradually stir in the yogurt with the garlic, lemon juice and seasoning. Bring to the boil, lower the heat and simmer gently for 10-15 minutes or until the fish is tender.
6 Taste and adjust the seasoning. Turn into a warmed serving dish and garnish with the prawns and coriander. Serve immediately.

COOK'S TIP

The firm, white flesh of the monkfish comes from the tail end, as a third of the length of the fish is taken up by a large unattractive head.

MONKFISH AND MUSSEL SKEWERS

SERVES 6

12 streaky bacon rashers, halved	60 ml (4 tbsp) chopped parsley
900 g (2 lb) monkfish, skinned, boned and cut into 2.5 cm (1 inch) cubes	finely grated rind and juice of 1 large lemon
36 cooked mussels, shelled	4 garlic cloves, crushed
25 g (1 oz) butter or margarine	salt and pepper
	shredded lettuce, to serve
	lemon slices, to garnish

1 Roll the bacon rashers up neatly. Thread the cubed fish, mussels and bacon alternately on to 12 oiled skewers.
2 Melt the butter or margarine in a saucepan, remove from the heat, then add the parsley, lemon rind and juice, and garlic. Season to taste; take care when adding salt as both the mussels and the bacon are naturally salty.
3 Place the skewers on an oiled grill rack. Brush with the parsley mixture, then cook under a preheated moderate grill for 15 minutes. Turn the skewers frequently during cooking and brush with the parsley mixture with each turn.
4 Arrange the hot skewers on a serving platter lined with shredded lettuce. Garnish with lemon slices and serve immediately.

VARIATION

Monkfish and Apricot Kebabs
Omit the mussels. Wrap each slice of bacon around a pre-soaked dried apricot. Thread on to skewers alternating with whole button mushrooms and squares of red and green pepper. Cook as above.

SMOKED HADDOCK IN CREAM PERNOD SAUCE

SERVES 4

4 smoked haddock fillets, about 700 g (1½ lb) total weight	2.5 ml (½ tsp) crushed fennel seeds
300 ml (½ pint) milk	150 ml (5 fl oz) double cream
few onion slices	15 g (½ oz) butter
2 bay leaves	60 ml (4 tbsp) Pernod
few black peppercorns	salt and pepper
	fennel sprigs, to garnish

1 Put the smoked haddock fillets in a large flameproof casserole. Pour in the milk and add the onion slices, bay leaves, peppercorns and fennel seeds. Pour in a little water if the liquid does not completely cover the smoked haddock.

2 Bring slowly to boiling point, then lower the heat, cover and simmer gently for 15 minutes or until the fish flakes easily when tested with a fork.

3 Remove the fish fillets from the cooking liquid and then flake into chunky pieces. Discard all skin and any bones.

4 Strain the cooking liquid and return to the rinsed-out pan. Boil to reduce slightly, then add the cream, butter and Pernod and boil again until the sauce thickens.

5 Return the fish to the liquid and heat through. Add salt and pepper to taste, taking care not to add too much salt as the fish is salty. Transfer to a warmed serving dish. Garnish with fennel sprigs and serve immediately.

COOK'S TIP

A rich and filling dinner party main course, best served with a plain accompaniment such as boiled rice or duchesse potatoes. If liked, the quantities may be halved and the dish served as a first course, with hot French bread.

COD IN A SPICY YOGURT CRUST

SERVES 4

30 ml (2 tbsp) chopped mint	10 ml (2 tsp) ground cumin
1 medium onion or 2 large spring onions, roughly chopped	10 ml (2 tsp) dried dill
2 garlic cloves, crushed	150 ml (5 fl oz) natural yogurt
5 ml (1 tsp) paprika	salt and pepper
30 ml (2 tbsp) coriander seeds	4 thick cod steaks or fillets, each about 225 g (8 oz)

1 First make the marinade mixture. Put the mint, onion, garlic, paprika, coriander, cumin, dill and yogurt in a blender or food processor and process until a thick paste is formed. Season the mixture to taste with salt and pepper.

2 Place the fish in a single layer in a shallow heatproof dish. Spread the paste all over the top of the fish and leave in a cool place to marinate for 2-3 hours.

3 Cook under a preheated hot grill, basting occasionally, until the fish is cooked and the yogurt mixture has formed a crust. Serve immediately.

VARIATION

Substitute haddock for cod in the above recipe. Steaks or fillets are equally suitable.

GOLDEN CRUMBED PLAICE

SERVES 4

450 g (1 lb) plaice fillets, skinned	50 g (2 oz) fresh brown breadcrumbs
dash of lemon juice	3 celery sticks, roughly chopped
bay leaf	25 g (1 oz) chopped walnuts
salt and pepper	30 ml (2 tbsp) chopped parsley
40 g (1½ oz) butter or margarine	parsley sprigs, to garnish

1 If necessary, divide each fish fillet in half, then roll up with the skinned side inside; secure with a cocktail stick.

2 Place the fish in a sauté pan, and add water to barely cover. Add the lemon juice, bay leaf and seasoning. Cover and simmer until tender, about 5 minutes.

3 Meanwhile melt the butter in a frying pan. Add the breadcrumbs and fry, stirring occasionally, until beginning to brown. Mix in the celery and walnuts and cook until the crumbs are golden. Stir in the parsley and seasoning.

4 Drain the fish on absorbent kitchen paper. Remove the cocktail sticks. Serve immediately, topped with the golden crumbs and garnished with parsley. Grilled tomatoes make an ideal accompaniment.

SWEET AND SOUR FISH

SERVES 4

4 cod fillets, each about 150 g (5 oz), skinned	15 ml (1 tbsp) vegetable oil
15 ml (1 tbsp) soy sauce	1 red pepper, seeded and sliced into strips
30 ml (2 tbsp) lemon juice	125 g (4 oz) spring onions, sliced
10 ml (2 tsp) white wine vinegar	125 g (4 oz) button mushrooms, halved or quartered
15 ml (1 tbsp) clear honey	
10 ml (2 tsp) tomato ketchup	125 g (4 oz) frozen green beans
1 clove garlic, crushed	
1.25 ml (¼ tsp) paprika	pepper

1 Divide each piece of fish in half. Roll up neatly with the skinned side inside.

2 Mix together the soy sauce, lemon juice, vinegar, honey, tomato ketchup, garlic and paprika. Place in a large sauté pan, add the fish and baste with the sauce. Bring to a very gentle simmer, cover and cook for 10-12 minutes, or until tender.

3 Meanwhile heat the oil in another sauté pan and stir-fry the vegetables over a high heat for 3-4 minutes until just tender. Season well with pepper.

4 Serve the fish with the sauce spooned over and accompanied by the stir-fried vegetables.

VARIATION

If you like fresh root ginger, grate a little into the pan as you stir-fry the vegetables.

PAN-FRIED SOLE WITH MARSALA

SERVES 4

8 sole quarter-cut fillets (two from each side of fish)	120 ml (8 tbsp) dry Marsala
plain flour, for coating	120 ml (8 tbsp) double cream
salt and pepper	chopped parsley and lemon wedges, to garnish
75 g (3 oz) butter	

1   Dip each of the eight sole fillets in the flour seasoned with salt and pepper. Coat both sides of the fish evenly, shaking off any excess.
2   Melt the butter in two large frying pans and fry the fish, all at once, for 2-3 minutes on each side until just cooked.
3   Sprinkle over the Marsala and cream, then add salt and pepper to taste. Shake the pans and let the sauce bubble for 2 minutes.
4   Serve immediately, garnished with chopped parsley, and lemon wedges.

SERVING SUGGESTION

Serve with new potatoes and mangetout or baby courgettes, and accompany with a chilled white wine.

MONKFISH WITH LIME AND PRAWNS

SERVES 4

550 g (1¼ lb) monkfish	150 ml (¼ pint) dry white wine
salt and pepper	finely grated rind and juice of 1 lime
15 ml (1 tbsp) plain wholemeal flour	pinch of raw cane sugar
30 ml (2 tbsp) vegetable oil	100 g (4 oz) cooked peeled prawns
1 small onion, chopped	lime slices, to garnish
1 garlic clove, chopped	
225 g (8 oz) tomatoes, skinned and chopped	

1   Using a sharp knife, skin the fish, if it is present then cut the fish into 2.5 cm (1 inch) chunks and toss in seasoned flour.
2   Heat the oil in a flameproof casserole and gently fry the onion and garlic for 5 minutes. Add the fish and fry until golden.
3   Stir in the tomatoes, wine, lime rind and juice, sugar, and salt and pepper to taste. Bring to the boil.
4   Cover and cook in the oven at 180°C (350°F) mark 4 for 15 minutes. Add the prawns and continue to cook for a further 15 minutes until the monkfish is tender. Garnish with lime slices and serve with rice, if liked.

SEAFOOD PILAKI

SERVES 8

30 ml (2 tbsp) olive oil	700 g (1½ lb) monkfish fillet, trimmed and cut into chunks
2 garlic cloves, crushed	
1 large onion, chopped	450 g (1 lb) cleaned squid, cut into rings
2 celery sticks, chopped	
3 large carrots, sliced	900 g (2 lb) mussels, cleaned
finely grated rind and juice of 1 lemon	30-45 ml (2-3 tbsp) chopped parsley
	salt and pepper
397 g (14 oz) can chopped tomatoes	chopped celery leaves, to garnish

1 Heat the oil in a large heavy-based pan. Add the garlic, onion, celery, carrots and lemon rind and cook for about 5 minutes, stirring all the time.

2 Add the lemon juice and the tomatoes with their juice, cover and cook on a low heat for about 25 minutes or until the vegetables are very tender. Stir occasionally and add a little water if the liquid is evaporating too rapidly.

3 Add the fish and squid and a little water. Re-cover and cook for 3-5 minutes. Arrange the mussels on the top, re-cover the pan and cook for about 5 minutes or until the fish is just tender, stirring occasionally. The mussels should have opened; discard any that remain shut. Stir in plenty of parsley and season to taste with salt and pepper. Serve hot or cold, garnished with torn celery leaves.

SEAFOOD STIR-FRY WITH BABY CORN

SERVES 4

2 celery sticks, trimmed	1 garlic clove, crushed
1 medium carrot, peeled	100 g (4 oz) cooked peeled prawns
350 g (12 oz) coley, haddock or cod fillet, skinned	
	425 g (15 oz) can whole baby corn cobs, drained
350 g (12 oz) Iceberg or Cos lettuce	salt and pepper
about 45 ml (3 tbsp) vegetable oil	

1 Slice the celery and carrot into thin matchsticks, 5 cm (2 inches) long. Cut the fish into 2.5 cm (1 inch) chunks.

2 Shred the lettuce finely with a sharp knife, discarding the core and any thick ribs.

3 Heat 15 ml (1 tbsp) of the oil in a wok or large frying pan until smoking. Add the lettuce and fry for about 30 seconds until lightly cooked. Transfer to a serving dish with a slotted spoon and keep warm.

4 Heat another 30 ml (2 tbsp) of oil in the pan until smoking. Add the celery, carrot, white fish and garlic and stir-fry over high heat for 2-3 minutes, adding more oil if necessary.

5 Lower the heat and add the prawns and baby corn. Toss well together for 2-3 minutes to heat through and coat all the ingredients in the sauce; the fish will flake apart.

6 Add salt and pepper to taste, spoon on top of the lettuce and serve immediately, with boiled rice if liked.

MIXED FISH STIR-FRY

SERVES 4

225 g (8 oz) monkfish fillet	1 small yellow pepper, seeded and finely sliced
225 g (8 oz) scallops, cleaned	1 medium onion, finely sliced
5 ml (1 tsp) flour	225 g (8 oz) tomatoes, skinned and cut into eighths
10 ml (2 tsp) ground coriander	125 g (4 oz) beansprouts
10 ml (2 tsp) ground cumin	75 ml (5 tbsp) dry white wine
30 ml (2 tbsp) vegetable oil	chopped coriander or parsley, to taste
1 small green pepper, seeded and finely sliced	salt and pepper

1 Slice the monkfish into thin strips and the scallops into thin rounds, removing their orange roe to cook separately. On a plate, mix the flour and spices together. Lightly coat all the fish in this mixture.

2 Heat 15 ml (1 tbsp) oil in each of two medium frying pans. Place the peppers and onion in one pan and stir-fry over a high heat until beginning to brown. Add the fish to the other pan and stir-fry for 2-3 minutes or until tender.

3 Add the tomatoes and bean sprouts to the vegetables and cook for 2-3 minutes or until the tomatoes begin to flop.

4 Stir the contents of both pans together. Mix in the wine with coriander and seasoning to taste and allow to bubble up. Serve with rice or noodles.

SPICED GRILLED MACKEREL

SERVES 4

4 mackerel, each about 275 g (10 oz), cleaned	5 ml (1 tsp) ground cumin
juice of 1 lemon	5 ml (1 tsp) chilli powder
60 ml (4 tbsp) chopped coriander	salt and pepper
10 ml (2 tsp) garam masala	30 ml (2 tbsp) vegetable oil
	lime wedges, to garnish

1 First bone the mackerel. With a sharp knife, cut of the heads just behind the gills. Extend the cut along the belly to both ends of the fish so that the fish can be opened out.

2 Place the fish on a board, skin side facing upwards. With the heel of your hand, press along the backbone to loosen it. Turn the fish over and lift out the backbone, using the tip of the knife if necessary to help pull the bone away from the flesh cleanly. Discard the bone.

3 Remove the tail and cut each fish in half lengthways, then wash under cold running water and pat dry. Score the skin side in several places with a knife.

4 Mix the lemon juice, half of the coriander, the garam masala, cumin, chilli powder and seasoning together.

5 Put the mackerel in a grill pan and pour over the marinade. Cover and leave at cool room temperature for 2 hours, turning once and brushing with the marinade.

6 When ready to cook, brush half the oil over the skin side of the mackerel. Cook under a preheated moderate grill for 5 minutes, then turn the fish over and brush with the remaining oil. Grill for a further 5 minutes.

7 Transfer the fish to a warmed serving platter and sprinkle with the remaining coriander. Serve immediately, garnished with lime wedges.

COOK'S TIP

Choose mackerel with rigid bodies and bright eyes and gills – indications of freshness. To save time, ask your fishmonger to bone the mackerel for you.

BOUILLABAISSE

SERVES 6

900 g (2 lb) fillets of mixed white fish and shellfish, eg whiting, conger eel, monkfish and prawns	2 garlic cloves, crushed
	1 bay leaf
60 ml (4 tbsp) olive oil	2.5 ml (½ tsp) dried thyme
2-3 onions, sliced	few parsley sprigs
1 celery stick, chopped	salt and pepper
225 g (8 oz) tomatoes	pinch of saffron strands
pared rind of 1 orange	cooked whole prawns, to garnish

1 Wash the fish and pat it dry with absorbent kitchen paper. Remove any skin, then cut the fish into fairly large, thick pieces.
2 Heat the oil in a large heavy-based saucepan and lightly fry the onions and celery for 5 minutes or until soft. Skin and slice the tomatoes.
3 Finely shred the orange rind, then stir half into the onion and celery with the garlic, herbs, salt and pepper. Infuse the saffron in a little hot water.
4 Put the fish into the pan with the vegetables. Add the saffron water, then pour in just enough cold water to cover the fish. Bring to the boil and simmer, uncovered, for 8 minutes.
5 Add the prawns and cook for a further 5-8 minutes. Serve garnished with the whole prawns and remaining orange rind.

COOK'S TIP

Saffron strands are the dried stigma of the autumn flowering crocus. Although they are very expensive to buy (saffron is the most expensive spice in the world), you should always use them in recipes like this one which calls for saffron water. They impart a superb delicate flavour.

SALMON KEDGEREE

SERVES 6

350 g (12 oz) salmon	salt and pepper
150 ml (¼ pint) dry white wine	350 g (12 oz) long grain rice
2 small onions, chopped	50 g (2 oz) butter
1 carrot, sliced	7.5 ml (1½ tsp) English mustard powder
1 celery stick, chopped	3 eggs, hard-boiled, shelled and quartered
15 ml (1 tbsp) lemon juice	cayenne pepper, to taste
6 peppercorns	celery leaves or parsley sprigs, to garnish
1 bouquet garni	

1 Put the salmon in a saucepan and pour in the wine and enough water to cover the fish. Add half of the chopped onions, the carrot, celery, lemon juice, peppercorns, bouquet garni and 5 ml (1 tsp) salt. Bring slowly to the boil, then remove from the heat. Cover tightly and cool.
2 Cook the rice in boiling salted water until tender.
3 Meanwhile, remove the salmon from the liquid and flake the flesh, discarding the skin and any bones. Strain the cooking liquid and reserve.
4 Melt half the butter in a large frying pan, add the remaining onion and fry gently for about 5 minutes or until soft. Drain the rice thoroughly, then add to the onion with the remaining butter. Toss to coat and stir in the mustard.
5 Add the flaked salmon and the hard-boiled eggs and a few spoonfuls of the strained cooking liquid to moisten. Heat through. Shake the pan and toss the ingredients gently so that the salmon and eggs do not break up.
6 Transfer to a warmed serving dish and sprinkle with cayenne to taste. Garnish with celery leaves or parsley sprigs and serve immediately.

FISH IN SPICY SAUCE WITH TOMATOES

SERVES 4

700 g (1½ lb) white fish (cod, halibut or haddock), skinned and filleted	5 ml (1 tsp) ground turmeric
60 ml (4 tbsp) ghee or vegetable oil	1.25 ml (¼ tsp) chilli powder
	5 ml (1 tsp) salt
7.5 ml (1½ tsp) coriander seeds	4 tomatoes, skinned and roughly chopped
5 ml (1 tsp) black peppercorns	2.5 ml (½ tsp) garam masala
1 garlic clove, crushed	chopped coriander and lime slices, to garnish

1 Wash the fish under cold running water and pat dry with absorbent kitchen paper. Cut into 2.5 cm (1 inch) cubes.
2 Heat the ghee or oil in a heavy-based frying pan. Add the fish, a few pieces at a time, and fry gently for 2-3 minutes. Remove the fish carefully from the pan with a slotted spoon and set aside on a plate.
3 Put the coriander seeds, peppercorns and garlic in a small electric mill or pestle and mortar and grind to a smooth paste.
4 Add the spice paste to the frying pan with the turmeric, chilli powder and salt, and fry gently for 2 minutes.
5 Stir in the tomatoes and 300 ml (½ pint) water. Bring, to the boil, then lower the heat and cook over a medium heat for 5 minutes. Add the fish and simmer, shaking the pan occasionally, for a further 10 minutes or until the fish is tender; do not stir. Remove from the heat.
6 Sprinkle the garam masala over the fish, cover the pan and let the fish stand for 2 minutes, then turn into a warmed serving dish. Garnish with chopped coriander and lime slices. Serve immediately.

INDONESIAN FISH CURRY

SERVES 4

1 small onion, chopped	700 g (1½ lb) haddock fillets, skinned and cut into bite-sized pieces
1 garlic clove, chopped	
2.5 cm (1 inch) piece fresh root ginger, chopped	225 g (8 oz) cooked peeled prawns
5 ml (1 tsp) turmeric	300 ml (½ pint) coconut milk
2. 5 ml (½ tsp) laos powder	juice of 1 lime
1.25 ml (¼ tsp) chilli powder	shredded coconut and lime wedges, to garnish
30 ml (2 tbsp) vegetable oil	
salt	

1 Put the onion, garlic, ginger, turmeric, laos powder, chilli powder and oil in a blender or food processor with 2.5 ml (½ tsp) salt and blend to a paste.
2 Transfer the mixture to a flameproof casserole and fry gently, stirring, for 5 minutes. Add the haddock pieces and prawns and fry for a few minutes more, tossing the fish to coat with the spice mixture.
3 Pour in the coconut milk, shake the pan and turn the fish gently in the liquid. (Take care not to break up the pieces of fish.) Bring slowly to the boil, then lower the heat, cover and simmer for 10 minutes or until tender.
4 Add the lime juice, taste and adjust the seasoning, then transfer to a warmed serving dish and sprinkle with coconut. Serve hot, garnished with lime wedges.

COOK'S TIP

Loas powder is used extensively in the cooking of South-East Asia. It comes from a root rather like ginger and has a peppery hot taste.
To make 300 ml (½ pint) coconut milk, break 100 g (4 oz) block creamed coconut into a jug and pour in 300 ml (½ pint) boiling water. Stir, then strain.

SEAFOOD CURRY

SERVES 4

45 ml (3 tbsp) vegetable oil	1 green chilli, seeded and finely chopped
2 onions, sliced into rings	150 ml (¼ pint) white wine
25 g (1 oz) desiccated coconut	25 g (1 oz) salted peanuts
15 ml (1 tbsp) plain flour	125 g (4 oz) frozen cooked peeled prawns, thawed and thoroughly drained
5 ml (1 tsp) ground coriander	salt and pepper
450 g (1 lb) haddock fillet, skinned and cut into chunks	coriander sprigs and shredded coconut, toasted, to garnish

1 Heat the oil in a large sauté pan, add the onion rings and fry until lightly browned.

2 Mix the coconut, flour and coriander together and toss with the haddock and chopped chilli. Add to the pan and fry gently for 5-10 minutes until golden, stirring.

3 Pour in the wine, bring to the boil and add the peanuts, prawns and seasoning. Cover tightly and simmer for 5-10 minutes or until the fish is tender. Serve immediately, garnished with coriander and coconut.

SCALLOPS IN CREAMY BASIL SAUCE

SERVES 4

900 g (2 lb) shelled scallops, thawed if frozen	150 ml (¼ pint) dry white wine
30 ml (2 tbsp) vegetable oil	20 ml (4 tsp) chopped basil
15 g (½ oz) butter	salt and pepper
1 small onion, finely chopped	150 ml (5 fl oz) double cream
2 garlic cloves, crushed	few basil sprigs, to garnish

1 Cut the scallops, including the coral, into fairly thick slices. Pat dry with absorbent kitchen paper and set aside.

2 Heat the oil and butter in a large frying pan, add the onion and garlic, and fry gently for 5 minutes or until soft and lightly coloured.

3 Add the scallops to the pan and toss to coat in the oil and butter. Stir in the wine and basil and season to taste.

4 Fry the scallops over a moderate heat for 5 minutes or until they are tender, turning them constantly so that they cook evenly on all sides. Do not overcook or they will become tough and rubbery.

5 Remove the scallops from the liquid with a slotted spoon and set aside on a plate. Boil the liquid until reduced by about half, then stir in the cream, a little at a time, and simmer until the sauce is thick.

6 Return the scallops to the pan and heat gently. Taste and adjust the seasoning and serve garnished with basil.

VARIATION

Scallops in Ginger Sauce

Replace the basil with a good pinch of powdered saffron. Add 15 ml (1 tbsp) finely chopped stem ginger to the pan with the scallops.

PRAWNS
IN COCONUT MILK

SERVES 4

700 g (1½ lb) medium raw prawns in the shell, or 900 g (2 lb) large frozen cooked prawns, thawed	45 ml (3 tbsp) ghee or vegetable oil
10 ml (2 tsp) wine vinegar	15 ml (1 tbsp) coriander seeds
5 ml (1 tsp) salt	10 ml (2 tsp) cumin seeds
2.5 cm (1 inch) piece fresh root ginger, peeled and finely chopped	5 ml (1 tsp) turmeric
	2.5 ml (½ tsp) chilli powder
2 garlic cloves, crushed	300 ml (½ pint) thick coconut milk
2 onions, roughly chopped	chopped coriander and sliced green chillies, to garnish

1 If using raw prawns, remove the shells, leaving on the tail. With the point of a sharp knife, cut down the back of each prawn and remove the dark vein. If using cooked prawns, remove the whole shell and de-vein.
2 Rinse the prawns and drain well. Place in a bowl with the vinegar and salt and leave to marinate for 30 minutes.
3 Place the ginger, garlic and onions in a blender or food processor and work to a smooth paste, adding a little water if the mixture sticks. Set aside.
4 Heat half of the ghee in a heavy-based frying pan and add the prawns, reserving the marinade. Toss raw prawns for 3-5 minutes until just turning pink; toss cooked prawns for 1-2 minutes only. Remove the prawns with a slotted spoon; replace in the marinade.
5 Heat the remaining ghee in the same pan and add the onion paste. Fry gently for 5 minutes until just turning golden brown. Stir in the coriander, cumin, turmeric and chilli powder and fry, stirring constantly, for 1 minute.
6 Add the prawns and marinade and stir well to coat, then pour in the coconut milk and mix well. Bring to the boil, then lower the heat and simmer for 5 minutes.
7 Turn into a warmed serving dish and garnish with the chopped coriander and chilli. Serve immediately.

PRAWNS
FRIED IN GARLIC

SERVES 2

50 g (2 oz) butter	60 ml (4 tbsp) brandy
30 ml (2 tbsp) olive oil	salt and pepper
12 raw jumbo prawns in the shell	lemon wedges and shredded lettuce, to serve
3 garlic cloves, crushed	

1 Melt the butter with the oil in a large heavy-based pan. Add the prawns and garlic and fry over high heat for 5 minutes, tossing the prawns constantly.
2 Sprinkle the brandy over the prawns with salt and pepper to taste. Serve immediately, garnished with lemon wedges and lettuce.

COOK'S TIP

In Italy the giant scampi used for this dish are caught in Mediterranean waters and are relatively easy to come by. The nearest equivalent in size is the Dublin Bay prawn, which is available at specialist fishmongers, but it is expensive. You can use smaller prawns if you wish, but the dish will lose its spectacular looks!
If your pan is not large enough to hold all of the prawns, cook them in two batches.

LEMON CHICKEN KEBABS

SERVES 4

4 boneless chicken thighs, about 450 g (1 lb) total weight	2 cloves garlic, crushed
	salt and pepper
50 g (2 oz) butter, melted	125 g (4 oz) cherry tomatoes
45 ml (3 tbsp) lemon juice	125 g (4 oz) onion, cut into large pieces
15 ml (1 tbsp) soft brown sugar	125 g (4 oz) courgettes, thickly sliced

1 Cut the chicken into 2 cm (¾ inch) cubes. Thread onto 4 wooden skewers and place in a foil-lined grill pan.

2 Whisk together the butter, lemon juice, sugar and garlic; season with a little salt and plenty of black pepper. Brush the sauce over the chicken.

3 Cook under a preheated high grill for about 8 minutes each side or until lightly browned and cooked through, basting occasionally.

4 Meanwhile, thread the vegetables onto 4 wooden skewers. Add to the grill pan for the last 5-6 minutes of the cooking time, basting with the lemon butter and turning occasionally until cooked through. Serve the chicken and vegetable kebabs with rice.

COOK'S TIP

Instead of plain rice, try a mixture of long grain and wild rice, flavoured with toasted pine nuts and grated lemon rind.

SPICED CHICKEN WITH GRAPES

SERVES 4

30 ml (2 tbsp) vegetable oil	pinch of turmeric
8 chicken thighs, about 800 g (1¾ lb) total weight	150 ml (¼ pint) chicken stock
175 g (6 oz) onion, chopped	salt and pepper
1 clove garlic, crushed	125 g (4 oz) seedless green grapes, halved
5 ml (1 tsp) ground coriander	150 ml (5 fl oz) natural yogurt
5 ml (1 tsp) ground cumin	

1 Heat the oil in a large sauté pan and brown the chicken on all sides. Remove with a slotted spoon and drain on absorbent kitchen paper.

2 Lower the heat and add the onion, garlic and spices to the pan. Cook for 2-3 minutes, stirring frequently.

3 Replace the chicken in the pan, add the stock and seasoning. Bring to the boil, cover and simmer gently for 20-25 minutes or until the chicken is cooked through.

4 Stir the grapes into the chicken juices with the yogurt. Heat gently and adjust the seasoning before serving with rice and spinach.

VARIATION

If you prefer, stir in two thinly sliced crisp apples, instead of the grapes at stage 4.

CHICKEN WITH SPICY YOGURT SAUCE

SERVES 4

4 large boneless chicken breasts	seeds of 3 green cardamoms, crushed
90 ml (6 tbsp) natural yogurt	salt
juice of 1 lime or lemon	30 ml (2 tbsp) ghee or vegetable oil
2 garlic cloves, crushed	2.5 ml (½ tsp) garam masala
2.5 ml (½ tsp) turmeric	30 ml (2 tbsp) chopped coriander
15 ml (1 tbsp) paprika	

1 Skin the chicken breasts and cut the flesh into strips about 1 cm (½ inch) wide. Put the chicken strips into a bowl with the yogurt, lime or lemon juice, garlic, turmeric, paprika, cardamom seeds and salt to taste. Mix well to coat.

2 Cover and leave to marinate in the refrigerator for at least 2 hours.

3 Heat the ghee or oil in a heavy frying pan or wok. Add the chicken and marinade and stir-fry for 10 minutes.

4 Lower the heat and add the garam masala and coriander. Stir-fry for a further 5-10 minutes until the chicken is tender. Transfer to a warmed serving dish and serve immediately, with lime wedges. Accompany the chicken with rice if liked.

CHICKEN WITH SPICY TOMATO SAUCE

SERVES 4

15 g (½ oz) butter or margarine	large pinch of chilli powder
15 ml (1 tbsp) vegetable oil	8 chicken thighs
1 medium onion, chopped	397 g (14 oz) can tomatoes
1 garlic clove, crushed	15 ml (1 tbsp) tomato purée
5 ml (1 tsp) ground cumin	salt and pepper
5 ml (1 tsp) ground coriander	30 ml (2 tbsp) chopped parsley

1 Heat the butter and oil in a large frying pan, add the onion and garlic, cover and cook for 4-5 minutes or until the onion is softened. Add the cumin, coriander and chilli powder and cook for 1 minute, stirring continously.

2 Push the onion to one side of the pan, then add the chicken and brown on both sides. Stir in the tomatoes and the tomato purée and season to taste.

3 Bring to the boil, stirring continuously. Cover and simmer gently for about 30 minutes or until the chicken is tender. Stir in the parsley and serve immediately.

COOK'S TIP

Meaty little chicken thighs make a good, inexpensive midweek meal. The tasty tomato sauce is well spiced with cumin and coriander, and a pinch of chilli powder adds a pleasant heat without being fiery.

SPICY CHICKEN
WITH CASHEWS

SERVES 4

25 g (1 oz) piece fresh root ginger, peeled and sliced	2 bay leaves
4 cloves garlic, or 10 ml (2 tsp) garlic paste	10 ml (2 tsp) ground cumin
50 g (2 oz) unsalted cashew nuts	small pinch of cayenne pepper
150 g (5 oz) natural yogurt	200 ml (7 fl oz) chicken stock
30 ml (2 tbsp) vegetable oil	salt and pepper
700 g (1½ lb) chicken thighs, skinned	30 ml (2 tsp) chopped coriander or parsley
125 g (4 oz) onion, chopped	coriander or parsley sprigs, to garnish

1 Put the ginger, garlic, nuts, and 30 ml (2 tbsp) yogurt in a food processor or blender and work to a rough paste.

2 Heat the oil in a large shallow flameproof casserole and brown the chicken evenly on all sides; remove from the pan with a slotted spoon.

3 Add the onion to the casserole with the nut paste, bay leaves and spices and cook, stirring, for 1-2 minutes. Pour in the remaining yogurt, stock and seasoning. Bring to the boil.

4 Replace the chicken in the casserole, cover and simmer, stirring occasionally, for 25-30 minutes, or until the chicken is quite tender.

5 Stir in the chopped coriander and adjust the seasoning. Garnish with sprigs of coriander or parsley and serve with rice and fine green beans.

BAKED CHICKEN
FILLETS WITH PESTO

SERVES 4

4 skinless chicken breast fillets, about 450 g (1 lb) total weight	30 ml (2 tbsp) pesto sauce
	salt and pepper
125 g (4 oz) low-fat soft cheese	4 thin slices of ham
	shredded basil leaves, to garnish

1 Make a deep cut horizontally in each chicken fillet to form a pocket.

2 Mix together the soft cheese and pesto; season with salt and pepper to taste. Spoon most of the mixture into the chicken 'pockets'. Wrap each fillet in a thin slice of ham.

3 Place the chicken fillets on individual pieces of foil, spoon over the remaining cheese mixture and fold each piece of foil to make a parcel.

4 Place on a baking sheet and cook in the oven at 200°C (400°F) mark 6 for 25-30 minutes or until the chicken is tender.

5 Serve garnished with shredded basil, and accompanied by baked potatoes and a mixed side salad.

CHICKEN WITH PARMA HAM AND CHEESE

SERVES 4

4 boneless chicken breasts, skinned	salt and pepper
4 slices of Parma ham or other prosciutto	30 ml (2 tbsp) olive oil
15 ml (1 tbsp) plain flour	25 g (1 oz) butter
5 ml (1 tsp) dried mixed herbs	100 g (4 oz) fontina cheese, grated
	150 ml (¼ pint) dry white or rosé wine

1 Put the chicken breasts between two sheets of grease-proof paper and flatten with a meat mallet or rolling pin.
2 Trim the slices of Parma ham to about the same size as the chicken breasts.
3 Put the flour and herbs on a large flat plate, add a liberal sprinkling of salt and pepper and stir well to mix. Coat the chicken pieces on both sides with the flour mixture.
4 Heat the oil with the butter in a large heavy-based frying pan. Add the chicken pieces and fry over moderate heat for 10 minutes, turning once.
5 Place one slice of ham on top of each chicken breast, then sprinkle the cheese over the top to cover the ham completely.
6 Pour the wine around the chicken and bring to boiling point. Cover the pan tightly, lower the heat to simmering and cook for a further 5 minutes until the cheese has melted. Transfer to warmed serving plates and pour the pan juices over the chicken. Serve immediately.

CHICKEN WITH SAFFRON

SERVES 6

salt and pepper	30 ml (2 tbsp) dry white wine
30 ml (2 tbsp) plain flour	large pinch of saffron strands
6 chicken breast fillets, each about 175 g (6 oz), skinned	2 egg yolks
40 g (1½ oz) butter	60 ml (4 tbsp) single cream
200 ml (7 fl oz) chicken stock	vegetable julienne, to garnish

1 Season the flour, add the chicken and turn until coated. Shake off and reserve any excess flour.
2 Melt the butter in a medium flameproof casserole, add the chicken pieces, half at a time, and fry for 5-10 minutes or until golden brown.
3 Return all the chicken pieces to the pan with any remaining flour and pour in the chicken stock and white wine.
4 Sprinkle in the saffron, pushing it down under the liquid. Bring to the boil, cover tightly and cook in the oven at 180°C (350°F) mark 4 for about 50 minutes or until cooked.
5 Lift the chicken out of the juices and place in a warmed serving dish. Cover and keep warm.
6 Strain the cooking juices into a small saucepan. Mix the egg yolks and cream together and stir into the cooking juices until evenly mixed.
7 Cook gently, stirring all the time, until the juices thicken slightly. Do not boil. To serve, adjust the seasoning of the sauce, spoon over the chicken and garnish with vegetable julienne. Serve immediately.

CHICKEN AND AVOCADO STROGANOFF

SERVES 4

4 chicken legs, about 800 g (1¾ lb) total weight	10 ml (2 tsp) wholegrain mustard
30 ml (2 tbsp) vegetable oil	salt and pepper
150 g (5 oz) small button mushrooms	1 avocado (ripe but firm)
150 ml (¼ pint) chicken stock	150 ml (5 fl oz) Greek-style natural yogurt
	parsley sprigs, to garnish

1 Separate the chicken legs into thighs and drumsticks.

2 Heat the oil in a large sauté pan and cook the chicken, turning, until deep golden on both sides. Lift out with a slotted spoon and drain on absorbent kitchen paper.

3 Lower the heat, add the mushrooms to the pan and cook, stirring, for 2-3 minutes. Add the stock, mustard and seasoning.

4 Replace the chicken in the pan, bring to the boil, then cover and simmer for about 30-35 minutes or until the chicken is cooked.

5 Peel the avocado, halve, stone and cut into chunks. Stir into the chicken juices with the yogurt. Increase the heat and allow to bubble for 2-3 minutes to reduce the liquid. Adjust the seasoning.

6 Serve immediately, garnished with parsley and accompanied by rice and steamed green beans.

SESAME CHICKEN STIR-FRY

SERVES 4

4 skinless chicken breast fillets, about 450 g (1 lb) total weight	200 ml (7 fl oz) orange juice
225 g (8 oz) broccoli	salt and pepper
225 g (8 oz) baby corn cobs	30 ml (2 tbsp) toasted sesame seeds
60 ml (4 tbsp) sesame oil	50 g (2 oz) unsalted peanuts in skins
30 ml (2 tbsp) soy sauce	

1 Cut the chicken into thin strips. Divide the broccoli into small florets and cut each baby corn into two or three pieces.

2 Heat the sesame oil in a large frying pan or wok. Add the chicken and stir-fry over a high heat for 5-6 minutes, until browned.

3 Stir in the broccoli and baby corn. Cook, stirring, for a further 1-2 minutes.

4 Pour over the soy sauce and orange juice and allow the juices to bubble for about 3-4 minutes. Adjust the seasoning.

5 Stir in the toasted sesame seeds and peanuts, and serve with the egg noodles.

CHICKEN WITH TARRAGON SAUCE

SERVES 6

75 g (3 oz) butter or margarine	5 ml (1 tsp) chopped fresh tarragon or 2.5 ml (½ tsp) dried
6 chicken breast fillets, skinned	45 ml (3 tbsp) grated Parmesan cheese
25 g (1 oz) plain flour	salt and pepper
450 ml (¾ pint) chicken stock	150 ml (5 fl oz) single cream
30 ml (2 tbsp) tarragon vinegar	tarragon sprigs, to garnish
10 ml (2 tsp) French mustard	

1 Melt 50 g (2 oz) butter in a frying pan, add the chicken, cover and cook gently for about 20 minutes or until tender, turning once. Drain.

2 Meanwhile, melt the remaining butter in a saucepan, stir in the flour and gradually add the stock and vinegar. Stir in the mustard, tarragon and cheese, then bring to the boil. Season to taste and simmer for 3 minutes.

3 Remove from the heat and add the cream. Heat gently without boiling. To serve, place the chicken on a warmed serving dish and spoon over the sauce. Garnish with tarragon sprigs.

FRENCH-STYLE ROAST CHICKEN

SERVES 3-4

1-1.4 kg (2¼-3 lb) oven-ready chicken	100 g (4 oz) butter, softened
	salt and pepper
5-6 sprigs tarragon or parsley or 5 ml (1 tsp) dried tarragon or parsley	150 ml (¼ pint) chicken stock
	watercress sprigs, to garnish

1 Wipe the inside of the chicken, then put the tarragon or parsley inside it, with 15 g (½ oz) of the butter and some pepper.

2 Place on one side in a roasting tin, smear all over with one third of the remaining butter and roast in the oven at 220°C (425°F) mark 7 for 15 minutes.

3 Turn the chicken onto the other side, smear with half the remaining butter and return to the oven. Roast for another 15 minutes.

4 Turn the chicken breast side up, smear with the rest of the butter, return to the oven and roast at 190°C (375°F) mark 5 for 20-30 minutes, or until tender.

5 Place the chicken on a serving dish and keep warm while making the gravy.

6 To make the gravy, place the roasting tin on top of the cooker and scrape any sediment sticking to the bottom. Add the stock and bring to the boil, then simmer for 2-3 minutes, stirring. Add seasoning to taste and pour into a warmed gravy boat. Garnish the chicken with watercress and serve immediately, with the gravy handed separately.

COOK'S TIP

The French have a unique way of cooking chicken which gives a wonderfully moist and succulent flesh. The secret lies in smearing the bird with plenty of butter and turning it over at regular intervals during roasting. Tarragon has a natural affinity with chicken, and is the most popular herb to cook with it in France, so try to use it if you want an authentic 'French' flavour – it grows very easily in the garden in summer.

QUICK CHICKEN AND MUSSEL PAELLA

SERVES 4-6

60 ml (4 tbsp) olive oil	1.2 litres (2¼ pints) boiling chicken stock
about 450 g (1 lb) boneless chicken meat, skinned and cut into bite-sized cubes	5 ml (1 tsp) paprika
1 onion, chopped	2.5 ml (½ tsp) powdered saffron
2 garlic cloves, crushed	salt and pepper
1 large red pepper, sliced into thin strips	two 150 g (5 oz) jars mussels, drained
3 tomatoes, skinned and chopped	lemon wedges, cooked peeled prawns and mussels (optional), to garnish
400 g (14 oz) Valencia or risotto rice	

1 Heat the oil in a large deep frying pan, add the cubes of chicken and fry over a moderate heat until golden brown on all sides. Remove from the pan and set aside.

2 Add the onion, garlic and red pepper to the oil remaining in the pan and fry gently for 5 minutes or until softened. Add the tomatoes and fry for a few more minutes or until the juices run, then add the rice and stir to combine.

3 Pour in 1 litre (1¾ pints) of the boiling stock, allow to bubble vigorously, then add half the paprika and the saffron powder. Season to taste. Stir well and add the chicken.

4 Simmer, uncovered, for 30 minutes or until the chicken is cooked through, stirring frequently during this time to prevent the rice from sticking. When the mixture becomes dry, stir in a few more tablespoons of boiling stock. Repeat as often as necessary to keep the paella moist.

5 To serve, fold in the mussels and heat through. Taste and adjust the seasoning, then garnish with lemon wedges, prawns, mussels if using, and a sprinkling of paprika.

CARIBBEAN CHICKEN

SERVES 4

4 boneless chicken breasts, skinned	salt and pepper
425 g (15 oz) can pineapple slices in natural juice	45 ml (3 tbsp) vegetable oil
15 ml (1 tbsp) vinegar	175 g (6 oz) long grain rice
10 ml (2 tsp) soft brown sugar	1½ green, red or yellow peppers, seeded and sliced
	Tabasco sauce, to taste
	60 ml (4 tbsp) dark rum

1 Cut the chicken into bite-sized pieces and place in a bowl. Drain the pineapple, reserving the juice. Mix together the vinegar, pineapple juice, sugar, 10 ml (2 tsp) salt, and pepper to taste. Pour over the chicken, cover and leave to marinate for 1-2 hours, turning the chicken occasionally.

2 Drain the chicken and reserve the marinade. Make the marinade up to 600 ml (1 pint) with water and set aside.

3 Heat the oil in a flameproof casserole, add the chicken and fry over moderate heat until turning colour on all sides. Add the rice and most of the pepper slices and fry for 5 minutes, stirring.

4 Pour in the marinade and bring slowly to the boil. Stir once, then shake in Tabasco sauce to taste and lower the heat. Cover and simmer for 20 minutes or until the chicken and rice are tender and most of the liquid has been absorbed.

5 Chop the pineapple and add to the casserole with the rum. Fold in gently and heat through. Adjust seasoning before serving. Garnish with the remaining pepper slices.

CHICKEN WITH NUTS AND MUSHROOMS

SERVES 4

4 chicken breast fillets, skinned and cut into thin strips	5 ml (1 tsp) five spice powder
5 cm (2 inch) piece fresh root ginger, peeled and thinly sliced	45 ml (3 tbsp) vegetable oil
	125 g (4 oz) mushrooms, halved
45 ml (3 tbsp) soy sauce	¼ cucumber, cut into chunks
60 ml (4 tbsp) dry sherry	75 g (3 oz) walnut pieces, roughly chopped
	pepper

1 Put the chicken in a bowl with the ginger, soy sauce, sherry and five spice powder. Stir well, cover and leave to marinate for at least 1 hour.

2 Remove the chicken from the marinade with a slotted spoon, reserving the marinade.

3 Heat the oil in a large frying pan or wok. Add the chicken and cook for 3-4 minutes, stirring continuously.

4 Add the mushrooms, cucumber and walnuts and continue to cook for 1-2 minutes, until the chicken is cooked and the vegetables are tender but still crisp.

5 Stir in the reserved marinade and cook for 1 minute, until hot. Season to taste with pepper. Serve immediately, with rice or noodles.

VARIATION

Replace the walnut pieces with cashew nuts and sprinkle with a little sesame oil before serving.

CHICKEN TERIYAKI

SERVES 4

4 boneless chicken breasts, skinned	2 garlic cloves, crushed
90 ml (6 tbsp) soy sauce, preferably shoyu	2.5 cm (1 inch) piece fresh root ginger, peeled and crushed
90 ml (6 tbsp) sake or dry sherry	salt and pepper
25 g (1 oz) sugar	15-30 ml (1-2 tbsp) vegetable oil

1 Cut the chicken breasts into bite-size pieces. Place the pieces in a shallow bowl.

2 Mix together half the soy sauce, sake and sugar, then add half the garlic and ginger, with salt and pepper to taste. Pour over the chicken, cover and leave to marinate for at least 1 hour, turning the chicken pieces occasionally.

3 Thread the cubes of chicken on to oiled kebab skewers. Brush with oil and grill under moderate heat for about 10 minutes until the chicken is tender; baste with the marinade and turn frequently during cooking.

4 While the chicken is cooking, put the remaining soy sauce, sake and sugar in a small pan with the remaining garlic and ginger. Add salt and pepper to taste and heat through.

5 Spoon the warmed soy sauce mixture over the chicken and serve with rice.

SERVING SUGGESTION

Spicy and sweet, this Japanese skewered chicken looks good on a bed of saffron rice. For an exotic touch, follow with a mixed salad of oriental vegetables such as beansprouts, bamboo shoots, spring onions and fresh root ginger.

STIR-FRIED CHICKEN WITH VEGETABLES

SERVES 4

4 skinned chicken breast fillets	175 g (6 oz) button mushrooms, finely sliced
30 ml (2 tbsp) vegetable oil	10 ml (2 tsp) cornflour
1 bunch of spring onions, trimmed and finely sliced	30 ml (2 tbsp) dry sherry
3 celery sticks, finely sliced	15 ml (1 tbsp) soy sauce
1 green pepper, seeded and cut into thin strips	15 ml (1 tbsp) hoisin sauce
100 g (4 oz) cauliflower florets, divided into tiny sprigs	5 ml (1 tsp) soft brown sugar
	50 g (2 oz) cashew nuts
2 carrots, grated	salt and pepper
	celery leaves, to garnish

1 With a sharp knife, cut the chicken into bite-sized strips, about 4 cm (1½ inches) long.

2 Heat the oil in a wok or deep frying pan, add all the prepared vegetables and stir-fry over a brisk heat for 3 minutes. Remove the vegetables with a slotted spoon and set aside.

3 In a jug, mix the cornflour to a paste with the sherry, soy sauce and hoisin sauce, then add the sugar and 150 ml (¼ pint) water.

4 Add the chicken strips to the pan and stir-fry over a moderate heat until lightly coloured on all sides. Pour the cornflour mixture into the pan and bring to the boil, stirring constantly, until thickened.

5 Return the vegetables to the pan. Add the cashew nuts and salt and pepper to taste, and stir-fry for a few minutes more. Serve immediately, garnished with celery leaves.

STIR-FRIED CHICKEN WITH COURGETTES

SERVES 4

30 ml (2 tbsp) vegetable oil	1 red pepper, seeded and cut into thin strips
1 garlic clove, crushed	45 ml (3 tbsp) dry sherry
450 g (1 lb) chicken breast fillets, skinned and cut into thin strips	15 ml (1 tbsp) soy sauce
	60 ml (4 tbsp) natural yogurt
450 g (1 lb) courgettes, cut into thin strips	pepper

1 Heat the oil in a large frying pan or a wok and fry the garlic for 1 minute. Add the chicken and cook for 3-4 minutes, stirring continuously.

2 Add the courgettes and pepper and continue to cook for 1-2 minutes, until the chicken is cooked and the vegetables are tender but still crisp.

3 Stir in the sherry and soy sauce and cook for 1 minute, until hot. Stir in the yogurt and season to taste with pepper. Serve immediately, with boiled rice or noodles.

VARIATION

This colourful stir-fry can be varied according to the vegetables in season. In winter, try substituting the courgettes with a mixture of sliced leeks and broccoli, divided into tiny florets.

TURKEY FRICASSEE

SERVES 4

65 g (2½ oz) butter or margarine	15 ml (1 tbsp) lemon juice
175 g (6 oz) button mushrooms, thinly sliced	700 g (1½ lb) cooked turkey, cut into bite-size pieces
50 g (2 oz) flour	salt and pepper
600 ml (1 pint) chicken or turkey stock	45 ml (3 tbsp) double cream
	lemon slices dipped in chopped parsley, to garnish

1 Melt 15 g (½ oz) butter in a frying pan and sauté the mushrooms for 5 minutes until they are soft. Remove and set aside.

2 Melt the remaining butter in a saucepan. Add the flour and cook, stirring, for 2 minutes. Remove from the heat and gradually stir in the stock. Bring to the boil and cook for about 5 minutes, stirring until the sauce thickens.

3 Add the lemon juice to the sauce with the turkey, mushrooms and seasoning. Heat gently, then stir in the cream. Serve hot, garnished with the lemon slices.

VARIATION

Sauté 1 red or green pepper, seeded and thinly sliced, with the sliced mushrooms. Chicken can be used instead of turkey.

TURKEY MOLE

SERVES 4

50 g (2 oz) butter	pinch of ground cloves
15ml (1 tbsp) vegetable oil	pinch of ground cinnamon
4 turkey escalopes	1.25 ml (¼ tsp) coriander seeds
salt and pepper	
450 ml (¾ pint) chicken stock	50 g (2 oz) plain chocolate, grated
1 green pepper, seeded and chopped	45 ml (3 tbsp) ground almonds
2.5 ml (½ tsp) aniseed	2.5 ml (½ tsp) chilli powder
15 ml (1 tbsp) sesame seeds	3 tomatoes, skinned
2 garlic cloves, crushed	

1 Heat the butter and oil in a frying pan and fry the turkey escalopes for 2-3 minutes until browned on all sides. Drain on absorbent kitchen paper, then place in an ovenproof casserole.

2 Place all the remaining ingredients in a blender or food processor and purée until smooth.

3 Pour the blended sauce over the turkey. Cover and bake in the oven at 180°C (350°F) mark 4 for 20 minutes until the turkey is tender.

COOK'S TIP

Don't be put off by the inclusion of chocolate in this recipe. It adds a delicious richness to the sauce.

TURKEY ESCALOPES WITH DAMSONS

SERVES 4

two 225 g (8 oz) turkey breast fillets, skinned and cut widthways into 5 cm (2 inch) slices	5 ml (1 tsp) chopped fresh thyme or 1.25 ml (½ tsp) dried
75 ml (5 tbsp) unsweetened apple juice	15 g (½ oz) butter or margarine
45 ml (3 tbsp) soy sauce	15 ml (1 tbsp) vegetable oil
45 ml (3 tbsp) dry sherry	225 g (8 oz) damsons, halved and stoned
1 small garlic clove, crushed	pepper

1 Place the turkey slices between two sheets of dampened greaseproof paper and beat out with a rolling pin or meat mallet until about 2.5 cm (1 inch) thick.
2 Place the turkey slices in a large shallow dish and pour over the apple juice, soy sauce, sherry, garlic and thyme. Cover and leave in the refrigerator to marinate for 3-4 hours if possible, or overnight.
3 Remove the turkey from the marinade, reserving the marinade. Heat the butter and oil in a frying pan, add the turkey and fry quickly until browned on both sides. Add the damsons, reserved marinade and pepper to taste.
4 Cover and simmer gently for 10-15 minutes or until tender, stirring occasionally. Serve immediately.

COOK'S TIP

If damsons are not available, substitute plums.

TURKEY SAUTE WITH LEMON AND WALNUTS

SERVES 4

450 g (1 lb) turkey breast fillets, skinned	30 ml (2 tbsp) lemon juice
30 ml (2 tbsp) cornflour	45 ml (3 tbsp) lemon marmalade
45 ml (3 tbsp) vegetable oil	5 ml (1 tsp) white wine vinegar
1 green pepper, seeded and thinly sliced	1.25 ml (¼ tsp) soy sauce
40 g (1½ oz) walnut halves or pieces	salt and pepper
60 ml (4 tbsp) chicken stock	lemon wedges and parsley sprigs, to garnish

1 Cut the turkey flesh into 5 cm (2 inch) pencil-thin strips. Add to the cornflour and toss until coated.
2 Heat half the oil in a large sauté or deep frying pan, add the pepper strips and walnuts and fry for 2-3 minutes. Remove from the pan with a slotted spoon.
3 Add the remaining oil to the pan and fry the turkey strips for 10 minutes or until golden. Add the stock and lemon juice, stirring well to scrape up any sediment at the bottom of the pan. Add the lemon marmalade, vinegar and soy sauce. Season to taste.
4 Return the walnuts and green pepper to the pan. Cook gently for a further 5 minutes or until the turkey is tender. Taste and adjust the seasoning and serve immediately, garnished with lemon wedges and pasley.

VARIATION

Turkey Sauté with Orange and Pine Nuts
Substitute 30 ml (2 tbsp) orange juice and 45 ml (3 tbsp) orange marmalade for the lemon juice and marmalade in the above recipe. Replace the walnuts with pine nuts. Garnish with thin slices or wedges of orange to serve.

TURKEY AND BACON KEBABS

SERVES 4

30 ml (2 tbsp) cranberry sauce	salt and pepper
90 ml (6 tbsp) vegetable oil	700 g (1½ lb) boneless turkey escalopes
45 ml (3 tbsp) fresh orange juice	1 small onion
1 garlic clove, crushed	6 streaky bacon rashers, halved
2.5 ml (½ tsp) ground allspice	1 large red pepper, cut into chunks

1 Put the cranberry sauce, oil and orange juice in a shallow dish with the garlic, allspice and seasoning to taste. Whisk with a fork until well combined.

2 Cut the turkey into bite-sized pieces and place in the dish. Stir to coat in the oil and orange juice mixture, then cover and leave to marinate for 4 hours if possible, stirring occasionally.

3 Cut the onion into squares or even-sized chunks. Form the bacon rashers into small rolls. Remove the turkey from the marinade, reserving the marinade.

4 Thread the turkey, onion and red pepper on to oiled skewers with the bacon, dividing the ingredients as evenly as possible.

5 Cook under a preheated moderate grill for about 20 minutes, turning the skewers frequently and basting with the remaining marinade. Serve hot.

COOK'S TIP

The longer the turkey is marinated, the more tender and succulent it will be. If marinating in the refrigerator overnight, allow the turkey to come to room temperature before grilling.

QUICK TURKEY CURRY

SERVES 4-6

30 ml (2 tbsp) vegetable oil	2.5 ml (½ tsp) chilli powder
3 bay leaves	salt and pepper
2 cardamom pods, crushed	50 g (2 oz) unsalted cashew nuts
1 cinnamon stick, broken into short lengths	700 g (1½ lb) turkey fillets, skinned and cut into bite-size pieces
1 medium onion, thinly sliced	2 medium potatoes, peeled and cut into chunks
1 green pepper, seeded and chopped (optional)	4 tomatoes, skinned and chopped, or 225 g (8 oz) can tomatoes
10 ml (2 tsp) paprika	bay leaves, to garnish
7.5 ml (1½ tsp) garam masala	
2.5 ml (½ tsp) turmeric	

1 Heat the oil in a flameproof casserole, add the bay leaves, cardamom and cinnamon and fry over moderate heat for 1-2 minutes. Add the onion and green pepper if using, with the spices and salt and pepper to taste. Pour in enough water to moisten, then cook, stirring, for 1 minute.

2 Add the cashews and turkey, cover and simmer for 10 minutes. Turn the turkey occasionally during this time to ensure even cooking.

3 Add the potatoes and tomatoes and continue cooking for a further 20 minutes until the turkey and potatoes are tender. Garnish with bay leaves. Serve with boiled rice.

DUCK
WITH MANGO

SERVES 4

1 ripe, but still firm mango	2.5 ml (½ tsp) ground allspice
4 duck breasts or lean duck portions	45 ml (3 tbsp) plum jam
	20 ml (4 tsp) wine vinegar
60 ml (4 tbsp) peanut oil	salt and pepper

1 Skin and thickly slice the mango on either side of the large central stone.

2 Remove any excess fat from the duck portions. Divide each portion into three and place in a saucepan. Cover with cold water and bring to the boil. Lower the heat and simmer gently for 15-20 minutes. Drain well and pat dry with absorbent kitchen paper. Trim the bones.

3 Heat the oil in a wok or large frying pan until hot and smoking. Add the duck pieces and allspice and cook until well browned on all sides.

4 Stir in the jam and vinegar. Cook for a further 2-3 minutes, stirring constantly, until well glazed. Stir in the mango slices and season to taste. Heat through, then turn into a warmed serving dish and serve immediately.

VARIATION

Tropical Duck

Other tropical fruits could be used instead of the mango in the above recipe. Try guava, papaya or lychees.

SWEET AND
SOUR DUCK JOINTS

SERVES 4

4 duck portions	45 ml (3 tbsp) wine or cider vinegar
salt and pepper	
60 ml (4 tbsp) soy sauce	30 ml (2 tbsp) dry sherry
45 ml (3 tbsp) soft brown sugar	juice of 1 orange
	2.5 ml (½ tsp) ground ginger
45 ml (3 tbsp) honey	few orange slices and watercress sprigs, to garnish

1 Prick the duck portions all over with a fork, then sprinkle the skin liberally with salt and pepper.

2 Place on a rack in a roasting tin and roast in the oven at 190°C (375°F) mark 5 for 45-60 minutes or until the skin is crisp and the juices run clear when the thickest part of each joint is pierced with a skewer.

3 Meanwhile, to make the sauce, mix together all the remaining ingredients in a saucepan, add 150 ml (¼ pint) water and bring to the boil. Simmer, stirring constantly, for about 5 minutes to allow the flavours to blend and the sauce to thicken slightly. Add salt and pepper to taste.

4 Trim the duck joints neatly by cutting off any knuckles or wing joints. Arrange the duck on a warmed serving platter and coat with some of the sauce. Garnish with orange and watercress.

VENISON ESCALOPES WITH RED WINE

SERVES 6

6 venison escalopes, cut from the haunch (leg), each about 175 g (6 oz)	300 ml (½ pint) dry red wine
1 small onion, finely chopped	15 g (½ oz) butter or margarine
1 bay leaf	15 ml (1 tbsp) vegetable oil
2 parsley sprigs	30 ml (2 tbsp) redcurrant jelly
8 juniper berries	salt and pepper

1 Put the venison escalopes in a large shallow dish and sprinkle with the onion, bay leaf, parsley and juniper berries. Pour on the wine, cover and leave to marinate in the refrigerator for 3-4 hours if possible or overnight, turning the escalopes occasionally.

2 Remove the escalopes from the marinade, reserving the marinade. Heat the butter and oil in a large frying pan and fry the escalopes for 3-4 minutes on each side. Transfer to a warmed serving dish and keep warm while making the sauce.

3 Strain the reserved marinade into the frying pan and stir to loosen any sediment. Increase the heat and boil rapidly for 3-4 minutes, until reduced. Stir in the redcurrant jelly and season the mixture to taste. Cook, stirring, for 1-2 minutes.

4 Pour the sauce over the escalopes to serve.

QUAIL COOKED WITH JUNIPER

SERVES 4

75 g (3 oz) butter	6 juniper berries, washed
8 quail	30 ml (2 tbsp) gin or brandy
salt	watercress sprigs, to garnish
300 ml (½ pint) chicken stock	

1 Melt the butter in a large frying pan and fry the quail until brown on all sides.

2 Sprinkle with salt. Cover the pan and cook over moderate heat for about 20 minutes. If preferred, the quail can be cooked in the oven at 180°C (350°F) mark 4.

3 When they are nearly cooked, add the stock, juniper berries and gin or brandy. Continue to cook for a further 10 minutes until the quail are tender.

4 To serve, put the quail on to a warmed large dish and pour the cooking liquid round them. Serve immediately, garnished with sprigs of watercress.

STEAK AU POIVRE

SERVES 4

30 ml (2 tbsp) black peppercorns	15 ml (1 tbsp) olive or vegetable oil
4 sirloin, rump or fillet steaks, each about 125-175 g (4-6 oz) and 2.5 cm (1 inch) thick	30 ml (2 tbsp) brandy
	150 ml (¼ pint) double cream
	salt
25 g (1 oz) butter	parsley sprigs, to garnish

1 Crush the peppercorns coarsely using a pestle and mortar, or on a wooden board with a rolling pin.
2 Trim the steaks, then place them on the peppercorn mixture. Press hard to encrust the surface of the meat. Turn over and repeat with the other side.
3 Melt the butter with the oil in a frying pan, add the steaks and fry until sealed on all sides. Reduce the heat and continue cooking for 7-10 minutes, or until the steaks are cooked to your liking. Remove the steaks from the pan and keep warm.
4 Stir the brandy into the pan, remove from the heat and set it alight. Keep the pan off the heat until the flames have died down.
5 Stir in the cream, add salt to taste, then return to the heat and heat through gently. Pour over the steaks and serve immediately, garnished with parsley.

STEAK DIANE

SERVES 4

25 g (1 oz) butter or margarine	15 ml (1 tbsp) Worcestershire sauce
15 ml (1 tbsp) vegetable oil	10 ml (2 tsp) meat glaze (optional)
4 minute steaks	45 ml (3 tbsp) bottled Italian-style tomato sauce
2 shallots, finely chopped	
30 ml (2 tbsp) brandy	30 ml (2 tbsp) chopped parsley

1 Melt the butter with the oil in a heavy-based frying pan. When foaming, add the steaks and fry for 1 minute on each side.
2 Add the shallots and pour in the brandy. Remove from the heat and ignite the pan juices. Let the flames die down and stir in the Worcestershire sauce, meat glaze if using, tomato sauce and 45 ml (3 tbsp) cold water.
3 Increase the heat and shake the pan to mix the sauces together. Add the parsley and bring to the boil. Serve immediately, straight from the pan.

SERVING SUGGESTION

Steak Diane is very quick to prepare – ideal for a midweek dinner party. For a really simple, but delicious meal, serve with buttered new potatoes and a tossed green salad.

STEAKS WITH TOMATO, GARLIC AND OLIVES

SERVES 4

30 ml (2 tbsp) olive oil, plus extra for frying	15 ml (1 tbsp) chopped fresh oregano or basil, or 5 ml (1 tsp) dried
2-3 garlic cloves, sliced	salt and pepper
700 g (1½ lb) ripe tomatoes, skinned and roughly chopped, or two 397 g (14 oz) cans chopped tomatoes, drained	4 rump steaks, each about 175 g (6 oz), trimmed
	100 g (4 oz) large black olives, stoned and roughly chopped

1 To make the sauce, heat the oil in a medium saucepan, add the garlic and cook gently for about 1 minute.

2 Add the tomatoes with the herbs and salt and pepper to taste. Simmer gently for 15 minutes, until the tomatoes have cooked down but are not completely disintegrated.

3 Heat a little olive oil in a large frying pan. Fry the steaks for 2 minutes on each side.

4 Coat the steaks with the sauce, add the olives and cook, covered, for 5 minutes. Serve immediately.

RUMP STEAK IN WHISKY

SERVES 6

1.1 kg (2½ lb) piece rump steak, about 2 cm (¾ inch) thick	90 ml (6 tbsp) whisky
	30 ml (2 tbsp) vegetable oil
1 small onion, thinly sliced	salt and pepper
2 garlic cloves	watercress sprigs, to garnish

1 Trim off any excess fat from the steak, then place the meat in an edged dish into which it will fit snugly. Scatter the onion over the meat.

2 To make the marinade, crush the garlic and mix with the whisky, oil and pepper. Pour over the meat. Cover and leave to marinate for at least 2 hours, or overnight if possible, turning and basting once.

3 Lift the meat out of the marinade and pat the surface dry with absorbent kitchen paper, then place on the rack of the grill pan.

4 Grill the rump steak under a high heat for about 6 minutes each side, depending on how you like your steak cooked.

5 Meanwhile, strain the marinade into a small saucepan and heat gently; adjust seasoning, adding salt at this stage if necessary.

6 Lift the steak on to a serving plate and spoon over the warmed liquid. To serve, garnish with watercress.

SMOKED MUSSEL STEAKS

SERVES 4

4 sirloin steaks, each about 175 g (6 oz) and 2 cm (¾ inch) thick	30 ml (2 tbsp) white wine vinegar
105 g (3⅔ oz) can smoked mussels	1 bunch watercress, roughly chopped
	salt and pepper

1 Trim the steaks of any excess fat. With a sharp knife, make a slit along the length of each steak to form a pocket.
2 Drain the mussels, reserving the oil. Chop the mussels roughly and place in a bowl with the wine vinegar. Add the watercress with salt and plenty of pepper.
3 Spoon a little of the mussel mixture into each steak. Place in a single layer in a shallow flameproof dish, or on a foil-lined grill pan.
4 Brush the steaks with the reserved oil from the mussels. Cook under a preheated hot grill for about 3-4 minutes each side for a medium steak, about 5-6 minutes each side for well done. Turn the steaks over carefully with tongs or a fish slice to prevent the filling dropping out. Serve hot.

STILTON STEAKS

SERVES 4

100 g (4 oz) Stilton cheese, crumbled	pepper
25 g (1 oz) butter, softened	4 sirloin or fillet steaks, each 100-175 g (4-6 oz)
50-75 g (2-3 oz) walnut pieces, finely chopped	

1 Put the cheese in a bowl and mash with a fork. Add the butter and walnuts and mix well. Season with pepper to taste.
2 Put the steaks on the grill rack and season with plenty of pepper. Cook under a preheated grill for 5-15 minutes, turning frequently, until the steaks are cooked to your liking.
3 Remove the steaks from under the grill, sprinkle the cheese and nut mixture evenly over them and press down with a palette knife. Grill for a further minute or until the topping is melted and bubbling. Serve hot.

SPICED STEAKS

SERVES 4

FONDUE BOURGUIGNONNE

SERVES 4-6

700 g (1½ lb) rump steak	2.5 ml (½ tsp) chilli powder
seeds of 6 green cardamoms	salt
4 cloves	50 ml (2 fl oz) ghee or vegetable oil
6 black peppercorns	
juice of 2 limes	lime slices or wedges, to serve
150 ml (¼ pint) natural yogurt	

1 Cut off the fat around the edge of the steak, then cut the meat into serving pieces. Beat with a mallet until flat and thin. Set aside.
2 Dry-fry the cardamom seeds, cloves and peppercorns in a heavy-based frying pan for 1 minute, then finely grind in a small electric mill or with a pestle and mortar. Transfer to a bowl and add half of the lime juice, the yogurt, chilli powder and salt to taste. Stir well to mix.
3 Place the pieces of steak on a large plate and brush with half of the marinade. Leave to stand at room temperature for 30 minutes if possible, then turn the steak pieces over and repeat on the other side.
4 When ready to cook, heat the ghee in a large, heavy-based frying pan until smoking hot. Add the steaks in batches and sear on both sides in the hot fat. Lower the heat and continue frying for about 8 minutes or until cooked to your liking, turning the steaks frequently.
5 Remove the steaks from the pan and arrange overlapping on a warmed serving dish. Pour the remaining lime juice into the residual fat and stir to combine over high heat. Drizzle the pan juices over the steak and garnish with lime slices or wedges to serve.

	FOR THE MUSTARD DIP
700 g-1.1 kg (1½-2 lb) fillet or rump steak, trimmed of excess fat	45 ml (3 tbsp) mayonnaise
	60-90 ml (4-6 tbsp) soured cream
olive or vegetable oil, for cooking	45 ml (3 tbsp) wholegrain mustard
	30 ml (2 tbsp) finely chopped gherkins

1 First make the dip. Put the mayonnaise and cream in a bowl and whisk together until blended. Stir in the mustard and gherkins. Cover the bowl and leave for 1 hour if possible for the flavours to develop.
2 Cut the steak into 2.5 cm (1 inch) cubes and arrange on individual plates. Cover until ready to serve.
3 Pour oil into a metal fondue pot until one-third full. Heat on a fondue burner on the table to 190°C (375°F).
4 Give each guest a two-pronged fondue fork or long-handled skewer for spearing the meat cubes, which they cook in the hot oil for a few minutes, then cool a little. The cooked meat is then dipped into the mustard dip before eating.

COOK'S TIP

For carefree entertaining, Fondue Bourguignonne is a good choice, but it is important to be well organised before guests sit down to the table. The oil must be at the correct temperature or the meat will not cook quickly.

VARIATION

For added variety – and to save time buy a selection of ready prepared dips to serve with the fondue.

PEPPERED BEEF SAUTE

SERVES 2-3

350 g (12 oz) sirloin steaks	175 g (6 oz) red onion, thinly sliced
10 ml (2 tsp) green peppercorns in brine, drained	90 ml (6 tbsp) single cream
30 ml (2 tbsp) olive oil	15 ml (1 tbsp) lemon juice
	salt
	lemon slices, to garnish

1 Cut the steaks into fine, thin strips. Finely chop the peppercorns.

2 Heat the oil in a medium-sized sauté pan. Add the onion and fry until just beginning to soften.

3 Stir in the beef and peppercorns and cook over a high heat for about 2-3 minutes or until the meat is tender, stirring frequently.

4 Lower the heat and stir in the cream and lemon juice with salt to taste. To serve, garnish with lemon slices and accompany with noodles.

STEAK AND KIDNEY KEBABS

SERVES 4

225 g (8 oz) button onions	300 ml (½ pint) red wine
salt and pepper	30 ml (2 tbsp) brandy
450 g (1 lb) rump steak	2 large garlic cloves, sliced
225 g (8 oz) lamb's kidneys, skinned, halved and cored	olive oil, for brushing
125 g (4 oz) button mushrooms	150 ml (¼ pint) beef stock
	15 ml (1 tbsp) cornflour
12 bay leaves	watercress sprigs, to garnish

1 Put the button onions in a saucepan, cover with cold, salted water, bring to the boil and cook until almost tender, about 10-15 minutes. Drain and refresh under cold running water.

2 Cut the rump steak and kidneys into bite-sized pieces.

3 Thread the steak, kidney, onions, mushrooms and bay leaves on to wooden skewers – don't pack the ingredients too tightly together. Place the skewers in a large non-metallic dish.

4 Pour over the wine and brandy and add the garlic and plenty of pepper. Cover tightly and leave to marinate for several hours if possible, turning occasionally.

5 Lift the skewers out of the marinade and place on a grill rack. Protect the ends of the skewers with foil to prevent them burning. Brush the kebabs with oil and grill, turning occasionally, until cooked through.

6 Pour the stock and marinade into a saucepan and simmer for about 10 minutes. Mix the cornflour to a smooth paste with a little water. Off the heat, stir into the pan juices, then bring to the boil, stirring all the time. Cook for 1 minute, then adjust seasoning.

7 Garnish the kebabs with watercress and serve with the sauce, rice and broad beans.

STEAK
AND STILTON PARCELS

SERVES 4

2 quick-fry steaks, about 450 g (1 lb) total weight	60 ml (4 tbsp) single cream
30 ml (2 tbsp) vegetable oil	pepper
75 g (3 oz) blue Stilton cheese	5 large sheets filo pastry, about 45 x 25 cm (18 x 10 inch) each
15 ml (1 tbsp) chopped fresh tarragon or 2.5 ml (½ tsp) dried	50 g (2 oz) butter, melted
	lemon juice, to serve

1 Halve each steak. Heat the oil in a frying pan, then seal the meat quickly in the hot oil; allow to cool.
2 Grate the cheese or soften with a fork. Mix with the tarragon, cream and black pepper (the Stilton should add sufficient salt). Spread the mixture over the cold steaks.
3 Brush one sheet of filo pastry with butter and wrap around one steak to enclose it completely like a parcel. Place on a baking sheet and brush with butter. Repeat with the rest of the steaks.
4 Brush the last sheet of filo with butter and fold it over and over to form a strip about 2.5 cm (1 inch) wide. Cut into diamond shapes and use to decorate the parcels. Brush with melted butter. Chill for about 20 minutes.
5 Bake in the oven at 220°C (425°F) mark 7 for 15-20 minutes or until well browned. Squeeze lemon juice over the parcels and serve accompanied by a mixed leaf salad.

BEEF KEBABS
WITH HORSERADISH

SERVES 6

700 g (1½ lb) lean minced beef	salt and pepper
250 g (9 oz) grated onion	1 egg, beaten
135 ml (9 tbsp) horseradish sauce	plain flour, for coating
45 ml (3 tbsp) chopped thyme	150 ml (¼ pint) natural yogurt
250 g (9 oz) fresh white breadcrumbs	120 ml (8 tbsp) finely chopped parsley
	parsley sprigs, to garnish

1 Put the minced beef in a large bowl and mix in the onion, 90 ml (6 tbsp) of the horseradish, the thyme and breadcrumbs. Season to taste.
2 Add enough egg to bind the mixture together and, with floured hands, shape into 18 even-sized sausages. Cover and chill in the refrigerator until required.
3 Thread the kebabs lengthways on to six oiled skewers. Cook under a preheated grill for about 20 minutes, turning frequently.
4 Meanwhile, mix the yogurt with the remaining horseradish and the parsley. Spoon into a serving dish.
5 Serve the kebabs hot, garnished with parsley and accompanied by the sauce, and brown or saffron rice if desired.

CHILLI BEEF WITH NOODLES

SERVES 4

450 g (1 lb) rump steak	10 ml (2 level tsp) dried oregano or dried mixed herbs
225 g (8 oz) red pepper, halved and seeded	50 g (2 oz) dried tagliarini (thin pasta noodles)
225 g (8 oz) broccoli	30 ml (2 tbsp) sherry or medium white wine
30 ml (2 tbsp) vegetable oil	
1 medium onion, roughly chopped	300 ml (½ pint) beef stock
2.5 ml (½ level tsp) chilli powder or few drops of Tabasco sauce	5 ml (1 tbsp) soy sauce
	pepper

1 Trim the steak of any excess fat. Cut into bite-sized pieces. Cut the pepper into similar-sized pieces. Thinly slice the broccoli stalks, and divide the remainder into small florets.

2 Heat the oil in a large sauté pan and brown the beef well on all sides for about 2-3 minutes. Remove with a slotted spoon. Add the vegetables, chilli powder and oregano. Sauté, stirring, for 1-2 minutes.

3 Mix in the tagliarini, sherry, stock and soy sauce. Cover and simmer for 5 minutes or until the noodles and broccoli are tender.

4 Return the beef to the pan. Bring to the boil and simmer for 1 minute to heat through. Adjust seasoning, adding pepper as necessary.

CHINESE BEEF AND VEGETABLE STIR-FRY

SERVES 4

350 g (12 oz) fillet or rump steak, sliced into very thin strips	75 ml (5 tbsp) sesame or vegetable oil
30 ml (2 tbsp) cornflour	1 onion, thinly sliced
60 ml (4 tbsp) soy sauce	1 garlic clove, crushed
90 ml (6 tbsp) dry sherry	2.5 cm (1 inch) piece fresh root ginger, crushed
30 ml (2 tbsp) dark soft brown sugar	2 celery sticks, thinly sliced
30 ml (2 tbsp) wine vinegar	1 red pepper, sliced into thin strips
salt and pepper	225 g (8 oz) mangetout, halved

1 Put the steak in a bowl. Mix together the cornflour, soy sauce, sherry, sugar, vinegar and seasoning. Pour over the steak, stir well to mix, then cover and leave to marinate for 1 hour if possible.

2 Heat 30 ml (2 tbsp) of the oil in a wok or large frying pan. Add the onion, garlic and ginger and fry gently, stirring, for 5 minutes or until soft.

3 Heat another 15 ml (1 tbsp) of the oil in the pan. Add the celery and red pepper and fry, stirring, for a further 5 minutes or until tender but still crisp. Remove the vegetables from the pan with a slotted spoon.

4 Remove the steak from the marinade. Heat the remaining oil in the pan, add the steak and stir-fry over high heat for 5 minutes. Remove with a slotted spoon and set aside.

5 Add the mangetout to the pan and stir-fry over high heat for 2-3 minutes. Return the steak and vegetables to the pan, then pour in the marinade and stir until bubbling and well mixed. Taste and adjust the seasoning. Serve immediately.

TAGLIATELLE BOLOGNESE

SERVES 4

30 ml (2 tbsp) olive oil, plus 5 ml (1 tsp)	15 ml (1 tbsp) tomato purée
1 onion, chopped	15 ml (1 tbsp) chopped fresh oregano or 5 ml (1 tsp) dried
1 garlic clove, crushed	15 ml (1 tbsp) chopped fresh mixed herbs or 5 ml (1 tsp) dried
2 rashers streaky bacon, rinded and chopped	1 bay leaf
450 g (1 lb) minced beef	pinch of sugar
396 g (14 oz) can chopped tomatoes	salt and pepper
300 ml (½ pint) beef stock	400 g (14 oz) tagliatelle
30 ml (2 tbsp) red or white wine or wine vinegar	freshly grated Parmesan cheese, to serve

1 Heat the 30 ml (2 tbsp) oil in a heavy-based pan, add the onion, garlic and bacon and fry gently for 5 minutes until softened.

2 Add the beef and fry for a further 5 minutes until browned, stirring constantly and pressing with a wooden spoon to break up any lumps.

3 Add the tomatoes, stock, wine or vinegar and tomato purée with the herbs, sugar and seasoning to taste. Bring to the boil, stirring, then lower the heat and simmer, half covered, for 20 minutes.

4 Meanwhile, cook the tagliatelle in plenty of boiling salted water, with the 5 ml (1 tsp) oil added to prevent sticking, until *al dente* (tender, but firm to the bite). Drain thoroughly and turn into a warmed serving dish.

5 Taste and adjust the seasoning of the Bolognese sauce, then pour over the tagliatelle. Serve immediately, with Parmesan cheese handed separately.

VEAL IN MARSALA

SERVES 6

6 veal escalopes, each about 75 g (3 oz)	175 g (6 oz) button mushrooms, sliced
salt and pepper	90 ml (6 tbsp) Marsala
plain flour, for coating	90 ml (6 tbsp) chicken stock
60 ml (4 tbsp) vegetable oil	5 ml (1 tsp) arrowroot
50 g (2 oz) butter	lemon wedges, to serve
1 onion, finely chopped	

1 Trim each escalope to remove any skin. Place well apart between two sheets of dampened greaseproof paper and beat out until very thin, using a meat mallet or rolling pin.

2 Season the flour, add the veal and toss until coated. Heat the oil and butter in a large sauté pan or deep frying pan, add the veal and cook until well browned on all sides.

3 Push the veal to the side of the pan and add the onion and mushrooms to the remaining fat. Cook until browned. Add the Marsala and stock, bring to the boil and season lightly.

4 Cover the pan and cook gently for 5-10 minutes or until the veal is quite tender. Transfer to a warmed serving dish, cover and keep warm.

5 Mix the arrowroot to a smooth paste with a little water. Stir into the pan juices off the heat, then bring slowly to the boil, stirring all the time. Cook for 1 minute, adjust the seasoning and spoon over the veal. Serve with lemon wedges.

VEAL ESCALOPES WITH HERBS

SERVES 4

4 veal escalopes, each about 100 g (4 oz)	100 ml (4 fl oz) dry white wine
salt and pepper	30 ml (2 tbsp) chopped herbs (parsley, chervil, tarragon and chives)
45 ml (3 tbsp) plain flour	
25 g (1 oz) butter or margarine	60 ml (4 tbsp) double cream
	lemon wedges, to serve

1 Place the veal escalopes between two sheets of dampened greaseproof paper and beat until thin with a rolling pin or meat mallet.
2 Season the flour with a little salt and pepper and use to coat the escalopes.
3 Melt the butter or margarine in a large frying pan, add the escalopes and fry over a high heat for 1-2 minutes on each side or until browned. (You may have to fry in two batches, depending on the size of the pan.) Lower the heat and continue to cook for a further 4 minutes on each side or until tender. Transfer the veal to a warmed serving dish, cover and keep hot.
4 Add the white wine to the pan and bring slowly to the boil, stirring to scrape up any sediment left in the pan. Stir in the herbs and cream and season to taste. Simmer very gently for about 5 minutes or until slightly thickened.
5 Pour the sauce over the veal escalopes and serve immediately, with lemon wedges.

WIENER SCHNITZEL

SERVES 4

4 veal escalopes, each about 100 g (4 oz)	FOR THE GARNISH
salt and pepper	1 hard-boiled egg
1 egg, size 2, beaten	lemon slices
150 g (5 oz) fresh breadcrumbs	parsley sprigs
75 g (3 oz) butter or margarine	
30 ml (2 tbsp) vegetable oil	

1 Place the veal escalopes between two sheets of dampened greaseproof paper and bat out thinly with a rolling pin or meat mallet.
2 Sprinkle the meat with salt and pepper to taste. Coat in the beaten egg, then in the breadcrumbs, pressing the crumbs on well.
3 Melt the butter with the oil in a large frying pan. Add the escalopes, two at a time, and fry for about 2 minutes on each side, until golden. Drain on absorbent kitchen paper and keep warm while cooking the remainder.
4 For the garnish, finely chop the egg white and yolk, keeping them separate.
5 Serve the schnitzels hot, garnished with the chopped egg, lemon slices and parsley.

SERVING SUGGESTION

In Vienna, Wiener Schnitzel is traditionally served with a mixed salad. Lettuce, tomato, cucumbers, radishes and asparagus are a favourite Austrian combination.

VEAL STEAKS
WITH GRUYERE

SERVES 4

40 g (1½ oz) butter or margarine	100 g (4 oz) gruyère cheese, grated
4 thick veal steaks, each about 175 g (6 oz)	5 ml (1 tsp) Dijon mustard
150 ml (¼ pint) dry white wine	5 ml (1 tsp) chopped tarragon (optional)
	salt and pepper

1 Melt the butter in a large frying pan and, when foaming, add the veal steaks. Fry briskly for 1-2 minutes on each side until browned.
2 Lower the heat, pour in the wine and bring to a gentle simmer. Cover the pan and simmer for about 15-20 minutes, or until the steaks are tender.
3 Uncover the pan and transfer the steaks to a foil-lined grill pan, reserving any pan juices. Mix the cheese and mustard together with the tarragon if using, and salt and pepper to taste.
4 Spread the cheese on top of the steaks, then cook under a preheated grill for 1-2 minutes until the cheese melts. Meanwhile, boil the pan juices rapidly until reduced by half.
5 Transfer the veal steaks to a warmed serving dish. Pour over the pan juices and serve immediately.

COOK'S TIP

Don't be confused between gruyère and emmental. Genuine gruyère from Switzerland has only a few small holes, whereas Swiss emmental has lots of large holes. The reason for the confusion between these two cheeses is that when they are made in other countries, particularly in the French alps, the size and number of the holes is sometimes reversed! For this recipe, you can use either gruyère or emmental, both of which have excellent melting qualities, and a nutty flavour which goes so well with veal.

VEAL ESCALOPES
WITH LEMON

SERVES 4

4 veal escalopes, each about 100 g (4 oz)	60 ml (4 tbsp) olive oil
30 ml (2 tbsp) plain flour	45 ml (3 tbsp) lemon juice
salt and pepper	90 ml (6 tbsp) dry white wine
50 g (2 oz) butter	lemon slices and parsley sprigs, to garnish

1 Put the veal escalopes between two sheets of greaseproof paper and bat out until thin with a meat mallet or rolling pin.
2 Trim the escalopes, then coat in the flour seasoned with salt and pepper. Make sure both sides are evenly coated.
3 Melt the butter with the oil in a large heavy-based frying pan. Add the escalopes and fry for 3-4 minutes on each side until tender. During cooking, press the escalopes constantly with a fish slice to help prevent shrinkage and keep them as flat as possible.
4 Transfer the escalopes to a warmed serving platter using a fish slice; cover and keep warm.
5 Add the lemon juice and wine to the pan and stir to combine with the cooking juices. Bubble vigorously for a minute or two, then add salt and pepper to taste. Pour over the escalopes, garnish with lemon slices and parsley sprigs and serve immediately.

COOK'S TIP

If you do not have a pan large enough to cook all four escalopes together, either use two frying pans or cook two first and keep them warm while you are cooking the others.

MEDALLIONS OF VEAL WITH GINGER

SERVES 4

22.5 ml (1½ tbsp) plain flour	15 ml (1 tbsp) olive oil
5 ml (1 tsp) ground ginger	3 pieces of stem ginger, with syrup
salt and pepper	100 ml (4 fl oz) dry white wine
8 veal medallions (see below)	
40 g (1½ oz) butter	150 ml (¼ pint) double cream

1 Mix the flour on a plate with the ground ginger and salt and pepper to taste. Coat the veal in the flour.

2 Melt 25 g (1 oz) of the butter with the oil in one or two large heavy-based frying pans. Add the veal and fry over moderate heat until lightly coloured, turning once.

3 Meanwhile, chop one of the pieces of stem ginger very finely. Mix with the syrup from all the pieces of ginger. Add the white wine, then pour over the veal.

4 Bring to the boil, then lower the heat, cover the pan tightly and simmer very gently for 15 minutes or until the veal is just tender, turning once during cooking.

5 Meanwhile, slice the remaining pieces of stem ginger into thin rings with a sharp knife.

6 When the veal is tender, transfer to a warmed dish, cover and keep hot in a low oven. Stir the cream into the sauce (combining them in one pan if two were used to cook the veal). Simmer until reduced, stirring constantly, then whisk in the remaining butter. Taste and adjust seasoning.

7 Place 2 medallions on each warmed serving plate and spoon over the sauce to coat the veal. Top with a few slices of stem ginger and serve immediately.

COOK'S TIP

Large supermarkets and high-class butchers usually sell medallions of veal. They are cut from the rump end of the fillet or loin, and are usually sold tied into a neat shape with string, sometimes with fat around to keep them moist during cooking. This fat should be removed before serving.

VEAL ESCALOPES WITH WINE AND FENNEL

SERVES 8

8 veal escalopes, each about 175 g (6 oz)	700 g (1½ lb) tomatoes, skinned
30 ml (2 tbsp) plain flour	50 g (2 oz) butter
salt and pepper	45 ml (3 tbsp) vegetable oil
450 g (1 lb) fennel	150 ml (¼ pint) dry white wine
1 large onion	
	30 ml (2 tbsp) tomato purée

1 Cut each escalope into 3 equal pieces. Place between two sheets of dampened greaseproof paper and bat out thinly with a rolling pin or meat mallet.

2 Spread the flour out on a plate and season with salt and pepper. Use to coat the pieces of meat.

3 Trim the fennel, reserving the feathery tops for garnish. Slice the fennel and onion thinly. Cut each of the tomatoes into 8 pieces.

4 Melt the butter with the oil in a large frying pan. When foaming, brown the veal, a few pieces at a time. Remove from the pan with a slotted spoon and transfer to a plate.

5 Add the fennel and onion to the fat remaining in the pan and brown lightly. Stir in the white wine, tomato purée and tomatoes, with salt and pepper to taste. Bring to the boil and replace the meat.

6 Cover the pan and simmer for about 5 minutes or until the meat is tender. Taste and adjust seasoning, then transfer to a warmed serving dish and garnish with the reserved fennel tops. Serve immediately.

SERVING SUGGESTION

Serve this Italian-style dish with rice and a salad of radicchio, lamb's lettuce and basil leaves.

PAN-FRIED VEAL WITH MUSTARD AND CREAM

SERVES 4

4 veal escalopes, each about 100-175 g (4-6 oz)	150 ml (¼ pint) single cream
40 g (1½ oz) butter or margarine	15 ml (1 tbsp) wholegrain mustard
150 ml (¼ pint) veal or chicken stock	juice of ½ lemon
	salt and pepper
	chopped parsley, to garnish

1 Cut the veal into thin, pencil-like strips about 6 cm (2½ inches) long. Melt the butter in a frying pan and, when foaming, add the veal. Fry over high heat for 2-3 minutes, stirring constantly, until lightly browned.

2 Lift the veal out of the pan with a slotted spoon and transfer to a plate.

3 Add the stock to the pan and boil until reduced by half, stirring continuously.

4 Stir in the cream, mustard, lemon juice and browned veal. Season to taste with salt and pepper and simmer for 5 minutes. Serve immediately, garnished with chopped parsley, accompanied with buttered noodles and a tossed mixed salad.

COOK'S TIP

The sharp pungency of mustard is particularly good with veal. Wholegrain mustard is specified because it is less strong than some of the smooth English and Dijon mustards, which would completely overpower the delicate flavour of the dish. Wholegrain mustards made from crushed black and yellow mustard seeds are usually French and vinegar-based, with a seasoning of pimentos, cloves and cinnamon. Look for the famous Moutarde de Meaux in delicatessens and good supermarkets; its granular texture adds interest to the sauce in this recipe, and it has just the right degree of 'hotness'.

SHEFTALIA

SERVES 4-6

450 g (1 lb) boneless leg or shoulder of lamb, minced	60 ml (4 tbsp) chopped parsley
225 g (8 oz) belly of pork, rinded	salt and pepper
1 large onion	lemon slices, to garnish

1 Put the lamb in a large bowl. Cut the pork into small pieces and the onion into quarters. Pass the pork and onion through a mincer into the bowl with the lamb. Alternatively, finely chop all the ingredients in a food processor. Add the parsley and salt and pepper to taste.

2 Knead the mixture thoroughly with your fingers until it is smooth and well mixed.

3 With dampened hands, shape into 12 sausage shapes, about 5 cm (2 inches) long. Thread on to 4 or 6 flat metal skewers. Chill in the refrigerator for 30 minutes.

4 Cook under a preheated grill or over a charcoal barbecue for about 15 minutes until cooked, turning frequently. Serve hot, garnished with lemon slices.

SERVING SUGGESTION

Sheftalia are usually served with pitta bread and rice for an informal meal. A typical Cypriot mixed salad to accompany these kebabs would be a combination of tomatoes, raw onions, lettuce, cucumber and large black olives, tossed in an oil and vinegar dressing with plenty of chopped fresh mint.

SPANISH PORK ESCALOPES

SERVES 4

450 g (1 lb) pork fillet	10 ml (2 tsp) plain flour
225 g (8 oz) tomatoes	100 ml (4 fl oz) red wine
15 ml (1 tbsp) vegetable oil	15 ml (1 tbsp) tomato purée
25 g (1 oz) butter or margarine	1 garlic clove, crushed
	salt and pepper
1 small onion, finely chopped	12 stuffed green olives, sliced

1 Cut the pork into 8 pieces and bat out thinly between two sheets of dampened greaseproof paper, using a rolling pin or meat mallet.
2 Skin and quarter the tomatoes. Put the seeds into a sieve over a bowl and press through the juices; discard the seeds. Roughly chop the tomato flesh.
3 Heat the oil and butter in a large frying pan, add half of the pork and fry until browned on both sides. Remove from the pan with a slotted spoon and set aside. Repeat with the remaining pork.
4 Add the onion to the pan and fry for about 5 minutes until lightly browned. Stir in the flour and cook for 1 minute, then gradually add the wine, chopped tomatoes and their juice, the tomato purée, garlic and salt and pepper to taste. Bring to the boil, stirring all the time.
5 Return the meat to the pan. Add the olives, cover and simmer for 10-15 minutes or until the pork is tender.

COOK'S TIP

There are two ways to skin tomatoes. The best method for firm tomatoes is to immerse them in a large bowl of boiling water for 10 seconds, then drain and plunge into cold water. Remove from the water one at a time and peel off the skin with your fingers. If you only have to skin a few ripe tomatoes and have a gas hob, use the following method. Hold the tomato in the stalk end with the prongs of a fork, and turn it constantly in the flames until the skin blisters and bursts. Leave until cool enough to handle, then peel away the skin.

PORK WITH CIDER AND CORIANDER

SERVES 4

450 g (1 lb) pork fillet	15 ml (1 tbsp) ground coriander
30 ml (2 tbsp) vegetable oil	15 ml (1 tbsp) plain flour
50 g (2 oz) butter	150 ml (¼ pint) dry cider
1 green pepper, seeded and sliced into rings	150 ml (¼ pint) chicken or vegetable stock
225 g (8 oz) celery, sliced	salt and pepper
100 g (4 oz) onion, chopped	

1 Trim excess fat from the pork fillet and slice into 5 mm (¼ inch) thick pieces. Place between two sheets of dampened greaseproof paper and beat out until thin with a rolling pin or meat mallet.
2 Heat the oil with half the butter in a large frying pan. Add the green pepper and celery and fry gently for 2-3 minutes. Lift out with a slotted spoon and keep warm on a serving plate.
3 Add the remaining butter to the pan, increase the heat to high, then add the pork, a few pieces at a time. Cook the pork until browned on all sides, then remove from the pan.
4 Add the onion to the fat remaining in the pan and fry until golden brown. Stir in the coriander and flour and cook for 1 minute. Gradually add the cider and stock and bring quickly to the boil, stirring constantly. Return the pork to the pan, season to taste and simmer for about 5 minutes. Serve hot, with the green pepper and celery.

PORK ESCALOPES WITH SAGE

SERVES 4

450 g (1 lb) pork fillet	grated rind of 1 lemon
100 g (4 oz) fresh brown breadcrumbs	1 egg, beaten
30 ml (2 tbsp) fresh sage or 10 ml (2 tsp) dried	75 g (3 oz) butter, melted
	lemon wedges, to serve

1 Using a sharp knife, trim any excess fat from the pork fillet and cut the meat into 5 mm (¼ inch) slices.

2 Beat out into even thinner slices between two sheets of greaseproof paper, using a meat mallet or rolling pin.

3 Mix together the breadcrumbs, sage and grated lemon rind. Dip the escalopes into the beaten egg, then coat with the breadcrumb mixture.

4 Lay the pork escalopes in the base of a grill pan lined with foil and brush with melted butter. Grill for about 3 minutes each side, turning once. Serve with lemon wedges.

COOK'S TIP

Unless you have a large grill pan, you will probably need to cook the pork in two batches. Keep the first batch warm in a low oven while cooking the remainder.

CRUMB-TOPPED PORK CHOPS

SERVES 4

4 lean pork loin chops	pinch of dried thyme
50 g (2 oz) fresh white breadcrumbs	finely grated rind of 1 lemon
15 ml (1 tbsp) chopped fresh parsley or 5 ml (1 tsp) dried	2.5 ml (½ tsp) coriander seeds, crushed
5 ml (1 tsp) chopped fresh mint or 2.5 ml (½ tsp) dried	1 egg, beaten
	salt and pepper

1 Cut the rind off the chops and put them in one layer in a baking tin.

2 Mix the remaining ingredients together and season to taste. Spread this mixture evenly over the chops with a palette knife.

3 Bake in the oven at 200°C (400°F) mark 6 for 45-50 minutes or until golden. Serve hot.

VARIATION

Crumb-topped Lamb Chops

Substitute four lamb chump chops for the pork and use rosemary instead of thyme in the crumb topping. Omit the coriander, if preferred.

GOLDEN GRILLED PORK STEAKS

SERVES 4

8 pork loin steaks, each about 75 g (3 oz)	4 dried apricots, shredded
finely grated rind and juice of 1 large orange	2 garlic cloves, sliced
45 ml (3 tbsp) dry sherry	vegetable oil, for brushing
2 bay leaves	300 ml (½ pint) stock
salt and pepper	5 ml (1 tsp) cornflour
1 bunch spring onions, trimmed and cut into 1 cm (½ inch) lengths	dash of soy sauce (optional)
	orange slices and fresh herbs, to garnish

1 Trim the pork steaks and shape into rough rounds, securing each with a cocktail stick. Place in a non-metallic dish.

2 Add the orange rind with the strained juice, sherry, bay leaves and seasoning.

3 Add the spring onions, apricots and garlic to the dish with the pork steaks and stir well. Cover tightly and refrigerate for at least 2 hours, preferably overnight.

4 Lift the pork onto a grill rack, reserving the marinade. Brush lightly with oil and grill for about 7 minutes each side or until tender and well browned. Remove cocktail sticks.

5 Meanwhile, simmer the marinade ingredients in a saucepan with the stock for 10 minutes. Mix the cornflour to a smooth paste with a little water, then off the heat, stir into the pan. Return to the heat and boil for 1-2 minutes, stirring all the time. Adjust seasoning, and add a dash of soy sauce, if using.

6 To serve, spoon the sauce over the pork steaks, garnish with orange slices and fresh herbs and serve with mashed potato and cabbage.

QUICK PORK CASSOULET

SERVES 4

450 g (1 lb) streaky pork rashers, about 2 cm (¾ inch) thick	5 ml (1 tsp) dried mixed herbs
15-30 ml (1-2 tbsp) vegetable oil	400 g (14 oz) can chopped tomatoes
350 g (12 oz) onion, sliced	450 ml (¾ pint) stock
1 green pepper, seeded and roughly chopped	salt and pepper
6 celery sticks, chopped	432 g (15¼ oz) can red kidney beans, drained
2.5 ml (½ tsp) chilli powder	fried white breadcrumbs, for topping (optional)
	chopped parsley, to garnish

1 Cut the rind and any excess fat off the pork rashers and then divide the flesh into bite-sized pieces. Heat a little oil in a flameproof casserole and lightly brown the pork.

2 Remove the pork from the casserole. Add the vegetables, with a little more oil if necessary, and stir-fry the mixture for about 2-3 minutes.

3 Add the chilli powder and cook for 1 minute before mixing in the herbs, tomatoes and juice, stock and seasoning. Return the meat to the casserole and bring to the boil. Cover tightly and simmer for about 45 minutes or until the meat is tender.

4 Uncover, stir in the kidney beans and simmer to reduce and thicken slightly. Adjust seasoning before serving, topped with fried breadcrumbs if desired. Garnish with chopped parsley.

PORK
FILLET WITH APPLE

SERVES 4

about 30 ml (2 tbsp) vegetable oil	75 g (3 oz) frozen baby onions
550 g (1¼ lb) pork fillet, thinly sliced	2 apples, peeled, cored and sliced
10 ml (2 tsp) ground coriander	45 ml (3 tbsp) chopped parsley
300 ml (½ pint) cider	150 ml (5 fl oz) single cream
150 ml (¼ pint) light stock	salt and pepper

1 Heat the oil in a large shallow sauté pan and brown the pork fillet in two batches, stirring constantly and adding a little more oil if necessary.
2 Return all the meat to the pan and add the coriander, cider, stock, frozen onions and apple slices. Bring to the boil and simmer for about 5 minutes or until the pork and onions are tender.
3 Stir in the chopped parsley and cream. Simmer gently for a further 1-2 minutes to heat through. Season well.
4 Serve accompanied with boiled rice and glazed carrots.

COOK'S TIP

Apples always combine well with pork as their fruitiness offsets the rich meat. Use firm, crisp apples such as Granny Smith's, or they may break up when cooking.

STIR-FRIED
PORK AND VEGETABLES

SERVES 4

450 g (1 lb) pork fillet, trimmed	1 bunch of spring onions, trimmed and finely chopped
60 ml (4 tbsp) dry sherry	1-2 garlic cloves, crushed
45 ml (3 tbsp) soy sauce	30 ml (2 tbsp) cornflour
10 ml (2 tsp) ground ginger	300 ml (½ pint) chicken stock
salt and pepper	175 g (6 oz) beansprouts
1 medium cucumber	spring onion tassels, to garnish (optional)
30 ml (2 tbsp) vegetable oil	

1 Cut the pork into thin strips and place in a bowl. Add the sherry, soy sauce, ginger and salt and pepper to taste, then stir well.
2 Cut the cucumber into strips, about 2.5 cm (1 inch) long, discarding the seeds.
3 Heat the oil in a wok or large heavy-based frying pan, add the spring onions and garlic and fry gently for about 5 minutes until softened, then remove from the pan with a slotted spoon and set aside.
4 Add the pork to the pan, increase the heat and stir-fry for 2-3 minutes until lightly coloured.
5 Mix the cornflour with a little of the cold chicken stock and set aside.
6 Add the cucumber, spring onions and beansprouts to the pork, with the cornflour and stock. Stir-fry until the juices thicken and the ingredients are well combined. Taste and adjust the seasoning, then turn into a warmed serving dish. Garnish with spring onion tassels if using. Serve immediately, with rice.

COOK'S TIP

Spring Onion Tassels
Trim the spring onions, discarding the dark ends, to 7.5 cm (3 inch) lengths. With a sharp knife, shred each end leaving about 2 cm (¾ inch) intact in the middle. Leave in a bowl of iced water to open out.

PORK AND PASTA STIR-FRY

SERVES 4

450 g (1 lb) pork fillet	salt and pepper
75 g (3 oz) streaky bacon, rinded and chopped	175 g (6 oz) green beans, halved
225 g (8 oz) onions, preferably red, finely sliced	1 green pepper, seeded and cut into strips
15 ml (1 tbsp) wholegrain mustard	75 g (3 oz) dried pasta shells or bows
100 ml (4 fl oz) dry cider	15 ml (1 tbsp) soy sauce
1 garlic clove, crushed	60 ml (4 tbsp) stock
45-60 ml (3-4 tbsp) vegetable oil	

1 Cut the pork into strips, about 5 cm x 5 mm (2 x ¼ inch), discarding skin and excess fat. Place in a bowl with the bacon and onions. Add the mustard, cider, garlic, 15 ml (1 tbsp) oil and seasoning. Stir well. Cover and leave to marinate in the refrigerator for at least 1 hour.
2 Blanch the green beans and pepper together in boiling salted water for 2 minutes, drain; run under cold water, cool.
3 Cook the pasta in boiling salted water until just cooked, about 7-10 minutes. Drain and toss in a little oil to prevent the pasta sticking.
4 Drain the meat and the onions from the marinade, reserving juices. Heat 30 ml (2 tbsp) oil in a large sauté or frying pan. Add the meat and onions and stir-fry over a high heat for 3-4 minutes or until the meat is lightly browned and the onions are beginning to soften.
5 Put the beans, pepper and pasta into the pan with the marinade, soy sauce, stock and seasoning. Bring to the boil, stirring, then simmer for about 5 minutes or until piping hot. Serve immediately.

SATAY-STYLE PORK

SERVES 4

450 g (1 lb) pork fillet, cubed	5 ml (1 tsp) ground cumin
90 ml (6 tbsp) Greek-style natural yogurt	15 ml (1 tbsp) vegetable oil
90 ml (6 tbsp) satay marinade (see below)	salt and pepper
15 ml (1 tbsp) lemon juice	lemon slices and mint sprigs, to garnish

1 Place the pork in a bowl and add the yogurt, satay marinade, lemon juice, cumin, oil and seasoning to taste. Stir well until the meat is evenly coated. Cover and leave to marinate for at least 15 minutes.
2 Thread the meat on to 4 wooden skewers and brush with the marinade. Cook under a preheated grill for about 10 minutes, or until cooked through, basting with some of the marinade and turning occasionally.
3 Place the remaining marinade in a small saucepan and heat very gently, taking care not to boil. Pour over the meat and serve, garnished with lemon slices and mint. Serve with a salad.

COOK'S TIP

Ready-prepared satay marinade is available bottled, from larger supermarkets and delicatessens.
If you have time, marinate the pork overnight as this gives extra flavour.

ITALIAN SAUSAGE CASSEROLE

SERVES 4

450 g (1 lb) Italian sausages (salsiccia)	90 ml (6 tbsp) chicken or beef stock
45 ml (3 tbsp) olive oil	60 ml (4 tbsp) dry white wine or water
25 g (1 oz) butter	5 ml (1 tsp) dried sage
1 large onion, chopped	5 ml (1 tsp) dried rosemary
3 peppers (1 green, 1 red, 1 yellow), seeded and sliced	salt and pepper
225 g (8 oz) can chopped tomatoes	chopped parsley, to garnish

1 Plunge the sausages into a large pan of boiling water and simmer for 10 minutes. Drain, leave until cool enough to handle, then remove the skin and cut the sausages into chunks.

2 Heat the oil with the butter in a flameproof casserole, add the onion and fry gently for 5 minutes until soft but not coloured.

3 Add the sausage and peppers and fry for a further 5 minutes, stirring constantly.

4 Add the tomatoes with their juice, the stock and wine. Bring slowly to the boil, then lower the heat, add the herbs and seasoning to taste and simmer uncovered for 10-15 minutes. Taste and adjust seasoning before serving, garnished with parsley.

COOK'S TIP

Italian frying sausage sold in specialist delicatessens is available as individual sausages, usually called *salamelle*, or in one long piece called *luganega* or *salsiccia a metro*, which is cut and sold by the kg (lb). Both types are suitable for this recipe, but check with the shopkeeper before buying as some varieties are peppery hot and may not be to your taste.

CHIPOLATAS AND BEANS

SERVES 4

30 ml (2 tbsp) vegetable oil	430 g (15 oz) can red kidney beans, drained and rinsed
450 g (1 lb) pork chipolata sausages	150 ml (¼ pint) beef stock
1 large onion, sliced	salt and pepper
4 rashers streaky bacon, chopped	chopped parsley, to garnish

1 Heat the oil in a flameproof casserole, add the sausages and fry until browned on all sides. Remove the sausages from the pan with a slotted spoon and set aside.

2 Add the onion and bacon to the pan and fry for about 5 minutes or until they begin to turn brown, stirring occasionally.

3 Cut each sausage into four pieces and return to the pan with the kidney beans and beef stock. Season to taste, cover and cook gently for about 15 minutes or until the sausages are tender. Serve hot, sprinkled with parsley.

GLAZED GAMMON STEAKS

SERVES 4

15 ml (1 tbsp) soy sauce	garlic salt
2.5 ml (½ tsp) mustard powder	pepper
15 ml (1 tbsp) golden syrup	15 ml (1 tbsp) cornflour
	15 ml (1 tbsp) lemon juice
1.25 ml (¼ tsp) ground ginger	8 bacon chops or 4 gammon steaks
90 ml (6 tbsp) orange juice	

1 In a small saucepan, combine the soy sauce, mustard, syrup, ginger and orange juice with garlic salt and pepper to taste.
2 Blend the cornflour with the lemon juice, stir in a little of the mixture from the pan and then stir into the pan. Bring to the boil, stirring all the time, until the mixture has thickened to a glaze. Remove from the heat.
3 Cut most of the fat from the bacon chops or gammon steaks and then brush half of the glaze on one side.
4 Cook under a preheated moderate grill for 15 minutes or until the meat is cooked right through, golden brown and bubbling. Turn several times and brush with the remaining glaze during cooking. Serve hot.

BACON CHOPS WITH GOOSEBERRY SAUCE

SERVES 4

15 ml (1 tbsp) soft brown sugar	15 g (½ oz) butter or margarine
5 ml (1 tsp) mustard powder	1 large onion, chopped
pepper	150 ml (¼ pint) vegetable stock
4 bacon chops, each 175 g (6 oz)	100 g (4 oz) gooseberries, topped and tailed

1 Mix together the brown sugar, mustard and pepper and rub into both sides of the bacon chops.
2 Melt the butter or margarine in a large frying pan or flameproof casserole and cook the onion for 2 minutes, then add the bacon chops, half the stock and the gooseberries. Simmer gently for 15 minutes.
3 Remove the chops from the pan. Purée the onions and gooseberries in a blender or food processor until smooth.
4 Return the chops and purée to the pan with the remaining stock. Simmer gently for 10 minutes, until the chops are tender and cooked through. Serve at once.

COOK'S TIP

At the start of the season gooseberries are too acid and hard to be eaten raw, but are perfect for cooking. Look for thick prime back bacon chops, good for gentle braising.

LAMB NOISETTES WITH RED WINE SAUCE

SERVES 6

12 lamb noisettes	225 g (8 oz) button mushrooms
flour, for coating	300 ml (½ pint) red wine
25 g (1 oz) butter	150 ml (¼ pint) chicken stock
60 ml (4 tbsp) vegetable oil	15 ml (1 tbsp) tomato purée
2 large onions, sliced	2 bay leaves
1 garlic clove, finely chopped	salt and pepper

1 Lightly coat the lamb noisettes with flour. Heat the butter and oil in a large flameproof casserole. Add the noisettes, a few at a time, and cook over a high heat until browned on both sides. Remove from the casserole with a slotted spoon and set aside.

2 Add the onions and garlic to the casserole and fry for about 5 minutes or until golden. Add the mushrooms and fry for a further 2-3 minutes. Stir in the red wine, stock, tomato purée and bay leaves. Season to taste.

3 Return the noisettes to the casserole and bring to the boil, then cover and simmer gently for about 30 minutes or until tender, turning the meat once during this time.

4 Lift the noisettes out of the sauce and remove the string. Place the noisettes on a warmed serving dish and keep warm. Boil the remaining sauce rapidly for 5-10 minutes to reduce. Taste and adjust the seasoning, remove the bay leaves, then pour the sauce over the noisettes. Serve immediately.

LAMB WITH ONION PUREE

SERVES 4

45 ml (3 tbsp) olive oil	2 medium onions, finely chopped
15 ml (1 tbsp) white wine vinegar	30 ml (2 tbsp) plain flour
1.25 ml (¼ tsp) dried sage	300 ml (½ pint) milk
1 garlic clove, crushed	1 clove
4 lamb chump chops, each about 225 g (8 oz)	30 ml (2 tbsp) single cream
	salt and pepper
	sage sprigs, to garnish

1 In a jug, whisk together the olive oil, vinegar, sage and crushed garlic.

2 Trim the chops of any excess fat. Place the chops flat in a shallow non-metallic dish. Pour over the marinade, cover and leave to marinate in a cool place for 1 hour.

3 Remove the chops from the marinade, using a slotted spoon, and place under a preheated hot grill. Cook for 7-10 minutes on each side.

4 Meanwhile, put the marinade and chopped onions in a small saucepan. Cover and cook over low heat, for about 10-15 minutes until the onions are soft and golden.

5 Stir in the flour, then the milk and clove. Bring to the boil and simmer for 2 minutes. Discard the clove, transfer to a blender or food processor and work until smooth. Return the onion purée to the rinsed-out pan. Add the cream and salt and pepper to taste and reheat gently.

6 Arrange the chops on a warmed serving dish and garnish with sprigs of sage. Serve the onion purée separately.

SERVING SUGGESTION

These grilled chump chops are served with a tasty onion purée. Jacket baked potatoes topped with soured cream would make a delicious accompaniment.

LAMB FILLETS IN GARLIC

SERVES 4

450 g (1 lb) lamb neck fillet	15-30 ml (1-2 tbsp) vegetable oil
2 large garlic cloves, thinly sliced	10 ml (2 tsp) flour
20 ml (4 tsp) chopped fresh rosemary or 5 ml (1 tsp) dried	300 ml (½ pint) lamb stock
	10 ml (2 tsp) Dijon mustard
salt and pepper	dash of gravy browning (optional)
8 rashers streaky bacon, rinded	lime wedges and herbs, to garnish

1 Trim the lamb fillet and divide into four pieces. Split horizontally, without cutting right through, and open out like a book.

2 Sprinkle with the garlic, rosemary and pepper. Close the fillets.

3 Stretch the bacon rashers with the back of a blunt-edged knife. Wrap around the fillets, securing with wooden cocktail sticks.

4 Heat the oil in a small roasting tin. Add the lamb and bake at 200°C (400°F) mark 6 for 30-35 minutes or until the lamb is tender.

5 Slice the lamb into 5 mm (¼ inch) thick pieces, discarding the cocktail sticks. Cover and keep warm.

6 Pour all but 30 ml (2 tbsp) juice out of the tin. Stir in the flour and cook until lightly browned. Add the stock, mustard, gravy browning if using, and seasoning and let bubble for a few minutes. Serve garnished with lime wedges and herbs. Accompany with potatoes and a salad.

LAMB CHOPS AND LEEKS WITH LENTILS

SERVES 4

4 loin lamb chops, about 450 g (1 lb) total weight and about 2.5 cm (1 inch) thick	450 g (1 lb) leeks, trimmed and cut into 1 cm (½ inch) slices
1 small onion, finely chopped	125 g (4 oz) split red lentils
100 ml (4 fl oz) fresh orange juice	5 ml (1 tsp) paprika
	300 ml (½ pint) lamb stock
salt and pepper	coriander sprigs, to garnish
15 ml (1 tbsp) vegetable oil	

1 Trim the chops of fat; place in a non-metallic dish. Sprinkle the onion over the lamb. Pour over the orange juice and season with pepper. Cover and leave to marinate in a cool place for at least 2 hours or preferably overnight, turning once.

2 Lift the chops out of the marinade; pat dry on absorbent kitchen paper. Heat the hot oil in a medium-sized sauté pan and brown the chops on both sides. Drain on kitchen paper.

3 Add the leeks, lentils and paprika to the pan and stir over a moderate heat for 1 minute. Place the chops on the lentils. Pour in the marinade and stock and bring to the boil.

4 Cover and simmer for 20 minutes. Adjust the seasoning. Serve garnished with coriander and accompanied by steamed or boiled potatoes.

ORIENTAL LAMB

SERVES 4

1.4 kg (3 lb) lean shoulder of lamb, boned	15 ml (1 tbsp) plain flour
30 ml (2 tbsp) vegetable oil	5 ml (1 tsp) ground ginger
25 g (1 oz) butter or margarine	300 ml (½ pint) chicken stock
450 g (1 lb) small new potatoes, scrubbed or scraped	15 ml (1 tbsp) Worcestershire sauce
	30 ml (2 tbsp) soy sauce
	salt and pepper
225 g (8 oz) small pickling onions, skinned	2 caps canned pimiento, diced

1 Cut the lamb into 2.5 cm (1 inch) pieces, about 5 mm (¼ inch) thick, discarding any excess fat.
2 Heat the oil and butter or margarine in a large sauté pan and add the meat, a few pieces at time. Fry until browned on all sides, turning frequently. Remove from the pan with a slotted spoon.
3 Add the potatoes and onions to the fat remaining in the pan and fry until lightly browned, turning frequently.
4 Return the meat to the pan, sprinkle in the flour and ginger and stir well. Cook gently, stirring, for 2 minutes.
5 Add the stock, Worcestershire sauce and soy sauce, and season to taste. Bring to the boil, stirring, then cover and simmer for 30 minutes or until the meat is tender.
6 Add the pimientos and stir over a low heat to warm through. Taste and adjust the seasoning, then transfer the lamb to a warmed serving dish. Serve hot.

TANGY LAMB CHOPS

SERVES 4

30 ml (2 tbsp) vegetable oil	30 ml (2 tbsp) chopped fresh parsley or 10 ml (2 tsp) dried
4 lamb chump chops	15 ml (1 tbsp) chopped fresh mint or 5 ml (1 tsp) dried
salt and pepper	5 ml (1 tsp) sugar
juice and finely grated rind of 1 lemon	150 ml (¼ pint) beef or chicken stock

1 Heat the oil in a frying pan, add the chops and fry over a brisk heat until browned on both sides. Lower the heat and season to taste.
2 Mix the lemon juice and rind with the herbs and sugar, then spoon this mixture over the chops and pour in the stock. Cover the pan tightly and simmer gently for 30 minutes or until the meat is tender. Serve hot with the juices poured over.

VARIATION

You can vary the herbs used in this dish, depending on what is available. Fresh rosemary is, of course, the classic herb to use with lamb.

LAMB ESCALOPES IN OATMEAL

SERVES 4

2 lamb leg steaks, about 550 g (1¼ lb) total weight (bone in) and about 2-2.5 cm (¾-1 inch) thick	salt and pepper
	1 egg, beaten
Dijon mustard, to taste	150 ml (5 fl oz) soured cream
about 150 g (5 oz) medium oatmeal	15-30 ml (1-2 tbsp) paprika
	45-60 ml (3-4 tbsp) vegetable oil
15 ml (1 tbsp) dried rubbed sage	25 g (1 oz) butter

1 Trim excess fat off lamb and cut out the bone. Place the meat between sheets of greaseproof paper and, using a rolling pin, bat out thinly to a 5 mm (¼ inch) thickness. Divide each steak into 5 pieces.
2 Spread a little mustard over one side of each piece of lamb. Mix the oatmeal, sage and seasoning together.
3 Brush the meat with beaten egg and coat with the oatmeal mixture; cover and chill for about 30 minutes.
4 Mix the soured cream and 15 ml (1 tbsp) mustard together in a small bowl. Sprinkle with a little paprika; cover and chill.
5 Heat a little oil in a frying pan. Mix in the butter and, when foaming, add about half the meat. Fry over a moderate heat until browned and tender, about 3 minutes each side. Drain on absorbent kitchen paper. Keep warm, covered, while frying the remaining lamb, adding more oil if necessary.
6 Serve the lamb with the soured cream sauce and accompanied by a green leaf, orange and onion salad.

LAMB FILLET AND PEPPER STIR-FRY

SERVES 4

30 ml (2 tbsp) vegetable oil	1 yellow pepper, seeded and sliced
450 g (1 lb) lamb fillet, thinly sliced	125 g (4 oz) mangetout
125 g (4 oz) carrots, sliced diagonally	1 large courgette, sliced
2 sticks celery, thinly sliced	45 ml (3 tbsp) garlic and spring onion sauce (see below)
1 red pepper, seeded and sliced	15 ml (1 tbsp) soy sauce
	salt and pepper

1 Heat the oil in a large sauté pan or wok and quickly stir-fry the lamb for about 5 minutes, or until cooked through and golden brown. Remove from the pan with a slotted spoon and drain on absorbent kitchen paper.
2 Add the carrots, celery and peppers to the pan and stir-fry for 3-4 minutes.
3 Add all the remaining ingredients together with the lamb. Cook for a further 2-3 minutes until the vegetables are just tender. Adjust the seasoning to serve.

COOK'S TIP

Bottled ready-prepared garlic and spring onion sauce is available from large supermarkets and delicatessens. If you haven't any to hand, replace with 30 ml (2 tbsp) sherry and 1 crushed garlic clove.

BOBOTIE

SERVES 4-6

1 thick slice white bread, crust removed	30 ml (2 tbsp) curry powder
300 ml (½ pint) milk	5 ml (1 tsp) sugar
25 g (1 oz) butter or margarine	salt and pepper
1 large onion, chopped	700 g (1½ lb) lean cooked minced lamb or beef
2 eating apples, peeled and chopped	2 eggs
	25 g (1 oz) flaked almonds
50 g (2 oz) seedless raisins, currants or sultanas	bay leaves, to garnish

1 Soak the bread in the milk for a few minutes, then squeeze the bread with your fingers, catching the milk in a bowl. Reserve the bread and milk separately.
2 Melt the butter in a flameproof dish, add the chopped onion and fry gently for 5 minutes until soft but not coloured.
3 Add the apples and raisins, the curry powder, sugar and salt and pepper to taste. Fry for a further 2 minutes, stirring, then add the lamb and the reserved bread. Stir to combine. Remove from the heat and level the surface.
4 Beat the eggs with the reserved milk and salt and pepper to taste. Pour slowly over the lamb, then sprinkle over the almonds. Cook in the oven at 180°C (350°F) mark 4 for 45 minutes to 1 hour until the custard is set. Serve from the dish, garnished with bay leaves.

HERB-COATED LAMB STEAKS

SERVES 4

15 ml (1 tbsp) chopped mint (optional)	1 egg, beaten
about 125 g (4 oz) sage and onion stuffing mix	about 30 ml (2 tbsp) vegetable oil
pepper	lemon slices and mint sprigs, to garnish
4 lamb steaks, about 550 g (1¼ lb) total weight, trimmed	

1 Stir the mint, if using, into the stuffing mix. Season with pepper.
2 Divide each steak into two or three pieces and bat out thinly between two sheets of damp greaseproof paper. Dip each piece of steak in beaten egg, then thoroughly coat in the dry stuffing mix.
3 Heat the oil in a heavy-based frying pan and cook the steaks for about 5 minutes each side or until tender and cooked through, adding a little more oil if necessary. Drain well on absorbent kitchen paper.
4 Serve the steaks immediately, garnished with lemon and mint. Accompany with steamed shredded cabbage.

COOK'S TIP

For this tasty dish, look out for thin lamb steaks which will need little batting out.

SPICED
LIVER SAUTE

SERVES 4

450 g (1 lb) lamb's liver	15 ml (1 tbsp) plain white flour
about 30 ml (2 tbsp) vegetable oil	5-10 ml (1-2 tsp) paprika
125 g (4 oz) onion, sliced	150 ml (¼ pint) light stock
125 g (4 oz) button mushrooms, sliced if large	dash of Tabasco sauce
	salt and pepper
125 g (4 oz) fine green beans	150 ml (5 fl oz) single cream

1 Trim the liver and cut into strips. Heat the oil in a large sauté pan and sauté the liver until evenly browned. Lift out with a slotted spoon and set aside; keep warm.

2 Add the onion, mushrooms and beans to the pan with a little more oil if necessary, and cook, stirring, until beginning to soften. Mix in the flour and paprika and cook for a further 1 minute.

3 Add the stock, liver, Tabasco and seasoning. Simmer, covered, for 5-10 minutes, or until the liver is cooked and the vegetables are just tender.

4 Stir in the cream, adjust the seasoning and bubble up quickly. Serve immediately, with rice or tagliatelle.

COOK'S TIP

If fresh fine green beans are not available, use frozen ones.

SAUTEED LIVER
WITH SAGE AND APPLE

SERVES 4

450 g (1 lb) thinly sliced calf's liver	5 ml (1 level tsp) dried rubbed sage or dried mixed herbs
25 g (1 oz) plain white flour	15 ml (1 level tbsp) mustard, preferably wholegrain
45 ml (3 tbsp) oil	150 ml (5 fl oz) single cream
125 g (4 oz) leeks, trimmed and sliced	300 ml (½ pint) apple juice
1 eating apple, cored and thinly sliced	salt and pepper

1 Cut the liver into slightly smaller slices. Sprinkle the flour onto a flat plate and coat the liver slices well on all sides.

2 Heat 30 ml (2 tbsp) oil in a large sauté pan (preferably non-stick) and brown the liver well for about 30 seconds on each side. Remove with a slotted spoon.

3 Heat the remaining oil in the pan. Add the leeks, apple and sage and sauté, stirring well, for 2-3 minutes. Mix in the mustard, cream and apple juice, then bring to the boil and allow to bubble for about 5 minutes or until the sauce is reduced by about half.

4 Return the liver to the pan, season and simmer very gently for 1-2 minutes or until hot through. Serve immediately, with creamed potatoes and steamed broccoli.

BACON AND LIVER ROULADES

SERVES 3-4

4 rashers streaky bacon, about 100 g (4 oz) total weight	30 ml (2 tbsp) brandy
	15 ml (1 tbsp) chopped fresh marjoram or oregano or 5 ml (1 tsp) dried
225 g (8 oz) lamb's liver	
60 ml (4 tbsp) orange juice	salt and pepper

1 Cut the rind off each rasher and stretch the rashers with a blunt-edged knife. Cut each rasher across into three pieces.

2 Divide the liver into 12 even-sized pieces, removing any skin and ducts.

3 Roll a piece of bacon around each piece of liver and secure with a cocktail stick. Place in the base of a foil-lined grill pan.

4 Mix the orange juice, brandy, herbs and seasoning together and spoon over the bacon rolls. Leave to marinate in a cool place for at least 1 hour.

5 Cook under a moderate grill for 12-15 minutes, turning and basting occasionally. Remove the cocktail sticks before serving.

CALF'S LIVER WITH ONIONS AND SAGE

SERVES 6

50 g (2 oz) butter	12 slices of calf's liver
45 ml (3 tbsp) olive or vegetable oil	salt and pepper
2 large onions, sliced	15 ml (1 tbsp) white wine vinegar
6 sage leaves	sage leaves and lemon wedges, to garnish

1 Heat the butter and oil in a frying pan. Add the onions and cook very gently for 20 minutes, stirring occasionally, until soft. Stir in the sage and cook for 2-3 minutes.

2 Add the liver to the pan. Increase the heat and fry for 2-3 minutes on each side.

3 Season the liver, then transfer to a warmed serving dish with the onions; cover and keep hot. Add the vinegar to the pan and boil briskly for 1-2 minutes, stirring to loosen the sediment from the base of the pan.

4 To serve, pour the vinegar mixture over the liver and garnish with sage and lemon.

LIVER STROGANOFF

SERVES 4

4 thin slices of lamb's liver, total weight 350 g (12 oz)	15 ml (1 tbsp) tomato purée
25 g (1 oz) butter or margarine	10 ml (2 tsp) Dijon mustard
1 medium onion, thinly sliced	30 ml (2 tbsp) brandy
	salt and pepper
225 g (8 oz) button mushrooms, thinly sliced	150 ml (¼ pint) soured cream
	chopped parsley, to garnish

1 Slice the liver into thin strips. Melt the butter in a large heavy-based frying pan, add the liver and fry over moderate heat for about 5 minutes, stirring constantly so that the strips become evenly and lightly coloured. Remove with a slotted spoon and set aside.

2 Add the sliced onion to the pan and fry over a moderate heat for about 5 minutes until soft but not coloured. Remove the onion with a slotted spoon and add to the liver.

3 Add the mushrooms to the pan, increase the heat and toss until the juices run. Remove and add to the liver and onions.

4 Stir the tomato purée and mustard into the pan juices, then the brandy. Stir over high heat, scraping up the sediment from the base of the pan.

5 Return the liver, onion and mushrooms to the pan and stir to combine with the juices. Add salt and pepper to taste, then remove from the heat.

6 Stir about half of the soured cream into the stroganoff. Turn the stroganoff into a warmed serving dish and drizzle with the remaining cream. Sprinkle with chopped parsley, and serve with noodles.

KIDNEY AND MUSHROOM SAUTE

SERVES 3-4

450 g (1 lb) lamb's kidneys, skinned, halved and cored	30 ml (2 tbsp) single cream
15 ml (1 tbsp) vegetable oil	10 ml (2 tsp) wholegrain mustard
25 g (1 oz) butter	1 garlic clove, crushed
225 g (8 oz) large flat mushrooms, sliced	salt and pepper
	chopped parsley, to garnish

1 Cut the kidney halves in half again.

2 Heat the oil and butter in a large frying pan, add the kidney pieces and fry quickly until browned on all sides, turning frequently.

3 Stir in the mushrooms and cook for 1 minute, shaking the pan from time to time. Lower the heat and add the cream, mustard and garlic. Season to taste and heat through gently. Serve immediately on a bed of rice, garnished with parsley.

GRANDMA'S CHEESE PUDDING

SERVES 8

1.1 litres (2 pints) milk	8 eggs
100 g (4 oz) fresh breadcrumbs	5 ml (1 tsp) French mustard
450 g (1 lb) Cheddar cheese, grated	salt and pepper

1 Put the milk in a saucepan and bring to the boil. Place the breadcrumbs in a bowl and pour the hot milk over. Stir in the cheese.
2 Lightly beat the eggs with the mustard and the milk and breadcrumb mixture. Season to taste.
3 Butter a shallow 2.8 litre (5 pint) ovenproof dish and pour in the cheese pudding mixture. Bake in the oven at 180°C (350°F) mark 4 for about 45 minutes or until lightly set and golden. Serve at once.

CAULIFLOWER SOUFFLES

SERVES 8

225 g (8 oz) small cauliflower florets	200 ml (7 fl oz) milk
salt and pepper	15 ml (1 tbsp) wholegrain mustard
40 g (1½ oz) butter or margarine	100 g (4 oz) mature Farmhouse Cheddar cheese, grated
45 ml (3 tbsp) plain flour	4 eggs, separated

1 Grease eight individual ramekin dishes.
2 Put the cauliflower in a saucepan and just cover with boiling salted water. Cover and simmer until tender, then drain.
3 Meanwhile, prepare a white sauce. Put the butter, flour and milk in a saucepan and heat, whisking continuously, until the sauce thickens, boils and is smooth. Simmer for 1-2 minutes. Add the mustard and season to taste.
4 Turn the sauce into a blender or food processor. Add the cauliflower and work to an almost smooth purée.
5 Turn into a large bowl and leave to cool slightly. Stir in the cheese with the egg yolks.
6 Whisk the egg whites until stiff but not dry and fold into the sauce mixture. Spoon into the ramekin dishes.
7 Bake in the oven at 180°C (350°F) mark 4 for 25 minutes or until browned and firm to the touch. Serve at once.

COOK'S TIP

The distinctive flavour of cauliflower lends itself to soufflés. This dish, like all soufflés, can be started ahead and finished off just before baking. If the sauce base is allowed to cool, allow about 10 minutes extra cooking time. Ensure people are ready to eat the soufflé as soon as it is done.

GOAT'S CHEESE WITH PEAR AND WALNUTS

SERVES 2

few salad leaves, such as Webb's lettuce and radicchio, torn into pieces	50 g (2 oz) walnuts, chopped
	½ bunch watercress
100 g (4 oz) goat's cheese, halved into 2 discs	30 ml (2 tbsp) lemon juice
	45 ml (3 tbsp) vegetable oil
2 ripe pears, cored and cut into chunks	

1 Arrange the salad leaves on two serving plates and top with the goat's cheese. Mix together the pears, walnuts and watercress.

2 Blend the lemon juice and oil together, add to the pear mixture and toss to coat. Spoon on to the cheese to serve.

VARIATION

If you prefer not to use goat's cheese, Caerphilly makes a delicious substitute, as do other white cheeses, such as Lancashire, Wensleydale or white Stilton.

MIXED VEGETABLE RING

SERVES 4

100 g (4 oz) butter	salt and pepper
1 large onion, sliced	215 ml (7½ fl oz) milk
50 g (2 oz) mushrooms	100 g (4 oz) plain flour
2 courgettes, sliced	3 eggs, beaten
175 g (6 oz) aubergine, quartered and sliced	40 g (1½ oz) walnut pieces, chopped
1 red pepper, seeded and sliced	100 g (4 oz) Double Gloucester cheese with chives, grated
3 tomatoes, skinned and chopped	

1 Melt 25 g (1 oz) of the butter in a large saucepan, add the onion and mushrooms and fry lightly for 5 minutes or until softened.

2 Add the courgettes, aubergine and red pepper and cook for 5 minutes, stirring occasionally. Add the tomatoes and season to taste.

3 Melt the remaining butter in a medium saucepan with the milk, then bring to the boil. Remove the pan from the heat, tip in all the flour and beat thoroughly with a wooden spoon. Allow to cool slightly, then beat in the eggs, a little at a time. Stir in the walnuts.

4 Pipe or spoon the mixture around the edge of a well-greased 900 ml (1½ pint) ovenproof serving dish. Fill the centre with the vegetables and bake in the oven at 200°C (400°F) mark 6 for 35-40 minutes or until the pastry is risen and golden. Sprinkle with the cheese, then return to the oven until the cheese has melted. Serve at once.

OEUFS GRUYERE

SERVES 4

40 g (1½ oz) butter or margarine	175 g (6 oz) gruyère cheese, grated
100 g (4 oz) button mushrooms, thinly sliced	1.25 ml (¼ tsp) ground mace
40 g (1½ oz) plain flour	salt and pepper
150 ml (¼ pint) milk	4 eggs, size 1 or 2
150 ml (¼ pint) dry white wine	30 ml (2 tbsp) grated Parmesan cheese
150 ml (¼ pint) double cream	2.5 ml (½ tsp) paprika
	about 60 ml (4 tbsp) dried breadcrumbs

1 Melt the butter in a saucepan, add the mushrooms and fry gently for 5 minutes. Remove with a slotted spoon and set aside.

2 Add the flour to the fat remaining in the pan and cook gently, stirring, for 1-2 minutes. Remove from the heat and gradually blend in the milk and wine. Bring to the boil, stirring constantly, then simmer for 3 minutes until thick and smooth.

3 Lower the heat, stir in the cream, 100 g (4 oz) of the Gruyère and cook gently until the cheese melts. Add the mace, salt and pepper, and remove from the heat. Stir in the mushrooms.

4 Pour half the sauce into individual gratin dishes. Break an egg into the centre of each dish. Cover with the remaining sauce.

5 Mix the remaining gruyère with the Parmesan and paprika and sprinkle over the sauce. Cover with the breadcrumbs. Bake in the oven at 190°C (375°F) mark 5 for 10-15 minutes. Serve immediately.

SERVING SUGGESTION

Oeufs Gruyère are deliciously creamy. Serve for a quick lunch or supper, with a tossed mixed salad.

CHEESE FONDUE

SERVES 6

450 g (1 lb) gruyère cheese	1 liqueur glass of kirsch (optional)
450 g (1 lb) emmental cheese	pepper
30 ml (2 tbsp) cornflour	pinch of grated nutmeg
1 garlic clove	1 loaf French bread, cubed
450 ml (¾ pint) dry white wine	

1 Grate the gruyère and emmental cheeses and mix together with the cornflour.

2 Rub the inside of a heavy-based flameproof dish with the garlic. Put the cheese mixture in the dish and add the wine.

3 Heat gently, stirring all the time until the cheese has melted. Add the kirsch, if using, and season with freshly ground pepper and nutmeg. Stir well together. When the mixture is of a thick creamy consistency, it is ready to serve.

4 Pile the bread cubes into a basket and serve with the fondue.

CHEESY BAKED PASTA AND MUSHROOMS

SERVES 2-3

225 g (8 oz) ribbon noodles	60 ml (4 tbsp) double cream
25 g (1 oz) butter	salt and pepper
1 garlic clove, crushed	1 egg, lightly beaten
225 g (8 oz) mushrooms, thinly sliced	100 g (4 oz) mozzarella cheese
50 g (2 oz) Stilton cheese	

1 Cook the noodles in a large pan of boiling salted water until just tender.

2 Meanwhile, melt the butter in a large frying pan, add the garlic and mushrooms and fry for about 5 minutes or until just softened, stirring frequently. Crumble in the Stilton cheese and cook for 1-2 minutes, stirring continuously. Stir in the cream and season to taste.

3 Drain the pasta and season with lots of pepper. Mix into the mushroom sauce. Stir in the egg and mix thoroughly.

4 Turn the mixture into a buttered ovenproof dish and grate the mozzarella on top. Cover with foil and bake in the oven at 180°C (350°F) mark 4 for 10 minutes, then remove the foil and bake at 220°C (425°F) mark 7 for a further 10-15 minutes or until brown and crusty on top.

TAGLIATELLE IN CURD CHEESE AND HERBS

SERVES 2

15 g (½ oz) butter or margarine	50 g (2 oz) cooked ham, diced (optional)
1 garlic clove, crushed	salt
50 g (2 oz) mushrooms, sliced	100 g (4 oz) tagliatelle, preferably wholewheat
5 ml (1 tsp) chopped sage	50 g (2 oz) curd cheese
	sage leaves, to garnish

1 Melt the butter or margarine in a frying pan and fry the garlic, mushrooms and sage for 2 minutes, then stir in the ham if using.

2 Cook the tagliatelle in a large pan of boiling salted water until just tender. Drain well and keep warm.

3 Gently heat the cheese with the mushroom mixture until melted, then stir in the noodles. Serve immediately, garnished with sage leaves.

CELERIAC AU GRATIN

SERVES 4-6

15 ml (1 tbsp) lemon juice	150 ml (¼ pint) dry white wine
2 heads of celeriac, total weight about 900 g (2 lb)	175 g (6 oz) gruyère cheese, grated
salt and pepper	75 g (3 oz) Parmesan cheese, freshly grated
100 g (4 oz) butter or margarine	

1 Fill a bowl with cold water and add the lemon juice. Peel the celeriac, then cut into chunky pieces. Place the pieces in the bowl of acidulated water as you prepare them, to prevent discoloration.
2 Drain the celeriac, then plunge quickly into a large pan of boiling salted water. Return to the boil and cook for 10 minutes. Drain thoroughly.
3 Melt the butter in a flameproof gratin dish. Add the celeriac and turn to coat in the butter. Stir in the wine. Mix together the gruyère and Parmesan cheeses and sprinkle over the top of the celeriac, with salt and pepper to taste. Bake in the oven at 190°C (375°F) mark 5 for 30 minutes until the celeriac is tender when pierced with a skewer and the topping is golden brown.

SERVING SUGGESTION

Serve for a vegetarian supper dish, with a colourful tomato or red pepper salad, and hot garlic or herb bread.

COOK'S TIP

From the same family as celery, which it resembles in flavour, celeriac is an unusual, quite ugly-looking vegetable, sometimes called 'turnip-rooted celery', which is an apt description. Only buy small celeriac, very large specimens tend to be woody and lacking in flavour.

TURMERIC AND WALNUT MUSHROOMS

SERVES 8

1.1 kg (2½ lb) button mushrooms	15 ml (1 tbsp) turmeric
300 ml (½ pint) olive oil	1 garlic clove, crushed
100 ml (4 fl oz) white wine vinegar	salt and pepper
5 ml (1 tsp) Dijon mustard	125 g (4 oz) walnut pieces
5 ml (1 tsp) sugar	350 g (12 oz) emmental cheese, cubed
	chopped parsley, to garnish

1 Leave the small button mushrooms whole and cut any larger ones in half. Place in a serving dish.
2 In a jug, whisk together the oil, vinegar, mustard, sugar, turmeric and garlic until well blended. Add salt and pepper to taste.
3 Pour the dressing over the mushrooms and mix thoroughly to coat. Cover and leave to marinate in the refrigerator for at least 8 hours.
4 To serve, stir the mushrooms well and mix in the walnut and emmental. Garnish with chopped parsley.

CAULIFLOWER IN CURRY SAUCE

SERVES 4

1 large cauliflower	5 ml (1 tsp) salt
90 ml (6 tbsp) ghee or vegetable oil	5 ml (1 tsp) turmeric
5 ml (1 tsp) black mustard seeds	3 tomatoes, skinned and finely chopped
5 ml (1 tsp) cumin seeds	1 small green chilli, seeded and finely chopped
5 cm (2 inch) piece fresh root ginger, peeled and finely chopped	2.5 ml (½ tsp) sugar
1 small onion, finely chopped	30 ml (2 tbsp) chopped coriander

1 Divide the cauliflower into small florets, discarding the green leaves and tough stalks.

2 Heat the ghee in a heavy-based saucepan or flameproof casserole. Add the mustard seeds and, when they begin to pop, stir in the cumin seeds, ginger, onion, salt and turmeric. Fry for 2-3 minutes, stirring constantly.

3 Add the cauliflower and mix well to coat with the spice mixture. Stir in the tomatoes, chopped green chilli, sugar and half of the chopped coriander. Cover the pan tightly with a lid and cook gently for 15 minutes or until the cauliflower is tender but not mushy.

4 Uncover the pan and boil rapidly for 1-2 minutes to reduce and thicken the sauce. Turn into a warmed serving dish and sprinkle with the remaining chopped coriander. Serve immediately.

VARIATIONS

This curry sauce can be used for other vegetables besides cauliflower. Potatoes are one of the best vegetables to curry, and peas, okra, mushrooms, carrots and aubergines are also good. They can all be cooked in the same way as the cauliflower in this recipe, although the cooking time in step 3 will vary according to the type of vegetable used. Why not choose three or four different vegetables and make a mixed vegetable curry?

TOFU AND VEGETABLES IN A SPICY SAUCE

SERVES 4

75 g (3 oz) creamed coconut	2.5 ml (½ tsp) chilli powder
225 g (8 oz) firm or pressed tofu	30 ml (2 tbsp) soy sauce
oil for deep-frying, plus 45 ml (3 tbsp)	4 medium carrots, cut into matchstick strips
6 spring onions, trimmed and finely chopped	225 g (8 oz) cauliflower florets, separated into small sprigs
2.5 cm (1 inch) piece fresh root ginger, peeled and finely chopped	175 g (6 oz) French beans, topped and tailed
1 garlic clove, crushed	175 g (6 oz) beansprouts
2.5 ml (½ tsp) turmeric	salt and pepper

1 To make the coconut milk, cut the creamed coconut into small pieces and place in a measuring jug. Pour in boiling water to the 900 ml (1½ pint) mark. Stir until dissolved, then strain through a muslin-lined sieve. Set aside.

2 Drain the tofu and cut into cubes. Pat thoroughly dry with absorbent kitchen paper. Heat the oil to 190°C (375°F) in a wok or deep-fat fryer. Deep-fry the cubes of tofu in the hot oil until golden brown on all sides, turning them frequently with a slotted spoon. Remove and drain on absorbent kitchen paper.

3 Heat the 45 ml (3 tbsp) oil in a heavy-based saucepan or flameproof casserole. Add the spring onions, ginger and garlic and fry gently for about 5 minutes until softened.

4 Add the turmeric and chilli powder and stir fry for 1-2 minutes, then add the coconut milk and soy sauce and bring to the boil, stirring all the time. Add the carrots and simmer, uncovered, for 10 minutes.

5 Add the cauliflower and French beans. Simmer for a further 5 minutes, then add the tofu and beansprouts and heat through. Season to taste, then turn into a warmed serving dish. Serve immediately, with rice or noodles.

MEXICAN
RE-FRIED BEANS

SERVES 4-6

30 ml (2 tbsp) vegetable oil	1 green chilli, seeded and finely chopped
1 medium onion, finely chopped	two 425 g (15 oz) cans red kidney or pinto beans, drained
1 garlic clove, crushed	

1 Heat the oil in a large frying pan, add the onion and fry gently for about 5 minutes until soft and lightly coloured. Stir in the garlic and chilli and continue cooking for 1-2 minutes. Remove from the heat.

2 Mash the beans in a bowl with a potato masher or the end of a rolling pin. Add to the frying pan with 150 ml (¼ pint) water and stir well to mix.

3 Return the pan to the heat and fry for about 5 minutes, stirring constantly until the beans resemble porridge, adding more water if necessary. Take care that the beans do not catch and burn. Serve hot, topped with grated Cheddar cheese, if liked.

COOK'S TIP

Re-fried beans can be re-fried again and again, with the addition of a little more water each time. The flavour improves with each frying.

CHEESE
AND NUT ROAST

SERVES 4-6

40 g (1½ oz) butter or margarine	50 g (2 oz) Brazil nuts, finely chopped
1 medium onion, finely chopped	125 g (4 oz) unsalted peanuts, finely chopped
125 g (4 oz) Sage Derby cheese, or Cheddar cheese plus 5 ml (1 tsp) rubbed sage	125 g (4 oz) fresh brown breadcrumbs
50 g (2 oz) hazelnuts, finely chopped	2 eggs
	salt and pepper

1 Grease and base-line a 900 ml (1½ pint) loaf tin.

2 Melt the butter in a saucepan, add the onion and fry gently for about 5 minutes or until soft and just beginning to brown. Transfer to a bowl.

3 Grate the cheese finely into the bowl. Stir to mix with the onion, adding the sage if needed. Add the nuts, breadcrumbs and eggs and mix well again. Season to taste with salt and pepper.

4 Press the nut mixture evenly into the prepared tin. Bake in the oven at 180°C (350°F) mark 4 for about 45 minutes, or until golden brown.

5 Leave the nut roast to cool in the tin for 2-3 minutes, then turn out on to a warmed serving dish. Cut into slices and serve hot.

COOK'S TIP

Serve this tasty vegetarian roast with one of the ready-prepared tomato sauces available from large supermarkets and delicatessens.

WALNUT CROQUETTES

SERVES 4

40 g (1½ oz) butter or margarine	5 ml (1 tsp) chopped fresh herbs, eg thyme, sage or chives, or pinch of dried mixed herbs
1 small onion, finely chopped	
5 ml (1 tsp) mild curry powder	1 egg
225 g (8 oz) walnut pieces, finely chopped	about 15 ml (1 tbsp) milk
75 g (3 oz) Cheddar cheese, coarsely grated	salt and pepper
	oil for shallow-frying
175 g (6 oz) fresh brown breadcrumbs	watercress sprigs, to garnish

1 Melt the butter in a medium saucepan and sauté the onion for 2-3 minutes until softened. Add the curry powder and cook, stirring, for a further minute. Remove from the heat.

2 Stir in the nuts, cheese, breadcrumbs, herbs and egg, with enough milk to bind to a firm mixture. Season. Shape into croquettes, about 5 cm (2 inches) long, 2.5 cm (1 inch) in diameter.

3 Heat the oil in a sauté pan and shallow-fry the croquettes in batches for 3-4 minutes until golden and hot through. Drain on absorbent kitchen paper.

4 Serve immediately, garnished with watercress.

COOK'S TIP

Serve these croquettes with a ready-prepared tomato sauce or ratatouille, available from larger supermarkets and delicatessens.

SPICED VEGETABLE COUSCOUS

SERVES 4

125 g (4 oz) spring onions	50 g (2 oz) creamed coconut
15 ml (1 tbsp) vegetable oil	15 ml (1 tbsp) tomato purée
225 g (8 oz) parsnips or carrots, chopped	400 g (14 oz) can spiced lentil dahl
350 g (12 oz) potato, preferably sweet potato, peeled and chopped	15 ml (1 tbsp) white wine vinegar
	salt and pepper
225 g (8 oz) frozen broad beans or French beans	225 g (8 oz) couscous (pre-cooked)

1 Roughly chop the spring onions, reserving the tops for garnish.

2 Heat the oil in a medium saucepan and sauté the spring onions, parsnips or carrots, and potato for 1 minute. Add all the remaining ingredients, except the couscous.

3 Stir in 150 ml (¼ pint) water. Bring to the boil, cover and simmer for about 20 minutes or until the vegetables are tender.

4 Meanwhile, cook the couscous in plenty of boiling salted water for 3-5 minutes or until tender. Drain well.

5 Serve the couscous topped with the spiced vegetables. Garnish with the spring onion tops.

VEGETABLE KEBABS WITH TOFU SAUCE

SERVES 2-4

297 g (10½ oz) silken tofu	4 small courgettes, trimmed
30 ml (2 tbsp) olive oil	6 baby corn cobs, halved crossways
20 ml (4 tsp) soy sauce	16 button mushrooms
about 30 ml (2 tbsp) lemon juice	12 cherry tomatoes or 3 medium tomatoes, quartered
1-2 garlic cloves, crushed	
15 ml (1 tbsp) sesame oil (optional)	12 bay leaves
salt and pepper	30 ml (2 tbsp) sesame seeds

1 Put the tofu in a blender or food processor with half the oil and soy sauce, the lemon juice, garlic and sesame oil (if using). Work until evenly combined, then add salt and pepper to taste and more lemon juice, if liked. Pour into a jug and chill.

2 Cut each courgette into 3 pieces. Blanch in boiling salted water for 1 minute, then drain. Thread the vegetables and bay leaves on to oiled skewers.

3 Mix the remaining oil and soy sauce with the sesame seeds. Brush over the kebabs. Cook under a preheated grill for about 10 minutes, turning and brushing frequently. Serve hot, on a bed of boiled rice, if liked, with the tofu sauce handed separately.

COOK'S TIP

Tofu is also known as soya bean curd. It is off-white in colour and is formed into soft blocks. Tofu can be bought by weight from Chinese stores or in cartons from healthfood shops. Of the three forms, silken tofu is the softest and ideal for sauces. Firm tofu is made from heavily pressed bean curd and soft tofu has a texture between the two.

Tofu is high in protein, fairly low in carbohydrate and fat and is a good source of calcium, iron and the B vitamins, thiamin and riboflavin.

BUCKWHEAT AND LENTIL CASSEROLE

SERVES 4

150 g (5 oz) buckwheat	225 g (8 oz) red lentils
salt and pepper, to taste	3 bay leaves
30 ml (2 tbsp) vegetable oil	30 ml (2 tbsp) lemon juice
1 red or green pepper, seeded and cut into strips	1 garlic clove, crushed
	2 rosemary sprigs
1 medium onion, finely chopped	5 ml (1 tsp) cumin seeds
350 g (12 oz) courgettes, sliced	600 ml (1 pint) vegetable stock
175 g (6 oz) mushrooms, sliced	chopped parsley, to garnish

1 Bring 450 ml (¾ pint) water to the boil in a saucepan, sprinkle in the buckwheat, add a pinch of salt and return to the boil. Boil rapidly for 1 minute. Lower the heat, cover and cook gently, without stirring, for 12 minutes or until the water has been absorbed. Transfer to a greased casserole.

2 Heat the oil in a flameproof casserole or saucepan and fry the pepper and onion for 5 minutes. Add the courgettes and mushrooms and fry for 5 minutes. Stir in the lentils, bay leaves, lemon juice, garlic, rosemary, cumin and stock. Add to the buckwheat and stir well.

3 Simmer for 45 minutes until the lentils are cooked, stirring occasionally. Adjust the seasoning and sprinkle with chopped parsley. Serve hot with boiled rice and grated cheese, if liked.

COOK'S TIP

Buckwheat consists of tiny brown seeds. They are high in protein and contain most of the B vitamins. The grains are gluten free.

HOT
SPICED CHICK PEAS

SERVES 4

15 ml (1 tbsp) vegetable oil	450 g (1 lb) tomatoes, skinned and roughly chopped
1 medium onion, roughly chopped	15 ml (1 tbsp) lemon juice
10 ml (2 tsp) ground turmeric	60 ml (4 tbsp) chopped coriander
15 ml (1 tbsp) cumin seeds	salt and pepper
two 400 g (14 oz) cans cooked chick peas, drained	coriander leaves, to garnish

1 Heat the oil in a medium saucepan and sauté the onion until golden brown.
2 Add the turmeric and cumin seeds. Cook, stirring, for 1-2 minutes, before adding all the remaining ingredients.
3 Sauté for 1-2 minutes, stirring frequently, then adjust the seasoning. Serve garnished with fresh coriander and accompanied by crusty wholemeal bread.

SPINACH AND
MUSHROOM OMELETTE

SERVES 2

225 g (8 oz) frozen chopped spinach, thawed	40 g (1½ oz) butter or margarine
4 eggs	125 g (4 oz) button mushrooms, sliced
1.25 ml (¼ tsp) freshly grated nutmeg	10 ml (2 tsp) wholegrain mustard
salt and pepper	142 ml (5 fl oz) soured cream

1 Press the spinach in a sieve or colander to remove excess liquid. Place in a blender with the eggs, nutmeg and seasoning. Blend until smooth.
2 Heat 25 g (1 oz) butter in a large non-stick frying pan. When foaming, add the spinach mixture. Cook until the base is set, then place under a hot grill for 1-2 minutes to cook the top.
3 Meanwhile, heat the remaining butter in a pan and sauté the mushrooms with the mustard. Add the soured cream and seasoning and bring to the boil.
4 Spoon the mushroom mixture over one half of the omelette, then flip over to enclose the filling. Serve immediately, cut into wedges.

COOK'S TIP

Meat eaters could sauté chopped bacon with the mushrooms.

VEGETABLE MEDLEY

SERVES 4

25 g (1 oz) butter or margarine	15 ml (1 tbsp) chopped fresh sage or 5 ml (1 tsp) dried
2 carrots, sliced	125 g (4 oz) lentils, cooked
1 large onion, chopped	15 ml (1 tbsp) raisins
1 green pepper, seeded and sliced	30 ml (2 tbsp) unsalted peanuts
2 tomatoes, skinned and chopped	salt and pepper
1 large cooking apple, peeled and chopped	300 ml (10 fl oz) natural yogurt
1 garlic clove, crushed	25 g (1 oz) soft cheese
	sage leaves, to garnish

1   Melt the butter in a large frying pan and lightly fry the carrots, onion, green pepper, tomatoes, apple, garlic and sage for 15 minutes, until softened.
2   Add the lentils, raisins and peanuts. Season to taste.
3   Stir the yogurt into the soft cheese and mix well to blend. Stir into the vegetable mixture. Reheat gently for 5 minutes. Serve at once, garnished with sage.

VEGETABLE CURRY

SERVES 4

30 ml (2 tbsp) vegetable oil	2 potatoes, roughly chopped
10 ml (2 tsp) ground coriander	2 carrots, sliced
5 ml (1 tsp) ground cumin	1 green pepper, seeded and chopped
2.5-5 ml (½-1 tsp) chilli powder	225 g (8 oz) tomatoes, roughly chopped
2.5 ml (½ tsp) turmeric	150 ml (5 fl oz) natural yogurt
2 garlic cloves, crushed	salt and pepper
1 medium onion, chopped	toasted flaked almonds, to garnish
1 small cauliflower, cut into small florets	

1   Heat the oil in a large saucepan, then add the coriander, cumin, chilli powder, turmeric, garlic and onion and fry for 2-3 minutes, stirring continuously.
2   Add the cauliflower, potatoes, carrots and green pepper and stir to coat in the spices. Stir in the tomatoes and 150 ml (¼ pint) water. Bring to the boil, cover and gently simmer for 25-30 minutes or until the vegetables are tender.
3   Remove from the heat, stir in the yogurt and season to taste. Serve garnished with toasted almonds and accompanied by rice and chutney.

COOK'S TIP

A subtle blend of spices gives this curry its flavour. Adjust the amount of chilli powder according to taste, and vary the vegetables according to what's in season.

COOKING FOR ONE OR TWO

On those occasions when you are eating on your own, or dining à deux, turn to the recipes in this section for inspiration. Ideas range from nourishing fast snacks which can be assembled in an instant, to main meals which are easy to prepare and quick to cook. Quantities can, of course, be increased to serve larger numbers.

CRAB NOODLE SOUP

SERVES 2

25 g (1 oz) transparent or cellophane noodles	2.5 ml (½ tsp) salt
80 g (3 oz) can crab meat, drained	2.5 ml (½ tsp) caster sugar
1 egg white, beaten	1 cm (½ inch) piece fresh root ginger, peeled and finely chopped
5 ml (1 tsp) sesame oil (optional)	450 ml (¾ pint) chicken stock
15 ml (1 tbsp) dry sherry	2 spring onions, trimmed and finely sliced (optional)
5 ml (1 tsp) cornflour	

1 Soak the noodles in boiling water for 5 minutes. Mix the crab meat with the egg white and set aside.
2 In a small bowl, mix together the sesame oil, sherry, cornflour, salt, sugar and ginger.
3 Drain the noodles thoroughly. Using kitchen scissors, snip into 2.5 cm (1 inch) lengths.
4 Bring the chicken stock to the boil in a medium saucepan, quickly stir in the crab and egg white mixture, then the sherry and cornflour mixture.
5 Bring to the boil, stirring continuously, then add the noodles and spring onions, if liked. Heat through and serve immediately.

TAGLIATELLE WITH ANCHOVIES

SERVES 1

75 g (3 oz) dried or fresh green tagliatelle	60 ml (4 tbsp) whipping cream
salt and pepper	30 ml (2 tbsp) chopped parsley
half a 50 g (2 oz) can anchovy fillets, with oil	

1 Cook the tagliatelle in a medium pan of boiling salted water for 8-12 minutes if using dried, 2-3 minutes if using fresh, until just tender.
2 Meanwhile, put the anchovies with their oil into a small saucepan and cook over very low heat, crushing the anchovies with the back of a spoon until they dissolve to a purée.
3 Add the cream and increase the heat to high. Cook, stirring, for 2-3 minutes until the sauce thickens slightly. Stir in the parsley and salt and pepper to taste.
4 Drain the tagliatelle well and add to the anchovy sauce, tossing to coat the pasta. Serve immediately.

COOK'S TIP

To serve two: **double the quantity of ingredients and follow the recipe above.**

EGG AND SPINACH CROUTE

SERVES 1

2.5 cm (1 inch) thick slice bread	150 ml (¼ pint) milk
50 g (2 oz) fresh spinach, washed and trimmed	freshly grated nutmeg
	salt and pepper
65 g (2½ oz) butter	1 garlic clove, crushed
15 ml (1 tbsp) plain flour	few drops of vinegar
	1 egg

1　With a 7.5 cm (3 inch) pastry cutter, stamp out a round from the slice of bread. Set aside.
2　Cook the spinach with only the water that clings to the leaves after washing for 3-4 minutes until wilted. Drain well and chop finely.
3　Melt 15 g (½ oz) of the butter in a small saucepan, add the flour and cook gently, stirring, for 1-2 minutes. Remove from the heat and gradually blend in the milk. Bring to the boil, stirring constantly, then simmer for 3 minutes until thick and smooth. Stir in the spinach and nutmeg, salt and pepper to taste. Keep hot.
4　Toast the bread round on one side only. Spread the untoasted side with the remaining butter mixed with the garlic. Grill again until golden. Place the croûte on a warmed serving plate and keep hot.
5　Half fill a frying pan with water and add a few drops of vinegar. Bring the water to the boil, break the egg into a cup, then slip it into the water. Cook gently for 3-4 minutes or until lightly set, then lift out of the water with a slotted spoon.
6　Top the toasted croûte with the poached egg and spoon over the spinach. Serve immediately.

COOK'S TIP

To serve two: double the amount of bread, spinach and eggs, but keep the remaining ingredients the same. Follow the recipe above.

BAKED EGG WITH MUSHROOMS

SERVES 1

40 g (1½ oz) butter	5 ml (1 tsp) chopped fresh tarragon or 2.5 ml (½ tsp) dried
75 g (3 oz) button mushrooms, finely chopped	
	salt and pepper
½ small onion, finely chopped	1 egg
	tarragon sprigs, to garnish

1　Melt half of the butter in a small frying pan, add the mushrooms and onion and fry until golden and all the excess moisture has evaporated. Add the herbs and salt and pepper to taste.
2　Spoon the mushroom mixture into a ramekin or cocotte dish and make a well in the centre.
3　Carefully break an egg into the hollow, then dot with the remaining butter.
4　Stand the ramekin in a roasting tin. Pour hot water into the tin to come halfway up the side of the ramekin.
5　Cover the roasting tin with foil and bake in the oven at 180°C (350°F) mark 4 for 12-15 minutes, or until the egg is just set. Serve at once, garnished with tarragon sprigs, and accompanied by toast.

COOK'S TIP

To serve two: double the quantity of ingredients, but use 50 g (2 oz) butter. Follow the recipe above, dividing the mixture between 2 ramekins.

OMELETTE NICOISE

SERVES 1

2 eggs	50 g (2 oz) cooked French beans, roughly chopped
salt and pepper	5 black olives, stoned
25 g (1 oz) unsalted butter	half a 99 g (3½ oz) can tuna, drained and flaked
1 tomato, skinned and roughly chopped	anchovy fillets and chopped parsley, to garnish

1 Whisk the eggs in a jug with 30 ml (2 tbsp) water and plenty of salt and pepper.
2 Melt the butter in a small non-stick frying pan. When the butter is foaming, pour in the whisked egg mixture.
3 Cook the omelette over moderate heat, lifting it up around the edges with a spatula or palette knife to allow the liquid egg to run underneath. When the omelette is almost set, but still runny on top, allow the underside to colour a little.
4 Spoon the chopped tomato, beans, olives and tuna fish on top of the omelette and sprinkle with salt and pepper to taste.
5 Place the pan under a preheated hot grill for 2-3 minutes to heat the filling.
6 Fold the omelette in half, then turn on to a warmed plate. Garnish with fine strips of anchovy and chopped parsley. Serve immediately.

COOK'S TIP

To serve two: double the quantity of ingredients but use 3 eggs and the same amount of butter. Make the omelette in a larger pan and cut the omelette in half before serving.

PEPPER AND TOMATO OMELETTE

SERVES 2

30 ml (2 tbsp) olive oil	4 tomatoes, skinned and sliced
1 onion, sliced	5 eggs
2 garlic cloves, crushed	pinch of dried mixed herbs, or to taste
1 green pepper, seeded and sliced	salt and pepper
1 red pepper, seeded and sliced	50 g (2 oz) hard mature cheese, eg Parmesan or Farmhouse Cheddar, grated

1 Heat the olive oil in a non-stick frying pan. Add the onion and garlic and fry gently for 5 minutes until soft.
2 Add the pepper slices and the tomatoes and fry for a further 2-3 minutes, stirring frequently.
3 In a jug, beat the eggs lightly with the herbs and seasoning to taste. Pour into the pan, allowing the egg to run to the sides.
4 Draw in the vegetable mixture with a palette knife so that the mixture runs on to the base of the pan. Cook over moderate heat for 5 minutes until the underside of the omelette is set.
5 Sprinkle the top of the omelette with the grated cheese, then put under a preheated hot grill for 2-3 minutes until set and browned. Slide onto a serving plate and cut into wedges to serve.

COOK'S TIP

This type of omelette is different from the classic French kind, which is cooked for a very short time and served folded over. It is more like the Spanish tortilla, a flat omelette which is cooked for a longer time, then browned under a hot grill so that both sides become firm.

LOVAGE AND BLUE CHEESE OMELETTE

SERVES 2

4 eggs	75 g (3 oz) blue Cheshire cheese
10 ml (2 tsp) chopped lovage	15 g (½ oz) butter or margarine
salt and pepper	lovage leaves, to garnish

1 Whisk together the eggs, lovage, 30 ml (2 tbsp) water and seasoning. Coarsely grate the cheese, or cut it into thin slivers and set aside.
2 Heat the butter in a 20 cm (8 inch) non-stick frying pan. When foaming, pour in the egg mixture all at once.
3 Cook over a moderately high heat for a few minutes, drawing a fork through the omelette to allow the unset egg mixture to run through to the edges.
4 When set underneath but still creamy on top, scatter the cheese over the surface of the omelette. Leave for a few moments until the cheese starts to melt, then fold the omelette into three.
5 To serve, slide the omelette on to a serving plate. Garnish with lovage leaves. Divide in two for serving.

VARIATION

Use blue Stilton or Wensleydale instead of Cheshire cheese.

SMOKED HADDOCK SCRAMBLE

SERVES 1

2 eggs	1 large slice white bread, crusts removed
15 ml (1 tbsp) milk	25 g (1 oz) butter or margarine
15 ml (1 tbsp) cream	
2.5 ml (½ tsp) lemon juice	50 g (2 oz) smoked haddock fillet, flaked
salt and pepper	
oil, for shallow frying	chopped parsley, to garnish

1 In a bowl, whisk together the eggs, milk, cream, lemon juice, and salt and pepper to taste. Set aside while frying the bread.
2 Heat the oil in a frying pan, add the bread and fry until golden brown on both sides. Remove and drain on absorbent kitchen paper.
3 Melt the butter in a saucepan and add the egg mixture with the fish. Cook slowly, stirring gently and continuously, until the egg mixture becomes very creamy in texture. Taste and adjust seasoning, then remove from the heat to prevent overcooking.
4 Place the croûte on a serving plate, spoon over the haddock scramble and sprinkle with chopped parsley. Serve immediately.

COOK'S TIP

To serve two: double the quantity of ingredients but use 3 eggs. Follow the recipe above.

PIZZA-IN-THE-PAN

SERVES 2

225 g (8 oz) self-raising flour	175 g (6 oz) Cheddar cheese, grated
salt and pepper	15 ml (1 tbsp) chopped herbs, eg parsley or basil
60 ml (4 tbsp) vegetable oil	few black olives
45 ml (3 tbsp) tomato purée	
397 g (14 oz) can chopped tomatoes, drained	

1 Sift the flour and seasoning into a bowl. Make a well in the centre and pour in 30 ml (2 tbsp) of the oil and 60 ml (4 tbsp) water. Mix to a soft dough – it will bind together very quickly, although you may need to add a little more water.
2 Knead the dough lightly on a floured surface, then roll out to a circle that will fit a medium frying pan.
3 Heat half the remaining oil in the pan. Add the circle of dough and fry gently for about 5 minutes until the base is cooked and lightly browned.
4 Turn the dough out onto a plate and flip it over.
5 Heat the remaining oil in the pan, then slide the dough back into the pan, browned side uppermost. Spread with the tomato purée, then top with the tomatoes and sprinkle with the grated cheese, herbs and black olives.
6 Cook for a further 5 minutes until the underside is done, then slide the pan under a preheated grill. Cook for 3-4 minutes until the cheese melts. Serve immediately.

COURGETTE PASTICCIO

SERVES 2

400 g (14 oz) courgettes, coarsely grated	4 egg whites, size 2
100 g (4 oz) Cheddar cheese, grated	225 g (8 oz) can chopped tomatoes
60 ml (4 tbsp) plain wholemeal flour	10 ml (2 tsp) tomato purée
5 ml (1 tsp) chopped fresh basil or 2.5 ml (½ tsp) dried	50 g (2 oz) button mushrooms, sliced
pepper, to taste	2.5 ml (½ tsp) dried oregano
	parsley sprigs, to garnish

1 Combine the courgettes, 75 g (3 oz) of the cheese, the flour, basil and pepper in a large bowl. Whisk the egg whites until frothy but not stiff, then fold into the courgette mixture.
2 Place the mixture in a 23 cm (9 inch) loose-bottomed sandwich cake tin and smooth the surface. Bake in the oven at 180°C (350°F) mark 4 for 25 minutes or until slightly browned.
3 Mix the tomatoes and tomato purée together and spread over the cooked base. Scatter over the mushrooms and sprinkle the remaining cheese and oregano on top. Return to the oven and cook for a further 5 minutes. Garnish with parsley. Cut into wedges and serve hot.

COOK'S TIP

A pasticcio is rather similar to a pizza. The grated courgettes are included in the pasticcio base.

CROQUE MONSIEUR

SERVES 1

2 slices white bread	40 g (1½ oz) gruyère cheese
25 g (1 oz) butter	salt and pepper
1 slice boiled ham	15 ml (1 tbsp) vegetable oil

1 Cut the crusts off the bread, then spread one side of each slice with some of the butter.

2 Place the ham on the buttered side of one slice of bread, cutting it to fit if necessary. Cover with the gruyère cheese. Sprinkle with salt and pepper to taste, then top with the remaining slice of bread, buttered side down.

3 Press the sandwich together firmly, then cut into 4 triangles and press the edges together.

4 Melt the remaining butter with the oil in a heavy-based frying pan, add the 4 triangles and fry over moderate heat until crisp and golden on both sides. Press with a fish slice to keep the sandwiches together and turn once during frying. Serve hot.

COOK'S TIP

To serve two: double the quantities of all the ingredients, except the oil, and follow the recipe above. If necessary, use two pans or cook in batches.

SERVING SUGGESTION

Toasted sandwiches are the ideal quick snack when you arrive home hungry and cannot wait to cook a proper meal. Serve with a simple mixed salad of shredded lettuce, slices of tomato and cucumber, and mustard and cress.

WELSH RAREBIT

SERVES 1

50 g (2 oz) Cheddar cheese, grated	1.25 ml (¼ tsp) mustard powder
25 g (1 oz) butter or margarine	salt and pepper
15 ml (1 tbsp) brown ale	1 slice bread, crusts removed

1 Place all the ingredients except the bread in a heavy-based saucepan. Heat very gently, stirring continuously, until a creamy mixture is obtained.

2 Lightly toast the bread on one side only. Pour the sauce over the uncooked side and cook under a preheated hot grill until it is golden and bubbling. Serve with a crisp salad.

COOK'S TIP

To serve two: use the same amount of butter, but double the other ingredients. Follow the recipe above.

VARIATION

To make Buck Rarebit top with a poached egg.

BACON, CHEESE AND APPLE SMOKIES

SERVES 1

2.5 cm (1 inch) thick slice crusty bread	50 g (2 oz) smoked Applewood or Edam cheese
15 g (½ oz) butter or margarine	2 lean rashers of streaky bacon, rinded
½ eating apple, cored and sliced	

1 Toast the bread lightly on both sides, then spread one side with the butter. Arrange the apple slices on top of the buttered toast.
2 Slice the cheese thinly and place on top of the apple slices to cover them completely.
3 Stretch the bacon rashers with the back of a knife and cut each rasher in half. Use the bacon to cover the cheese.
4 Place the toast under a moderate grill for about 5 minutes, or until the bacon is golden and the cheese is beginning to melt, turning the bacon halfway through cooking. Serve immediately.

COOK'S TIP

Applewood is a mature Cheddar which has been smoked with an outer coating of paprika. There is another similar English smoked cheese called Charwood. Both can be obtained from good supermarkets and specialist cheese shops. They will give this tasty snack an unusual 'smoky' flavour.
To serve two: double the quantity of ingredients and follow the recipe above.

FRENCH BREAD PIZZA

SERVES 1

50 g (2 oz) salami, sliced, rinded and chopped	pepper
1 large ripe tomato, skinned and chopped	½ small French loaf
3 black olives, stoned and sliced	50 g (2 oz) butter or margarine
50 g (2 oz) mozzarella or bel paese cheese, grated	15 ml (1 tbsp) snipped fresh chives or 5 ml (1 tsp) dried mixed herbs

1 In a bowl, combine the salami, tomato, olives and half of the cheese. Season with pepper.
2 Trim the end off the French bread and split in half lengthwise. Toast both pieces on each side.
3 Spread generously with the butter and scatter the chives on top.
4 Spoon on the salami mixture, then top with the rest of the grated cheese. Cook under a hot grill for 2 minutes or until the cheese melts. Serve immediately.

COOK'S TIP

To serve two: double the quantity of ingredients and follow the recipe above.

HOT PITTA PACKET

SERVES 1

30 ml (2 tbsp) vegetable oil	2.5 ml (½ tsp) granulated sugar
1 cooked chicken leg, skinned, boned and shredded	5 ml (1 tsp) sesame oil (optional)
75 g (3 oz) button mushrooms, sliced	salt and pepper
½ small red pepper, seeded and finely sliced	1 medium carrot, grated
2.5 ml (½ tsp) chilli seasoning	50 g (2 oz) cabbage, finely sliced
15 ml (1 tbsp) soy sauce	1 wholemeal pitta bread

1 Heat the oil in a frying pan, add the chicken, mushrooms and red pepper and fry, stirring continuously, for 2-3 minutes.

2 In a jug, mix the chilli seasoning with the soy sauce, sugar, oil if using, and salt and pepper to taste. Add to the chicken with the remaining vegetables and cook over high heat for a further 2 minutes, stirring all the time.

3 Grill the pitta bread under a moderate heat on each side for about 2 minutes.

4 Using a sharp knife, make a slit along one edge of the pitta bread. Open the bread up carefully to form a pocket.

5 Spoon the chicken and vegetable mixture carefully into the pitta packet and serve immediately.

COOK'S TIP

With its filling of chicken and vegetables, this pitta packet is substantial enough to be served on its own.

To serve two: double the quantity of ingredients and follow the recipe above.

GLAZED SPICY SAUSAGES

SERVES 1

finely grated rind and juice of 1 small orange	5 ml (1 tsp) salt
90 ml (6 tbsp) mild chilli sauce	5 ml (1 tsp) Worcestershire sauce
30 ml (2 tbsp) clear honey	pepper
	2 pork sausages

1 To make the glaze, mix the orange rind and juice with the chilli sauce, honey, salt, Worcestershire sauce and pepper to taste. (This glaze will keep for up to 2 weeks in a screw-top jar in the refrigerator.)

2 Slash the sausages diagonally in 4 places and place in a foil-lined grill pan.

3 Brush the sausages generously with the glaze. Cook the sausages under a moderate grill for 10-15 minutes or until cooked through, turning and basting occasionally with more chilli glaze. Serve immediately, in long bread rolls as 'hot dogs' if preferred.

COOK'S TIP

Chilli sauce is used extensively in Chinese food, both as a dip and in cooking; it can be bought at oriental specialist stores and some large supermarkets. It is bright red in colour, made from a mixture of hot chillies, vinegar, sugar and salt. Some brands are fiery hot, so experiment with a few different ones until you find one that suits your taste. Treat any chilli sauce with caution, however, and add sparingly at first, until you are sure of its strength! If liked, you can use Tabasco as a substitute, but in this recipe you will only need a few drops.

To serve two: double the number of sausages and use the same amount of glaze.

SPICY PRAWN RISOTTO

SERVES 1

30 ml (2 tbsp) olive oil	2.5 ml (½ tsp) powdered saffron or turmeric
15 g (½ oz) butter	salt and pepper
1 small onion, finely chopped	75 g (3 oz) cooked peeled prawns
1 garlic clove, crushed	30 ml (2 tbsp) chopped coriander or mint
1 small red chilli, seeded and finely chopped, or ½ dried red chilli, crushed	cooked whole prawns, to garnish (optional)
75 g (3 oz) Italian risotto rice	
350 ml (12 fl oz) hot chicken stock	

1 Heat the oil with the butter in a heavy-based saucepan. Add the onion, garlic and chilli and fry gently for about 5 minutes until soft but not coloured.
2 Add the rice and stir gently until coated in the onion mixture. Add about one third of the hot stock, the saffron or turmeric and salt and pepper to taste. Stir over gentle heat until the liquid has been absorbed.
3 Continue adding more stock and stirring until all the liquid has been absorbed and the rice is *al dente* (tender, but firm to the bite). The total cooking time should be about 20 minutes.
4 Add the prawns and coriander and fold gently to mix with the rice. Heat through, then adjust seasoning. Serve hot, garnished with whole prawns, if liked.

COOK'S TIP

To serve two: follow the recipe above, doubling the quantity of rice, stock, prawns and coriander.

SERVING SUGGESTION

Serve with a refreshing side salad of thinly sliced cucumber dressed in olive oil, wine vinegar and chopped fresh coriander or mint.

FISH IN SOURED CREAM WITH TOMATO

SERVES 1

175 g (6 oz) whiting fillet	75 ml (5 tbsp) soured cream
salt and pepper	50 g (2 oz) gruyère cheese, grated
knob of butter	sprigs of herbs, to garnish (optional)
1 medium, firm tomato	
15 ml (1 tbsp) chopped parsley and chives, mixed	

1 To skin the whiting, dip your fingers in salt to get a good grip, then loosen a corner and pull firmly so the skin comes off cleanly.
2 Choose a shallow serving dish that fits under the grill and is just large enough to take the fish in a single layer. Put a knob of butter in the dish and grill until melted.
3 Remove the dish from the grill and put in the fish. Turn the fish so it is buttered side up, then sprinkle with salt and pepper to taste. Grill for 2-3 minutes.
4 Meanwhile, chop the tomato finely, place in a bowl and combine with the herbs and soured cream. Add 40 g (1½ oz) of the gruyère cheese, salt and pepper to taste, and mix again.
5 When the fish has cooked for about 3 minutes, spoon the cream mixture on top. Grate over a little more cheese and grill for a further 2 minutes, until bubbling. Serve at once, garnished with sprigs of herbs, if liked.

COOK'S TIP

Whiting is a member of the cod family, and is fished in North Atlantic waters. It is a small, round white fish which has a distinctive flavour and soft texture, but it is often overlooked for the more common cod and haddock.
To serve two: double the quantity of ingredients and follow the recipe above.

BUTTERED SALMON STEAKS

SERVES 2

100 g (4 oz) butter, softened	2 salmon steaks, each about 175 g (6 oz)
finely grated rind and juice of ½ lemon	75 ml (5 tbsp) dry white wine
10 ml (2 tsp) chopped fresh tarragon or 5 ml (1 tsp) dried	pepper
	tarragon sprigs and lemon wedges, to serve

1 In a small bowl, cream together the butter, lemon rind and juice, and the tarragon.
2 Cut 2 pieces of foil, each one large enough to wrap around a salmon steak. Grease the foil with half of the butter mixture.
3 Place the salmon steaks on the buttered foil and dot with the remaining butter. Spoon the wine over the steaks and sprinkle with pepper to taste.
4 Fold the foil around the steaks, keeping the parcels quite loose. Place the parcels on a baking sheet and bake in the oven at 170°C (325°F) mark 3 for 20 minutes, or until the fish is firm.
5 Unwrap the salmon steaks, transfer to warmed individual serving plates and pour over the juices from the foil packets. Serve immediately, garnished with tarragon sprigs and lemon wedges.

SERVING SUGGESTION

Serve with buttered new potatoes and mangetout, petits pois or broccoli. The ideal wine to serve would be a crisp, dry white such as a Muscadet or Italian Verdicchio.

SKEWERED SCALLOPS WITH BACON

SERVES 2

8 large fresh or frozen scallops, thawed	30 ml (2 tbsp) olive or vegetable oil
4 rashers streaky bacon, rinded	2 medium tomatoes, skinned
15 ml (1 tbsp) chopped fresh basil or tarragon or 5 ml (1 tsp) dried	5 ml (1 tsp) wine vinegar
	salt and pepper
	basil sprigs, to garnish

1 If necessary, remove and discard the tough white 'muscle' from each scallop, which is found opposite the orange coral. Separate the corals.
2 With a sharp knife, lightly score the scallops on each side in a lattice pattern.
3 Stretch the bacon rashers with the back of a knife and divide each rasher in two.
4 Wrap the bacon around the corals. Thread the scallops horizontally and corals alternately on to 2 kebab skewers. Place in a foil-lined grill pan.
5 Mix the basil with 15 ml (1 tbsp) of the oil and brush over the scallops and bacon. Cook under a hot grill for 5 minutes on each side until the scallops are just cooked and the bacon golden, brushing with more oil and basil when turning the skewers over.
6 Slice each tomato into 6 wedges and arrange on the side of a serving platter. Whisk the remaining oil and the vinegar together, with salt and pepper to taste.
7 When the scallops are cooked, place the skewers on the platters and spoon the dressing over the tomatoes. Garnish with sprigs of basil and serve immediately.

SERVING SUGGESTION

Serve on a bed of saffron rice, with a side salad of curly endive, radicchio and chopped red or green pepper. A chilled dry white Bordeaux wine goes well with scallops.

PAN-GRILLED CHICKEN WITH HERBS

SERVES 1

1 boneless chicken breast, about 175 g (6 oz), skinned	5 ml (1 tsp) chopped fresh tarragon or 2.5 ml (½ tsp) dried
25 g (1 oz) butter	5 ml (1 tsp) chopped fresh fennel or 2.5 ml (½ tsp) dried
15 ml (1 tbsp) olive oil	
1 garlic clove, crushed	salt and pepper
juice of ½ lemon	lemon slices and watercress sprigs, to garnish (optional)

1   Trim the chicken breast as necessary.

2   Melt the butter with the oil in a small saucepan. Remove from the heat and add the garlic, lemon juice and herbs.

3   Brush the base of the grill pan with a little of the melted mixture. Place the chicken in the pan and brush with more of the mixture.

4   Put the pan under a preheated moderate grill and cook for 15-20 minutes. Turn the chicken several times and brush with the herb mixture during grilling. Sprinkle with salt and pepper to taste at the end of the cooking time.

5   Serve hot, garnished with lemon slices and sprigs of watercress, if liked.

SERVING SUGGESTION

To serve two: follow the recipe above, doubling the quantities of all the ingredients except the herbs, which should only be increased by half.

FLAMBEED VEAL ESCALOPES

SERVES 2

2 veal escalopes	2 crisp dessert apples
25 g (1 oz) butter	60 ml (4 tbsp) dry white wine
15 ml (1 tbsp) olive oil	30 ml (2 tbsp) double cream
30 ml (2 tbsp) Calvados or brandy	salt and pepper
	parsley sprigs, to garnish

1   Cut each veal escalope in half and place between two sheets of dampened greaseproof paper. Beat out thinly with a meat mallet or rolling pin.

2   Melt the butter with the oil in a large heavy-based frying pan. Add the escalopes and fry over moderate heat for 5-7 minutes until the meat is tender, turning once.

3   Warm the Calvados or brandy gently in a ladle or small saucepan. Remove the pan of escalopes from the heat. Ignite the Calvados or brandy and pour over the escalopes while still flaming.

4   When the flames have died down, remove the escalopes from the pan with a fish slice. Place on a warmed serving plate, cover and keep hot in a low oven.

5   Quarter and core the apples, then slice thickly. Add the white wine to the pan and stir to scrape up the sediment with the pan juices. Add the apple slices and toss over high heat for about 5 minutes until tender and lightly coloured.

6   With a slotted spoon, remove the apple slices from the pan juices and arrange with the veal. Stir the cream into the pan juices and heat through. Add salt and pepper to taste, then pour over the veal and apples. Serve promptly, garnished with parsley.

COOK'S TIP

Calvados is an apple brandy from Normandy in north-western France. It is one of the most highly prized of French brandies, with its own *appellation contrôlée.*

ROQUEFORT RUMPBURGER

SERVES 1

175 g (6 oz) piece of rump steak, with surrounding fat	salt and pepper
¼ small onion, skinned	25-40 g (1-1½ oz) Roquefort cheese
few parsley sprigs	vegetable oil, for brushing

1 Work the steak, onion and parsley through a mincer, or in a food processor until finely minced. Season well with salt and pepper.

2 Place half of the meat mixture on a board and form into a flat burger shape. Cut the Roquefort into slices to fit on top of the burger.

3 Form the remaining meat mixture into a burger shape and place over the cheese. Press down well and make sure that the meat covers the cheese completely.

4 Place the burger on the rack in the grill pan and brush lightly with oil. Grill under a preheated moderate grill for 3-5 minutes or until cooked to your liking.

5 Turn the burger over, brush with more oil and grill the other side for a further 3-5 minutes. Serve hot.

COOK'S TIP

To serve two: double the quantity of all the ingredients and follow the recipe above.

STIR-FRIED BEEF IN OYSTER SAUCE

SERVES 2

25 g (1 oz) Chinese dried mushrooms	1 small onion, thinly sliced
175-225 g (6-8 oz) rump steak	1 garlic clove, crushed
30 ml (2 tbsp) oyster sauce	2 carrots
30 ml (2 tbsp) dry sherry	2.5 cm (1 inch) piece fresh root ginger, peeled and shredded
salt and pepper	10 ml (2 tsp) cornflour
30 ml (2 tbsp) vegetable oil	

1 Put the dried mushrooms in a bowl, pour in boiling water to cover and leave to soak for about 20 minutes.

2 Meanwhile, cut the steak into thin strips, place in a bowl and add the oyster sauce, sherry and salt and pepper to taste. Stir well to mix, then cover and leave to marinate in a cool place while the mushrooms are soaking.

3 Heat the oil in a wok or deep heavy-based frying pan. Add the onion and garlic and fry gently for about 5 minutes until soft but not coloured, stirring occasionally.

4 Meanwhile, drain the mushrooms and reserve 60 ml (4 tbsp) soaking liquid. Squeeze the mushrooms dry, then slice thinly, discarding any hard stalks. Cut the carrots into thin matchstick strips.

5 Add the mushrooms, ginger and carrots to the wok and stir-fry over moderate heat for about 5 minutes until slightly softened. Add the meat and marinade and stir-fry for a few minutes more, until the beef is tender.

6 Mix the cornflour to a paste with the reserved mushroom liquid. Pour into the wok and stir-fry until the sauce is thickened. Adjust seasoning before serving.

COOK'S TIP

Look for packets of Chinese dried mushrooms in specialist oriental shops; although expensive, they are only used in small quantities because of their strong flavour. They must be softened in warm water for 20 minutes before use.

PORK BROCHETTES

SERVES 1

175-225 g (6-8 oz) pork fillet	1.25 ml (¼ tsp) cayenne pepper
15 ml (1 tbsp) lemon juice	pinch of ground cumin
15 ml (1 tbsp) olive or vegetable oil	pinch of ground coriander
2.5 ml (½ tsp) paprika	salt and pepper
1.25 ml (¼ tsp) dried oregano	

1 Trim the pork of any fat or gristle and cut into 2 cm (¾ inch) cubes.
2 In a bowl, mix together the lemon juice, oil, paprika, oregano, cayenne, cumin, coriander and salt and pepper to taste. Add the cubed pork and mix well to coat. Cover and leave to marinate in the refrigerator for at least 1 hour.
3 Thread the pork cubes on to kebab skewers. Cook under a preheated hot grill for about 12 minutes, turning the brochettes occasionally to ensure even cooking. Baste occasionally during cooking with any remaining marinade. Serve immediately, with rice.

COOK'S TIP

To serve two: double the quantity of ingredients and use the same amount of cayenne but 1.25 ml (¼ tsp) cumin and coriander. Follow the recipe above.

VARIATION

This recipe could equally well be made with lamb fillet, or even with cubes of boneless chicken breast meat.

FETTUCCINE IN CREAMY MUSHROOM SAUCE

SERVES 1

100-175 g (4-6 oz) fresh or dried fettuccine or tagliatelle	1 slice smoked ham, cut into fine strips
salt and pepper	freshly grated nutmeg
25 g (1 oz) butter or margarine	75 ml (5 tbsp) double cream
40 g (1½ oz) button mushrooms, finely sliced	25 g (1 oz) freshly grated Parmesan cheese

1 Cook the pasta in a large pan of boiling salted water for 8-12 minutes if using dried pasta, 2-3 minutes if using fresh.
2 Meanwhile, melt the butter in a small saucepan, add the mushrooms and fry for 2-3 minutes. Add the strips of ham and nutmeg, salt and pepper to taste. Stir in the cream and simmer for 2 minutes or until slightly thickened.
3 Drain the pasta and stir in the sauce and Parmesan cheese, coating the pasta evenly. Serve immediately.

COOK'S TIP

To serve two: double the quantity of ingredients and follow the recipe above.

SERVING SUGGESTION

Serve with extra grated Parmesan cheese and plenty of freshly ground black pepper. An Italian style salad of cold French beans, tomato, onion, garlic and black olives tossed in a dressing of olive oil, lemon juice, chopped fresh basil and salt and pepper would go well with the pasta.

CALF'S LIVER WITH SAGE AND AVOCADO

SERVES 2

2 thin slices of calf's liver, each weighing 75-100 g (3-4 oz)	50 g (2 oz) butter
15 ml (1 tbsp) plain flour	1 ripe avocado
10 ml (2 tsp) rubbed fresh sage or 5 ml (1 tsp) dried	juice of 1 lime
salt and pepper	60 ml (4 tbsp) dry vermouth
	lime slices, to garnish

1 Cut the liver into small serving pieces, then coat in the flour mixed with half of the sage and pepper to taste. (Do not add salt as this will toughen the liver.)

2 Melt the butter in a heavy-based frying pan, add the liver and fry over moderate heat for 2-3 minutes on each side. Remove the pan from the heat and lift out the liver with a fish slice. Place on a warmed serving plate, cover and keep hot in a low oven.

3 Peel, halve and stone the avocado. Cut the flesh into thin slices. Reheat the butter in the frying pan, add the avocado slices and fry for 1-2 minutes until heated through. Remove from the pan with a slotted spoon and arrange with the liver.

4 Pour the lime juice and vermouth into the pan, increase the heat and boil to reduce, stirring vigorously to scrape up any sediment. Add the remaining sage, taste and adjust the seasoning, then pour over the liver. Serve immediately, garnished with the lime slices.

COOK'S TIP

Take great care when cooking calf's liver. It has a very delicate texture and should be cooked for the minimum amount of time as in this recipe, so that the centre is still moist and slightly pink. Never overcook calf's liver or it will be tough and rubbery.

CHICKEN LIVERS IN SHERRY SAUCE

SERVES 2

225 g (8 oz) chicken livers, thawed if frozen	75 ml (3 fl oz) sherry
25 g (1 oz) plain flour	50 ml (2 fl oz) chicken stock
salt and pepper	50 g (2 oz) black or green seedless grapes, halved
25 g (1 oz) butter or margarine	90 ml (3 fl oz) soured cream

1 Coat the livers in well-seasoned flour.

2 Melt the butter in a medium frying pan and fry the livers with any remaining flour for about 4 minutes, stirring once or twice. Gradually stir in the sherry and stock and simmer for 1-2 minutes.

3 Add the grapes and soured cream. Heat through gently and serve hot, with rice.

COOK'S TIP

Rich chicken livers have a very moist, crumbly texture. This quick dish is ideal served as a lunch or fast supper. If grapes are not available, substitute with 25 g (1 oz) sultanas.

MICROWAVE DISHES

A microwave oven is an invaluable time-saver, reducing cooking times – and washing up – to a minimum. This varied collection of soups, starters and delicious main meals has been created specifically for microwave cooking. Fish is particularly good cooked by microwave and you will find plenty of tasty fast fish dishes to choose from here.

CHILLED COURGETTE AND YOGURT SOUP

SERVES 4-6

1 medium onion, finely chopped	30 ml (2 tbsp) chopped mint
1 large potato, peeled and grated	150 ml (¼ pint) natural yogurt
600 ml (1 pint) boiling vegetable or chicken stock	salt and pepper
450 g (1 lb) courgettes, coarsely grated	courgette slices and mint sprigs, to garnish

1 Put the onion, potato and half the stock into a large bowl. Cover and cook on HIGH for 8-10 minutes or until very soft.
2 Add the courgettes, re-cover and continue to cook on HIGH for 4 minutes or until the courgettes are soft.
3 Rub through a sieve or purée in a blender or food processor until smooth. Add the remaining stock, the mint and the yogurt and season to taste with salt and pepper.
4 Cover and chill in the refrigerator for at least 4 hours before serving, garnished with courgette slices and mint.

SERVING SUGGESTION

A deliciously refreshing soup to serve as a summer starter.

SPICED CRANBERRY SOUP

SERVES 4

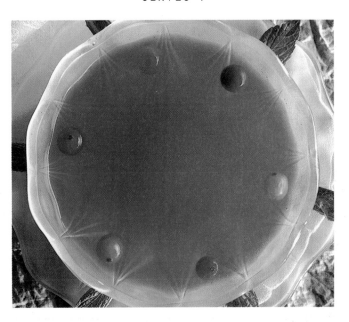

350 g (12 oz) cranberries	45 ml (3 tbsp) clear honey
4 whole cloves	15 ml (1 tbsp) crème de cassis
1 cinnamon stick	few cranberries and mint leaves, to garnish

1 Put the cranberries, cloves, cinnamon and honey into a large bowl with 600 ml (1 pint) water. Cover and cook on HIGH for 10-12 minutes or until the cranberries are tender.
2 Cool slightly, then pass the soup through a sieve. Stir in the crème de cassis, cover and chill in the refrigerator for at least 4 hours before serving.
3 To serve, spoon the soup into individual bowls and garnish each with a few cranberries and mint leaves.

SERVING SUGGESTION

An unusual chilled soup to serve as a starter during the cranberry season.

CHILLED PEA
AND MINT SOUP

SERVES 4-6

50 g (2 oz) butter or margarine	2 large mint sprigs
1 medium onion, roughly chopped	pinch of caster sugar
450 g (1 lb) peas	salt and pepper
600 ml (1 pint) milk	150 ml (¼ pint) natural yogurt
600 ml (1 pint) boiling chicken stock	mint sprigs, to garnish

1 Put the butter into a large bowl and cook on HIGH for 45 seconds or until melted.
2 Add the onion, cover and cook on HIGH for 5-7 minutes or until softened.
3 Add the peas, milk, stock, mint sprigs and the sugar. Re-cover and cook on HIGH for about 8 minutes or until boiling. Reduce the setting and continue cooking on LOW for 15 minutes, or until the peas are really tender. Season well with salt and pepper and allow to cool slightly.
4 Using a slotted spoon, remove about 45 ml (3 tbsp) peas from the soup and put them aside for the garnish. Purée the soup in a blender or food processor until quite smooth.
5 Pour the soup into a large serving bowl. Adjust the seasoning and leave to cool for 30 minutes. Stir in the yogurt, cover and chill for 2-3 hours before serving.
6 Serve garnished with the reserved peas and mint.

WATERZOOI

SERVES 6

15 ml (1 tbsp) vegetable oil	700 g (1½ lb) freshwater fish fillets, such as bream, carp, pike or eel, skinned
2.5 ml (½ tsp) ground cloves	
2 celery sticks, chopped	salt and pepper
2 leeks, sliced	2 egg yolks
2 large carrots, thinly sliced	150 ml (¼ pint) milk
1 bouquet garni	6 slices of toast
2 strips of lemon rind	30 ml (2 tbsp) chopped parsley
600 ml (1 pint) boiling fish or vegetable stock	

1 Put the oil, cloves, celery, leeks, carrots, bouquet garni, lemon rind and half the stock into a large bowl. Cover and cook on HIGH for 12-14 minutes or until the vegetables are softened.
2 Meanwhile, skin the fish if necessary and cut into bite-sized pieces. Discard the skin.
3 Add the fish, remaining stock and salt and pepper to taste to the soup. Re-cover and cook on HIGH for 6-7 minutes or until cooked.
4 Meanwhile, blend the egg yolks and milk together. When the fish is cooked, spoon a little of the liquid on to the egg yolk mixture and mix together. Pour back into the soup.
5 Re-cover and cook on medium for 1-2 minutes or until thickened, stirring once; do not allow the soup to boil or it will curdle. Discard the lemon rind and bouquet garni.
6 To serve, place the toast in six soup bowls, carefully spoon over the soup and garnish with chopped parsley. Serve immediately.

PASTINA AND SUMMER VEGETABLE SOUP

SERVES 4

15 ml (1 tbsp) olive oil	900 ml (1½ pints) boiling vegetable stock
100 g (4 oz) new carrots, sliced	30 ml (2 tbsp) chopped mint
100 g (4 oz) French beans, cut in half	4 lettuce leaves, finely shredded
225 g (8 oz) young peas	salt and pepper
50 g (2 oz) pastina (tiny pasta shapes)	

1 Put the oil, carrots, beans and peas into a large bowl. Cover and cook on HIGH for 2 minutes, stirring once.

2 Add the pastina and stock. Re-cover and cook on HIGH for 10 minutes or until the pasta and vegetables are tender.

3 Stir in the mint and lettuce and season to taste. Cook on HIGH for 1 minute or until the lettuce is just wilted. Serve hot.

PRAWNS AND LETTUCE IN BRANDY AND CREAM

SERVES 1

175 g (6 oz) medium raw prawns, in the shell	25 ml (1½ tbsp) brandy
15 g (½ oz) butter or margarine	45 ml (3 tbsp) double cream
salt and pepper	4 green Cos lettuce leaves, shredded
	lime twists, to garnish

1 To prepare the prawns, remove the shells, leaving the tail shells intact. Then, with kitchen scissors, split the prawns along the inner curve, stopping at the tail shell, and cutting deep enough to expose the dark vein. Spread each prawn wide open, remove the dark vein, then rinse under cold running water.

2 Put the butter into a medium bowl and cook on HIGH for 30 seconds or until melted. Stir in the prawns and cook on HIGH for 1½-2½ minutes or until the prawns just turn pink, stirring frequently. Remove with a slotted spoon and set aside.

3 Season the butter with salt and pepper and quickly stir in the brandy and the cream. Cook on HIGH for 4-4½ minutes or until the mixture is thickened and reduced.

4 Stir in the prawns and lettuce and mix together carefully. Cook on HIGH for 30-45 seconds or until the prawns are just heated through. Garnish with lime twists and serve immediately.

COOK'S TIP

If you find it difficult to buy raw prawns, buy the best quality cooked prawns in the shell and omit step 1.

BUCKWHEAT SPAGHETTI WITH SMOKED SALMON

SERVES 2

225 g (8 oz) buckwheat spaghetti	75 ml (3 fl oz) buttermilk
75 g (3 oz) smoked salmon trimmings	30 ml (2 tbsp) snipped chives
	1 egg, beaten
finely grated rind and juice of ½ small lemon	pepper
	chives, to garnish

1   Break the spaghetti in half and put into a large bowl. Pour over boiling water to cover by about 2.5 cm (1 inch) and stir. Cover and cook on HIGH for 5-6 minutes or until almost tender. Leave to stand, covered, for 5 minutes while making the sauce. Do not drain.

2   Cut the salmon into neat pieces and put into a serving bowl with the remaining ingredients and pepper to taste. Cook on HIGH for 1 minute or until slightly warmed, stirring once.

3   Drain the pasta and rinse with boiling water. Quickly stir into the sauce and toss together to mix. Garnish with chives and serve immediately, with a mixed salad.

PASTA WITH COURGETTES AND SMOKED TROUT

SERVES 4

2 medium courgettes	1 smoked trout, about 225 g (8 oz)
15 ml (1 tbsp) olive oil	
pinch of saffron	150 ml (¼ pint) crème fraîche or double cream
225 g (8 oz) fresh spinach pasta, such as tagliatelle	30 ml (2 tbsp) black lumpfish roe
salt and pepper	herb sprigs, to garnish

1   Cut the courgettes into very thin diagonal slices. Put the courgettes, oil and saffron into a medium bowl and cook on HIGH for 1 minute, stirring once.

2   Put the spinach pasta and salt to taste into a large bowl. Pour over enough boiling water to cover by about 2.5 cm (1 inch). Cover and cook on HIGH for 3-4 minutes. Stand, covered, while finishing the sauce. Do not drain.

3   To finish the sauce, remove and discard the skin and bones from the trout. Flake the flesh and stir into the courgettes with the crème fraîche and seasoning. Cook on HIGH for 2 minutes or until hot and slightly thickened.

4   Drain the pasta and return to the large bowl. Pour over the sauce and toss together to mix. If necessary, reheat the sauce and pasta together on HIGH for about 2 minutes. Transfer the pasta to four plates, top each with a spoonful of lumpfish roe and garnish with herbs.

TAGLIATELLE WITH FRESH FIGS

SERVES 1

75 g (3 oz) dried tagliatelle	1.25 ml (¼ tsp) medium curry powder
salt and pepper	30 ml (2 tbsp) soured cream
3 large ripe fresh figs	30 ml (2 tbsp) grated Parmesan cheese
15 g (½ oz) butter or margarine	herbs, to garnish

1 Put the tagliatelle and salt to taste in a medium bowl and pour over 600 ml (1 pint) boiling water. Stir, cover and microwave on HIGH for 3-4 minutes or until almost tender, stirring frequently. Leave to stand, covered, but do not drain.

2 Meanwhile, cut one of the figs in half lengthways. Reserve one of the halves to garnish, then peel and roughly chop the remainder.

3 Put the butter, chopped figs and curry powder in a shallow dish and microwave on HIGH for 2 minutes, stirring occasionally.

4 Drain the pasta and stir into the fig mixture with the soured cream and Parmesan cheese. Season well with salt and pepper. Carefully mix together with two forks and microwave on HIGH for 1-2 minutes or until hot.

5 Garnish with herbs and the reserved fig half and serve immediately.

SUMMER PASTA

SERVES 4

350 g (12 oz) Brie	2-3 large garlic cloves, crushed
3 large ripe beefsteak tomatoes	salt and pepper
1 large handful of basil leaves	450 g (1 lb) dried spaghetti
	45 ml (3 tbsp) olive oil

1 Remove and discard the thick outer rind from the Brie, leaving the top and bottom rind on. Cut the cheese into small pieces. Coarsely chop the tomatoes and basil. Carefully mix the cheese, tomatoes and basil with the garlic and season generously with black pepper and a little salt. Cover and leave for 30 minutes-1 hour to let the flavours develop, stirring occasionally.

2 Put the spaghetti and salt to taste into a large bowl and pour over enough boiling water to cover the pasta by about 2.5 cm (1 inch). Stir, cover and cook on HIGH for 7-10 minutes or until tender. Leave to stand, covered, for 5 minutes. Do not drain.

3 Drain the pasta and return to the rinsed-out bowl or serving dish with the oil. Cook on HIGH for 2 minutes or until hot. Add the cheese and tomato mixture and toss together. Serve immediately.

AUBERGINE AND YOGURT PUREE

SERVES 4

1 aubergine, total weight about 450 g (1 lb)	6 black olives, stoned and roughly chopped
5 ml (1 tsp) vegetable oil	juice of ½ lemon
1-2 garlic cloves, crushed	150 ml (¼ pint) natural yogurt

1 Rub the aubergine with the oil and prick well all over with a fork. Place on absorbent kitchen paper. Microwave on HIGH for 8 minutes or until tender, turning over once during cooking.

2 Leave to stand for 5 minutes then chop roughly, discarding the stalk. Put in a blender or food processor with the remaining ingredients and work until smooth.

3 Turn the purée into a bowl and leave to cool. Serve with wholemeal pitta bread, toast or crudités.

COOK'S TIP

Whole aubergines cook to perfection in the microwave and instead of turning brown, as in conventional cooking, they retain their delicate colour. Serve this interesting purée as a pâté or dip.

HERB AND MUSHROOM PATE

SERVES 6-8

25 g (1 oz) butter or margarine	60 ml (4 tbsp) chopped mixed herbs, eg thyme, sage, parsley, chervil
1 garlic clove, crushed	lemon juice, to taste
2 juniper berries, crushed	salt and pepper
700 g (1½ lb) mushrooms, roughly chopped	herbs, to garnish
75 g (3 oz) fresh brown breadcrumbs	

1 Put the butter, garlic and juniper berries into a large bowl and cook on HIGH for 1 minute.

2 Add the mushrooms and cook on HIGH for 10-12 minutes or until the mushrooms are really soft and most of the liquid has evaporated, stirring frequently.

3 Add the breadcrumbs and herbs, and lemon juice, salt and pepper to taste. Beat thoroughly together, then turn into a serving dish, cover and chill before serving. Garnish with fresh herbs and serve with melba toast.

TRICOLOUR PATE TRIO

SERVES 6

1 large red pepper	salt and pepper
175 g (6 oz) cauliflower florets	1 ripe avocado
300 ml (½ pint) natural yogurt	15 ml (1 tbsp) lemon juice
300 ml (½ pint) single cream	herbs and black olives, to garnish

1 Cut the pepper in half lengthways and remove the seeds. Place, cut side down, on a double sheet of absorbent kitchen paper and cook on HIGH for 5-6 minutes or until the pepper is soft.
2 Meanwhile, cut the cauliflower into very small florets and put into a large bowl with 15 ml (1 tbsp) water.
3 When the pepper is cooked, cook the cauliflower on HIGH for 6-7 minutes or until very tender, stirring occasionally.
4 Meanwhile, carefully peel the skin from the pepper and discard. Put the pepper, a third of the yogurt and a third of the cream in a blender or food processor and purée until smooth. Season to taste with salt and pepper.
5 Drain the cauliflower and put into the rinsed-out bowl of the blender or food processor with half of the remaining yogurt and half of the remaining cream, and purée until smooth. Season to taste with salt and pepper.
6 Halve the avocado and discard the skin and the stone. Put into the rinsed-out bowl of the blender or food processor with the remaining yogurt, cream and the lemon juice. Purée until smooth. Season to taste with salt and pepper. Leave all the pâtés to cool before serving.
7 To serve, put a large spoonful of each pâté side by side into six individual serving bowls. Shake each bowl gently from side to side allowing the pâtés to merge into one another but leaving three distinctive sections of colour. Sprinkle with a few fresh herbs and black olives. Serve immediately, with melba toast.

HERBY AUBERGINE CHEESE TERRINE

SERVES 6

2 large aubergines, each about 450 g (1 lb), finely chopped	100 g (4 oz) curd cheese
450 ml (¾ pint) boiling vegetable stock	60 ml (4 tbsp) chopped mixed herbs
2 eggs	salt and pepper
100 g (4 oz) breadcrumbs	coarsely chopped herbs, to garnish

1 Put the aubergines and the stock in a large bowl, cover and cook on HIGH for 20-25 minutes or until the aubergine is very soft.
2 Beat thoroughly to make a purée then stir in the eggs, breadcrumbs, curd cheese and herbs. Season with salt and pepper.
3 Grease a deep 20 cm (8 inch) round dish and line the base with greaseproof paper. Spoon the mixture into the dish and level the surface. Cook on MEDIUM for 20-25 minutes or until just firm to the touch.
4 Turn out on to a serving plate and press coarsely chopped herbs on to the sides and top. Serve hot or cold with salad and warm bread rolls.

RISOTTO ALLA MILANESE

SERVES 4

75 g (3 oz) butter or margarine	750 ml (1¼ pints) boiling vegetable stock
1 small onion, finely chopped	2.5 ml (½ tsp) saffron powder or large pinch of saffron strands
450 g (1 lb) arborio rice	
150 ml (¼ pint) dry white wine	75 g (3 oz) freshly grated Parmesan cheese
	salt and pepper

1 Put half the butter and the onion in a large bowl. Cover and cook on HIGH for 3-4 minutes or until the onion is softened. Add the rice, wine, stock and saffron, re-cover and cook on HIGH for 13-15 minutes or until the rice is tender and the water absorbed.

2 Stir in the remaining butter and half of the cheese, then season generously with pepper and a little salt. Serve immediately, with the remaining Parmesan handed round separately and accompanied by a mixed salad.

STUFFED SPINACH PASTA SHELLS

SERVE 4

20 large pasta shells	freshly grated nutmeg, ground mixed spice or ground mace
salt and pepper	
900 g (2 lb) fresh spinach, washed, trimmed and chopped, or a 226 g (8 oz) packet frozen chopped spinach	150 ml (¼ pint) olive oil
	30 ml (2 tbsp) lemon juice
	10 ml (2 tsp) tomato purée
450 g (1 lb) ricotta cheese	salt and pepper
	herbs, to garnish

1 Put the pasta shells into a large bowl with salt to taste and pour over enough boiling water to cover by about 2.5 cm (1 inch). Stir once, then cover and cook on HIGH for 18-20 minutes or until almost tender, stirring once during cooking. Do not drain, but leave to stand, covered, for 5 minutes.

2 Drain the pasta and rinse in cold water, then leave to drain again.

3 If using fresh spinach, put it into a large bowl, cover and cook on HIGH for 3-4 minutes or until just cooked. If using frozen spinach, cook on HIGH for 8-9 minutes or until thawed. Drain and return to the bowl.

4 Stir in the ricotta cheese and mix thoroughly together. Season to taste with nutmeg, mixed spice or mace and salt and pepper.

5 Use the spinach and cheese mixture to stuff the pasta shells and arrange upright on a serving dish.

6 To make the tomato vinaigrette, whisk the oil, lemon juice and tomato purée together and season to taste with salt and pepper. Drizzle over the pasta shells and serve immediately, garnished with fresh herbs.

WARM SALMON AND SCALLOP SALAD

SERVES 4

225 g (8 oz) salmon steak or cutlet	45 ml (3 tbsp) crème fraîche or soured cream
8 large shelled scallops	10 ml (2 tsp) wholegrain mustard
selection of salad leaves, eg curly endive, Webb's lettuce, radicchio and watercress	15 ml (1 tbsp) lemon juice
	salt and pepper
2 stale bridge rolls	few chopped fresh herbs, eg parsley, chives, dill and tarragon
45 ml (3 tbsp) olive or nut oil	

1 Skin the salmon and remove the bone, if necessary. Cut across the grain into very thin strips. If necessary, remove and discard from each scallop the tough white 'muscle' which is found opposite the coral. Separate the corals from the scallops. Slice the scallops into three or four pieces vertically. Cut the corals in half if large.
2 Heat a browning dish on HIGH for 5-8 minutes or according to the manufacturer's instructions.
3 Meanwhile, tear the salad leaves into small pieces, if necessary, and arrange on four plates. Cut the rolls into thin slices.
4 Add 30 ml (2 tbsp) of the oil to the browning dish and swirl to coat the bottom of the dish. Quickly add the sliced rolls and cook on HIGH for 2 minutes. Turn over and cook on HIGH for a further 1 minute or until crisp. Remove from the dish and set aside.
5 Add the remaining oil and the scallops, corals and salmon to the dish and cook on HIGH for 1½ minutes or until the fish looks opaque, stirring once.
6 Using a slotted spoon, remove the fish from the dish, and arrange on top of the salad leaves.
7 Put the crème fraîche or soured cream, mustard, lemon juice, and salt and pepper to taste into the browning dish and cook on HIGH for 1-2 minutes or until hot. Stir thoroughly and pour over the fish. Sprinkle with the croûtons and herbs, and serve immediately.

OYSTER MUSHROOM SALAD

SERVES 6

25 g (1 oz) butter or margarine	15 ml (1 tbsp) white wine vinegar
30 ml (2 tbsp) vegetable oil	salt and pepper
15 ml (1 tbsp) lemon juice	1 small red onion, finely chopped
450 g (1 lb) oyster mushrooms	45 ml (3 tbsp) chopped mixed herbs
mixed salad leaves, eg curly endive, radicchio, lamb's lettuce	

1 Put the butter, oil and lemon juice into a large shallow dish and cook on HIGH for 45 seconds or until the butter is melted. Add the mushrooms, cover and cook on HIGH for 2-3 minutes or until the mushrooms are tender.
2 Meanwhile, arrange the salad leaves on six plates.
3 When the mushrooms are cooked, remove them with a slotted spoon and arrange on top of the salad.
4 Quickly add the vinegar to the liquid remaining in the dish and cook on HIGH for 1 minute. Season to taste with salt and pepper. Pour over the mushrooms and sprinkle with the onion and the herbs. Serve immediately.

PIQUANT PURPLE SALAD

SERVES 4

450 g (1 lb) small new potatoes, scrubbed	½ cucumber
60 ml (4 tbsp) olive oil	175 g (6 oz) cooked beetroot
30 ml (2 tbsp) white wine vinegar	selection of red salad leaves, such as radicchio, oak leaf lettuce
salt and pepper	30 ml (2 tbsp) capers
450 g (1 lb) whiting fillets, skinned	6 anchovy fillets
30 ml (2 tbsp) milk	30 ml (2 tbsp) chopped dill
2 large pickled dill cucumbers or 4 gherkins	

1 Put the potatoes into a medium bowl with 30 ml (2 tbsp) water. Cover and cook on HIGH for 8-10 minutes or until tender, stirring occasionally.

2 While the potatoes are cooking, make the dressing. Whisk the oil and vinegar together and season to taste with salt and pepper. When the potatoes are cooked, drain well and pour the dressing over them. Leave to cool, stirring occasionally.

3 Cut the fish into small strips about 1 cm (½ inch) wide and 7.5 cm (3 inches) long and put into a shallow dish with the milk. Cover and cook on HIGH for 3-4 minutes or until just cooked. Do not overcook or the fish will break up and spoil the appearance of the salad. Leave to cool.

4 When the potatoes and fish are cold, slice the pickled dill cucumbers or gherkins and the cucumber and mix with the potatoes. Peel the beetroot and cut into chunks.

5 Arrange the salad leaves on a serving platter. Spoon over the potato mixture, then the fish and then the beetroot. Mix lightly together. Sprinkle with the capers, anchovies and dill. Serve with crusty bread.

AVOCADO, PRAWN AND POTATO SALAD

SERVES 4

350 g (12 oz) small new potatoes, scrubbed and quartered	salt and pepper
1 small ripe avocado	225 g (8 oz) cooked peeled prawns
150 ml (¼ pint) natural yogurt	4 large radishes, thinly sliced
15 ml (1 tbsp) lemon juice	2 spring onions, thinly sliced
5 ml (1 tsp) wholegrain mustard	few lettuce leaves, to garnish

1 Put the potatoes into a medium bowl with 30 ml (2 tbsp) water. Cover and cook on HIGH for 7-8 minutes or until tender, stirring occasionally.

2 Meanwhile, cut the avocado in half and remove the stone. Peel. Mash half the flesh with the yogurt, lemon juice, mustard and salt and pepper to taste.

3 Pour the dressing over the potatoes and toss together with the prawns. Cut the remaining avocado into cubes and mix into the salad with the radishes and spring onions. Serve garnished with lettuce leaves.

HOT BAGUETTE WITH SALAMI AND RED PEPPER

SERVES 2

15 ml (1 tbsp) olive or vegetable oil	150 ml (¼ pint) chicken stock
1 small onion, chopped	225 g (8 oz) mozzarella cheese
5 ml (1 tsp) paprika	4 thin slices Danish salami
2.5 ml (½ tsp) sugar	1 small baguette, about 30 cm (12 inches) long
pinch of cayenne pepper	salt and pepper
1 small red pepper, seeded and chopped	few black olives, stoned (optional)
15 ml (1 tbsp) plain flour	

1 Put the oil, onion, paprika, sugar, cayenne pepper and chopped red pepper into a medium bowl. Cover and cook on HIGH for 5-7 minutes or until the vegetables are softened, stirring occasionally.

2 Stir in the flour and cook on HIGH for 30 seconds. Then gradually stir in the chicken stock and cook on HIGH for 5-6 minutes, stirring frequently, until the pepper is softened and the sauce has thickened.

3 Meanwhile, cut the mozzarella into thin slices and remove the rind from the salami. Cut the baguette in half widthways, then cut each piece in half lengthways. Arrange a layer of mozzarella on two halves. Top with a layer of salami. Season with pepper.

4 When the sauce is cooked, let it cool a little, then work in a blender or food processor until smooth. Spoon on top of the salami. Top with a few olives, if using. Put the other half of the baguette on top of each half to make two sandwiches.

5 Wrap each sandwich in greaseproof paper and heat on HIGH for 1-1½ minutes or until the sandwiches are just warmed through. Serve immediately.

CROISSANTS WITH SMOKED MACKEREL

SERVES 4

50 g (2 oz) butter	2 smoked mackerel fillets
finely grated rind and juice of ½ lemon	salt and pepper
½ small bunch of watercress	cayenne pepper (optional)
	4 croissants

1 Put the butter into a medium bowl and cook on LOW for 1-2 minutes until slightly softened. Beat until smooth, then gradually beat in the lemon rind and juice.

2 Finely chop half the watercress, discarding any tough stems, and beat into the butter.

3 Flake the fish and mix carefully into the butter being careful not to mash the flakes of fish. Season to taste with salt, pepper and cayenne pepper.

4 Cut each croissant in half horizontally and spread the fish butter on one side of each. Lay the remaining sprigs of watercress on top of the butter.

5 Sandwich the croissants together again, wrap each one loosely in a napkin and cook on HIGH for 1-2 minutes until warm. (Note: one croissant will take 30 seconds.) Serve immediately, wrapped in the napkin.

COOK'S TIP

These deliciously rich croissants are just as good if made in advance and stored overnight in the refrigerator. If cooking them straight from the refrigerator, increase the cooking time in step 5 to 2-3 minutes.

135

SCRAMBLED EGGS WITH SMOKED SALMON

SERVES 2

4 eggs	50 g (2 oz) smoked salmon trimmings
60 ml (4 tbsp) milk or cream	salt and pepper
25 g (1 oz) butter or margarine	chopped parsley, to garnish

1 Put the eggs, milk and butter into a medium bowl and whisk together with a balloon whisk.

2 Cook on HIGH for 2 minutes or until the mixture just begins to set around the edge. Whisk vigorously to incorporate the set egg mixture, then cook on HIGH for a further 1-2 minutes or until the eggs are just set, whisking every minute.

3 Using kitchen scissors, snip the salmon trimmings into the egg mixture and mix gently together. Season to taste with salt and pepper, then serve immediately with hot buttered toast. Garnish with chopped parsley.

EGG NOODLES WITH SQUID AND SHRIMPS

SERVES 4-6

250 g (9 oz) packet thin egg noodles	450 g (1 lb) squid, cleaned
45 ml (3 tbsp) hoisin sauce	50 g (2 oz) blanched almonds
15 ml (1 tbsp) lemon juice	100 g (4 oz) cooked peeled shrimps or prawns
30 ml (2 tbsp) soy sauce	100 g (4 oz) beansprouts
15 ml (1 tbsp) sweet chilli sauce	3 spring onions, roughly chopped
45 ml (3 tbsp) sesame oil	black pepper
30 ml (2 tbsp) vegetable oil	shredded lettuce and lemon wedges, to garnish
1 garlic clove, crushed	

1 Put the noodles into a large bowl and pour over boiling water to cover by about 2.5 cm (1 inch). Cover and cook on HIGH for 2 minutes. Leave to stand, covered, for 5 minutes while cooking the fish. Do not strain.

2 Put the hoisin sauce, lemon juice, soy sauce, chilli sauce, oils and garlic into a large bowl. Cut the squid into small pieces or rings and mix into the sauce with the almonds. Cook on HIGH for 5 minutes or until the squid looks just opaque, stirring once.

3 Add the shrimps or prawns, beansprouts and drained noodles and mix thoroughly together. Cover and cook on HIGH for 2-3 minutes or until hot, stirring once. Stir the spring onions into the noodle mixture. Season to taste with black pepper.

4 To serve, spoon on to plates and top each portion with a pile of shredded lettuce and a lemon wedge. Serve immediately.

SWEET COOKED CLAMS

SERVES 2

450 g (1 lb) venus clams in the shell	15 ml (1 tbsp) caster sugar
2.5 cm (1 inch) piece fresh root ginger, peeled and grated	45 ml (3 tbsp) soy sauce
	10 ml (2 tsp) cornflour
	2.5 cm (1 inch) piece cucumber
60 ml (4 tbsp) sake or dry sherry	1 spring onion, trimmed

1 Thoroughly scrub the clams.
2 Put the ginger, sake or sherry, sugar and soy sauce into a large bowl and cook on HIGH for 2-3 minutes or until hot. Stir until the sugar is dissolved. Blend the cornflour with 60 ml (4 tbsp) water and stir into the sauce. Cook on HIGH for 2 minutes or until boiling and thickened, stirring once.
3 Add the clams and stir to coat in the sauce. Cook on HIGH for 4-5 minutes or until the clams have opened, stirring occasionally. Discard any clams which do not open.
4 Meanwhile, cut the cucumber and spring onion into very thin strips.
5 Spoon the clams and sauce on to individual serving plates. Sprinkle with the cucumber and spring onion and serve immediately.

MOULES MARINIERE

SERVES 2

1 small onion, finely chopped	900 g (2 lb) mussels, cleaned
1 garlic clove, crushed	25 g (1 oz) butter, diced
150 ml (¼ pint) dry white wine	salt and pepper
15 ml (1 tbsp) chopped parsley	chopped parsley, to garnish

1 Put the onion, garlic, wine, parsley and 45 ml (3 tbsp) water into a large bowl and cook on HIGH for 2-3 minutes or until hot.
2 Stir in the mussels, cover and cook on HIGH for 3-5 minutes or until all the mussels have opened, taking out the mussels on the top as they open and shaking the bowl occasionally. Discard any mussels which do not open.
3 Drain the mussels in a sieve over the bowl. Put the mussels into two large soup bowls.
4 Stir the butter into the cooking liquid. Cook on HIGH for 1-2 minutes or until hot, stirring frequently. Season to taste.
5 Pour the sauce over the mussels. Garnish with plenty of chopped parsley and serve immediately with French bread to mop up the juices.

MALAYSIAN
PRAWNS

SERVES 4

1 small onion, finely chopped	2.5 ml (½ tsp) ground cumin
1 garlic clove, chopped	15 ml (1 tbsp) red wine vinegar
3 large tomatoes, roughly chopped	5 ml (1 tsp) tomato purée
2.5 cm (½ inch) piece fresh root ginger, peeled and crushed	50 g (2 oz) creamed coconut, crumbled
2.5 ml (½ tsp) turmeric	450 g (1 lb) cooked peeled prawns
	salt and pepper

1   Put the onion, garlic, tomatoes, ginger, turmeric, cumin, vinegar, tomato purée, coconut and 150 ml (¼ pint) boiling water into a medium bowl. Cook on HIGH for 8 minutes or until thickened, stirring occasionally.

2   Add the prawns and stir together. Cover and cook on HIGH for 2-3 minutes or until the prawns are heated through, stirring once. Season to taste with salt and pepper. Serve with rice and poppadums.

COOK'S TIP

To cook poppadums in the microwave, brush on one side with a little oil. Cook one poppadum at a time on HIGH for 1 minute or until crisp and puffed up all over.

CEYLON
PRAWN CURRY

SERVES 4

50 g (2 oz) butter or margarine	5 ml (1 tsp) salt
1 large onion, finely chopped	5 ml (1 tsp) sugar
1 garlic clove, crushed	50 g (2 oz) creamed coconut
15 ml (1 tbsp) flour	450 ml (¾ pint) chicken stock
10 ml (2 tsp) turmeric	450 g (1 lb) cooked peeled prawns or 12 cooked Dublin Bay prawns, peeled
2.5 ml (½ tsp) ground cloves	5 ml (1 tsp) lemon juice
5 ml (1 tsp) ground cinnamon	coriander sprigs, to garnish

1   Put the butter into a shallow ovenproof dish and microwave on HIGH for 1 minute until the butter melts; stir in the onion and garlic. Cover and microwave on HIGH for 5-7 minutes until the onion softens.

2   Stir the flour, spices, salt and sugar into the onion. Microwave on HIGH for 2 minutes. Stir in the creamed coconut and stock. Microwave on HIGH for 6-8 minutes until boiling, stirring frequently.

3   Add the prawns and lemon juice to the sauce and adjust the seasoning. Microwave on HIGH for 1-2 minutes until the prawns are heated through. Garnish with the coriander and serve with rice and chutney.

FISH WITH CORIANDER MASALA

SERVES 2-3

1 medium onion, chopped	juice of 2 limes
2 garlic cloves	30 ml (2 tbsp) vegetable oil
1 green chilli, seeded (optional)	4 large tomatoes, finely chopped
2.5 cm (1 inch) piece fresh root ginger, peeled	15 ml (1 tbsp) garam masala
15 ml (1 tbsp) coriander seeds	salt
5 ml (1 tsp) turmeric	1 whiting, codling or pollack, about 700-900 g (1½-2 lb), scaled and cleaned
5 ml (1 tsp) fenugreek seeds	coriander sprigs, to garnish
45 ml (3 tbsp) chopped fresh coriander	

1 Put the onion, garlic, chilli, ginger, coriander seeds, turmeric, fenugreek seeds, fresh coriander and lime juice in a blender or food processor and process until smooth.

2 Put the oil in a large shallow dish (large enough to hold the fish) and cook on HIGH for 1 minute until hot. Add the spice paste and cook on HIGH for 5 minutes, or until the onion is softened, stirring occasionally.

3 Add the tomatoes, garam masala and salt to taste and cook on HIGH for 3-4 minutes until the sauce is reduced and slightly thickened, stirring occasionally.

4 Meanwhile, using a sharp knife, make deep cuts in a criss-cross pattern on each side of the fish. If the fish is too large for the microwave, push a long bamboo skewer through the tail and then into the body of the fish so that the tail is curved upwards. Alternatively remove the head and tail.

5 Lay the fish in the dish containing the sauce and spoon the sauce over the fish to coat it. Cover and cook on HIGH for 10-15 minutes depending on the thickness of the fish, until tender. Serve garnished with coriander.

HAKE AND LIME KEBABS

SERVES 4

700 g (1½ lb) hake fillets, skinned	salt and pepper
2 limes	mint sprigs, to garnish

1 Cut the hake into 2.5 cm (1 inch) cubes. Thinly slice 1½ limes. Thread the lime slices and the hake on to four wooden skewers. Arrange the kebabs in a single layer in a large shallow dish. Squeeze the juice from the remaining half lime over the kebabs.

2 Cover the kebabs and cook on HIGH for 4-5 minutes or until the fish is cooked, repositioning the kebabs once during cooking. Season to taste with salt and pepper. Serve hot, with rice or cracked wheat. Garnish with mint.

STUFFED HERRINGS

SERVES 4

4 herrings or mackerel, each about 225 g (8 oz), cleaned and scaled	50 g (2 oz) walnut halves, finely chopped
15 ml (1 tbsp) chopped rosemary	25 g (1 oz) fresh white breadcrumbs
15 ml (1 tbsp) snipped chives	salt and pepper
15 ml (1 tbsp) chopped sage	30 ml (2 tbsp) olive oil
2 garlic cloves, chopped	30 ml (2 tbsp) lemon juice

1 Remove the head and fins from each herring, then cut completely along the underside. Open the fish out and lay cut side down on a board. Press lightly along the middle of the back to loosen the bone.

2 Turn the fish over and ease out the backbone and as many small bones as possible. Wash and dry the fish.

3 Arrange the fish, skin side down, in a large shallow dish, placing the wider end towards the outside. Sprinkle the fish with the herbs, garlic, walnuts and half the breadcrumbs. Season generously with pepper and a little salt. Carefully fold each fish in half.

4 Mix the oil and lemon juice together and pour over the fish. Sprinkle with the remaining breadcrumbs. Cover and cook on HIGH for 8-10 minutes or until the fish is tender.

5 Serve the stuffed herrings with a little of the cooking liquid spooned over.

DEVILLED HERRINGS IN OATMEAL

SERVES 2

10 ml (2 tsp) tomato purée	4 small herring fillets
2.5 ml (½ tsp) mild mustard	60 ml (4 tbsp) medium oatmeal
2.5 ml (½ tsp) soft light brown sugar	15 ml (1 tbsp) vegetable oil
dash of Worcestershire sauce	15 g (½ oz) butter or margarine
pinch of cayenne pepper	lemon wedges and mustard and cress, to garnish
salt and pepper	

1 Heat a browning dish on HIGH for 5-8 minutes or according to manufacturer's instructions.

2 Meanwhile, mix the tomato purée, mustard, sugar, Worcestershire sauce and cayenne pepper together. Season to taste with salt and pepper. Spread the paste thinly on to both sides of each herring fillet, then coat in the oatmeal.

3 Put the oil and butter in the browning dish and swirl it around to coat the base of the dish.

4 Quickly add the herring fillets, skin side down, and cook on HIGH for 1½ minutes. Turn over and cook on HIGH for 1-2 minutes or until the fish is cooked. Serve garnished with lemon wedges and mustard and cress.

LEAF-WRAPPED MULLET

SERVES 4

4 red mullet, each about 275 g (10 oz), cleaned and scaled	30 ml (2 tbsp) white wine vinegar
3-4 garlic cloves	salt and pepper
45 ml (3 tbsp) olive oil	8 large Swiss chard or spinach leaves, trimmed

1 Using a sharp knife, slash the mullet three times on each side. Roughly chop the garlic and sprinkle into the slashes. Whisk the oil and vinegar together and season to taste with salt and pepper.
2 Put the fish into a shallow dish and pour over the oil and vinegar. Leave in a cool place for 30 minutes to marinate.
3 Remove the fish from the marinade and wrap each of them in two of the chard or spinach leaves. Return the wrapped fish to the dish containing the marinade.
4 Cover and cook on HIGH for 6-8 minutes or until the fish is tender, rearranging once and basting with the marinade during cooking.
5 Serve the fish in their leaf parcels, with a little of the marinade spooned over.

COOK'S TIP

Swiss chard makes a good wrapping for fish as the leaves are large and pliable and retain their bright green colour when cooked. It is a member of the beetroot family and is also known as seakale beet or silver beet.

SOLE AND SPINACH ROULADES

SERVES 4

12 sole fillets, each about 75 g (3 oz), skinned	12 spinach or sorrel leaves, washed
5 ml (1 tsp) fennel seeds, lightly crushed	15 ml (1 tbsp) dry white wine
salt and pepper	45 ml (3 tbsp) Greek strained yogurt
	pinch of turmeric

1 Place the sole fillets, skinned side up, on a chopping board. Sprinkle with the fennel seeds and season to taste with salt and pepper. Lay a spinach or sorrel leaf, vein side up, on top of each fillet, then roll up and secure with a wooden cocktail stick.
2 Arrange the fish in a circle around the edge of a large shallow dish and pour over the wine. Cover and cook on HIGH for 6-7 minutes or until tender.
3 Remove the fish from the cooking liquid, using a slotted spoon, and transfer to a serving plate.
4 Gradually stir the yogurt and turmeric into the cooking liquid. Season to taste with salt and pepper and cook on HIGH for 1-2 minutes or until slightly thickened, stirring occasionally. Serve the roulades with a little of the sauce poured over.

TROUT
WITH SESAME CREAM

SERVES 2-4

2 trout, total weight about 275 g (10 oz)	1 garlic clove, crushed (optional)
15 ml (1 tbsp) vegetable oil	30 ml (2 tbsp) finely chopped parsley
60 ml (4 tbsp) tahini (sesame seed paste)	salt and pepper
30 ml (2 tbsp) lemon juice	tarragon or parsley, lemon rind strips and black olives, to garnish
150 ml (¼ pint) soured cream	

1 Brush the trout with the oil and arrange in a single layer in a shallow dish. Cover and cook on HIGH for 5-7 minutes or until tender. Carefully peel off the skin, leaving the head and tail intact. Leave to cool.
2 To make the sauce, put the tahini, lemon juice, soured cream, garlic if using, and parsley into a bowl and mix together. Season to taste with salt and pepper.
3 Carefully transfer the fish to two plates. Coat in some of the sauce leaving the head and tail exposed. Garnish with tarragon or parsley leaves, lemon rind and olives. Serve with the remaining sauce and a salad or rice pilaff.

SERVING SUGGESTION

This unusual way of serving cold poached trout makes a delicious main course dish served with a salad or rice pilaff.

STUFFED
TROUT

SERVES 4

25 g (1 oz) butter or margarine	finely grated rind and juice of 1 lemon
1 medium onion, finely chopped	salt and pepper
75 g (3 oz) fresh breadcrumbs	4 whole trout, each about 225 g (8 oz), cleaned
30 ml (2 tbsp) chopped parsley	lemon wedges and chopped parsley or tarragon, to garnish

1 Put the butter into a medium bowl and microwave on HIGH for 1 minute until the butter melts. Stir in the onion. Cover and microwave on HIGH for 5-7 minutes until the onion softens. Stir in the breadcrumbs, parsley, lemon rind and juice, salt and pepper, and mix together well.
2 Fill each trout with the stuffing, then slash the skin twice on each side. Place the trout side by side in a large ovenproof dish.
3 Cover and microwave on HIGH for 8-10 minutes, turning the trout over and re-positioning them halfway through cooking. Stand for 5 minutes before serving, garnished with lemon wedges and parsley or tarragon.

FISH EN PAPILLOTE

SERVES 2

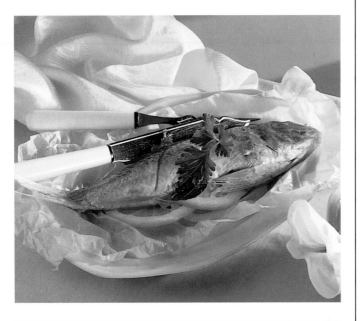

2 red mullet, each about 175 g (6 oz), cleaned and scaled	½ small onion, thinly sliced
	2 parsley sprigs
salt and pepper	2 bay leaves
	4 lemon slices

1 Slash the fish on each side using a sharp knife. Season the insides with salt and pepper to taste. Use the onion, parsley, bay leaves and lemon slices to stuff the fish.
2 Cut two 30 cm (12 inch) squares of greaseproof paper. Place a fish on each piece and fold it to make a neat parcel, twisting the ends together to seal. Place the parcels on a large flat plate.
3 Microwave on HIGH for 3-4 minutes or until the fish is tender. Serve the fish in their parcels.

COOK'S TIP

This simple method of cooking fish in greaseproof paper parcels works just as well with any other small, whole fish.

SPICED RED SNAPPER WITH ROOT VEGETABLES

SERVES 4

1 green chilli	225 g (8 oz) carrots
5 ml (1 tsp) ground aniseed	4 red snapper or red mullet, each about 275 g (10 oz), cleaned and scaled
2 allspice berries	
60 ml (4 tbsp) vegetable oil	salt and pepper
225 g (8 oz) celeriac	parsley sprigs, to garnish
225 g (8 oz) parsnips	

1 Remove the seeds from the chilli and discard. Finely chop the chilli and put into a small bowl with the aniseed. Crush the allspice berries and add with the oil. Cook on HIGH for 1-2 minutes or until hot, then leave to infuse while cooking the vegetables.
2 Cut the celeriac, parsnips and carrots into neat strips about 7.5 cm (3 inches) long and 1 cm (½ inch) wide. Put all of the vegetables into a medium bowl with 45 ml (3 tbsp) water. Cover and cook on HIGH for 5-6 minutes or until slightly softened, stirring once.
3 Slash the fish twice on each side and arrange in a single layer in a large dish. Brush with a little of the spiced oil, cover and put into the cooker on top of the bowl containing the vegetables. Cook on HIGH for 7-8 minutes or until tender, re-arranging the fish once during cooking.
4 Cook the remaining spiced oil on HIGH for 1 minute or until hot, then drain the vegetables and toss in half the hot oil. Season to taste with salt and pepper.
5 Arrange the vegetables on a platter with the fish. Spoon over the remaining oil, garnish with parsley and serve immediately.

PARCHMENT BAKED SALMON

SERVES 2

25 g (1 oz) butter or margarine	1.25 ml (¼ tsp) fennel seeds
½ small cucumber, thinly sliced	salt and pepper
2 spring onions, finely chopped	2 salmon steaks, each about 175 g (6 oz)
60 ml (4 tbsp) dry white wine	45 ml (3 tbsp) mayonnaise
10 ml (2 tsp) chopped dill	30 ml (2 tbsp) natural yogurt
	1.25 ml (¼ tsp) lemon juice
	dill sprigs, to garnish

1 Put half of the butter in a small bowl and microwave on HIGH for 30 seconds or until melted. Set aside 6 cucumber slices. Add the rest of the cucumber to the butter with the spring onions.

2 Cover and microwave on HIGH for 4-5 minutes or until tender. Stir in half of the wine and half of the fresh dill, and microwave uncovered on HIGH for 2 minutes. Leave to cool.

3 Meanwhile, put the remaining butter, the fennel seeds and the remaining wine in a small bowl and microwave on HIGH for 2 minutes or until reduced by half. Season with salt and pepper.

4 Cut two 28 cm (11 inch) squares of non-stick baking parchment or greaseproof paper and place a salmon steak on each. Arrange the reserved cucumber slices on top and pour over the butter, wine and fennel seeds. Fold the paper to make two neat parcels.

5 Place the parcels on an ovenproof plate and microwave on HIGH for 4-5 minutes or until the fish is tender.

6 While the fish is cooking, finish the sauce. Purée the cooled cucumber and onion mixture in a blender or food processor with the mayonnaise, yogurt, lemon juice, remaining dill, salt and pepper. Garnish the salmon with dill and serve warm, with the cucumber sauce.

MIXED SEAFOOD WITH SAFFRON SAUCE

SERVES 4

large pinch of saffron strands	4 cooked jumbo prawns in the shell (optional)
50 ml (2 fl oz) dry white wine	15 ml (1 tbsp) Greek strained yogurt
strip of orange rind	salt and pepper
1 bay leaf	herbs, to garnish
450 g (1 lb) cod fillet, skinned	
4 quarter-cut plaice fillets, each weighing about 50 g (2 oz), skinned	

1 Put the saffron, wine, orange rind and bay leaf into a small bowl. Cook on HIGH for 2-3 minutes or until boiling. Set aside to infuse while cooking the fish.

2 Cut the cod fillet into large chunks, and cut each plaice fillet in half. Arrange the fish and prawns, if using, in a single layer in a large shallow dish, placing the thinner pieces and the prawns towards the centre.

3 Pour over 30 ml (2 tbsp) of the infused sauce. Cover and cook on HIGH for 5-6 minutes or until the fish is tender. Transfer the fish to four warmed serving plates.

4 Strain the remaining wine mixture into the cooking juices remaining in the dish and stir in the yogurt. Season to taste with salt and pepper. Cook on HIGH for 1-2 minutes or until hot. Pour over the fish, garnish with herbs and serve immediately.

KIPPER KEDGEREE

SERVES 6

225 g (8 oz) smoked kipper fillet	1 egg, hard-boiled and chopped
30 ml (2 tbsp) milk	175 g (6 oz) cooked peeled prawns
15 ml (1 tbsp) vegetable oil	30 ml (2 tbsp) chopped parsley
l medium onion, chopped	10 ml (2 tsp) lemon juice
5 ml (1 tsp) mild curry powder	pepper
225 g (8 oz) long-grain brown rice, cooked	chopped parsley and lemon wedges, to garnish

1 Put the kipper fillet and milk into a large shallow dish. Cover and cook on HIGH for 3-4 minutes or until the fish flakes easily when tested with a fork. Set aside.

2 Put the oil and onion into a serving dish and cook on HIGH for 5-7 minutes or until softened. Stir in the curry powder and cook on HIGH for 1 minute.

3 Add the rice to the onion with the egg, prawns, parsley, lemon juice and pepper to taste.

4 Remove the fish from the poaching liquid using a slotted spoon. Flake the kipper and stir carefully into the rice mixture with 30 ml (2 tbsp) of the poaching liquid.

5 Cook on HIGH for 2-3 minutes or until heated through, stirring once. Serve hot, garnished with chopped parsley and lemon wedges.

MEDITERRANEAN CHICKEN

SERVES 2

2 chicken breast fillets, skinned	1 small onion, thinly sliced into rings
1 garlic clove, crushed	salt and pepper
10 ml (2 tsp) lemon juice	1 small red pepper
pinch of sugar	1 small yellow pepper
45 ml (3 tbsp) olive or vegetable oil	50 g (2 oz) black olives, halved and stoned
15 ml (1 tbsp) chopped fresh marjoram or 5 ml (1 tsp) dried	15 ml (1 tbsp) capers

1 Cut the chicken breasts in half crossways and place in a shallow dish.

2 Put the garlic, lemon juice and sugar into a small bowl and blend together. Gradually whisk in the oil. Stir in the marjoram and onion rings and salt and pepper to taste. Pour over the chicken, cover and leave to marinate for at least 30 minutes.

3 Meanwhile, seed the peppers and cut into large chunks. Put into a shallow dish with 30 ml (2 tbsp) water, cover and cook on HIGH for 5-6 minutes or until the peppers are just soft, stirring occasionally. Drain and set aside.

4 Cook the chicken, covered, on HIGH for 5-6 minutes or until tender, turning once.

5 Add the peppers, olives and capers and cook on HIGH for 1-2 minutes or until heated through, stirring once. Serve immediately.

CHICKEN AND PRUNE KEBABS

SERVES 4

16 prunes, stoned	15 ml (1 tbsp) vegetable oil
75 ml (5 tbsp) chicken stock	450 g (1 lb) leeks, thinly sliced
1 small garlic clove, crushed	
15 ml (1 tbsp) dry sherry	30 ml (2 tbsp) soured cream or smetana
4 chicken breast fillets, skinned and cut into 2.5 cm (1 inch) cubes	salt and pepper
	chopped parsley, to garnish

1 Put the prunes, chicken stock, garlic and sherry into a medium bowl. Cover and cook on HIGH for 2 minutes to plump the prunes.

2 Stir in the chicken and mix thoroughly together. Set aside while cooking the leeks.

3 Put the oil and leeks into a large shallow dish and stir to coat the leeks in the oil. Cover and cook on HIGH for 10-12 minutes until the leeks are really tender, stirring occasionally.

4 Meanwhile, thread the chicken and prunes on to eight wooden skewers. Place the kebabs on top of the leeks. Cover and cook on HIGH for 5-7 minutes until the chicken is tender, re-positioning once.

5 Stir the soured cream or smetana into the leeks and season with salt and pepper to taste. Spoon on to four warmed serving plates, then arrange the kebabs on top. Garnish with chopped parsley and serve immediately.

CHICKEN WITH PEANUT SAUCE

SERVES 4

60 ml (4 tbsp) olive oil	2 large tomatoes, skinned and chopped
30 ml (2 tbsp) herb vinegar	
10 ml (2 tsp) Dijon mustard	1 garlic clove, chopped
grated rind and juice of ½ lemon	15 ml (1 tbsp) tomato purée
	1.25-2.5 ml (¼ -½ tsp) cayenne pepper
15 ml (1 tbsp) soy sauce	
1 garlic clove, crushed	75 ml (3 fl oz) chicken stock
salt and pepper	15 ml (1 tbsp) soy sauce
4 chicken breast fillets, skinned	60 ml (4 tbsp) peanut butter
FOR THE SAUCE	TO GARNISH
1 small onion, chopped	lemon and lime slices

1 To make the marinade, whisk together the oil, vinegar, mustard, lemon rind and juice, soy sauce, garlic and seasoning until well blended.

2 Cut the chicken into 2.5 cm (1 inch) cubes and thread on to 8 wooden kebab sticks. Place these in a shallow ovenproof dish and pour the marinade over. Cover and leave to stand for 2 hours or overnight.

3 In a blender or food processor, blend all the ingredients for the sauce until smooth. Pour the sauce into a bowl, cover and set aside until it is needed.

4 Place the covered chicken in the oven and microwave on HIGH for about 10-12 minutes, or until the chicken is cooked, turning and repositioning at least twice during the cooking time.

5 Arrange the chicken in a serving dish. Reserve the cooking liquid and keep it hot while heating the sauce.

6 Add the reserved cooking liquid to the sauce mixture, cover and microwave on HIGH for 5-6 minutes, until boiling, stirring frequently.

7 Garnish the chicken with lemon and lime slices. Hand the sauce around separately.

CHICKEN IN CURRIED MAYONNAISE

SERVES 2

1 medium onion, chopped	1 small green pepper
2 chicken breast fillets, skinned	1 small red apple
60 ml (4 tbsp) dry white wine	10 ml (2 tsp) lemon juice
1 bay leaf	90 ml (6 tbsp) mayonnaise
large pinch of dried mixed herbs	15ml (1 tbsp) apricot jam
20 ml (4 tsp) mild curry powder	salt and pepper
	few lettuce leaves, to serve

1 Put the onion, chicken breasts, wine, bay leaf and mixed herbs into a shallow dish. Cover and cook on HIGH for 5-6 minutes or until tender.

2 Cut the chicken into bite-sized pieces and set aside. Stir the curry powder into the cooking liquid and cook on HIGH for 2-3 minutes or until slightly reduced.

3 Meanwhile, core, seed and dice the green pepper and core and thinly slice the apple. Mix with the chicken, stir in the lemon juice and set aside.

4 Stir the mayonnaise and apricot jam into the cooking liquid and season with salt and pepper. Pour over the chicken mixture and mix together until thoroughly coated.

5 Line a serving dish with lettuce leaves and pile in the chicken mayonnaise. Chill for 20 minutes before serving.

SHREDDED TURKEY WITH COURGETTES

SERVES 4

450 g (1 lb) turkey or chicken breast fillets	45 ml (3 tbsp) dry sherry
450 g (1 lb) courgettes	15 ml (1 tbsp) soy sauce
1 red pepper, seeded and thinly sliced	salt and pepper
45 ml (3 tbsp) vegetable oil	60 ml (4 tbsp) natural yogurt or soured cream

1 Cut all the ingredients into fine strips to ensure even cooking.

2 Place all the ingredients except the yogurt in a 2.3 litre (4 pint) microwave dish, season and stir well to mix.

3 Cover and microwave on HIGH for 4 minutes.

4 Leave to stand for 5 minutes, then add the yogurt, adjust the seasoning and serve.

LAMB WITH AUBERGINE AND MINT

SERVES 4

1 large aubergine, about 400 g (14 oz)	30 ml (2 tbsp) olive oil
salt and pepper	397 g (14 oz) can tomatoes, drained
450 g (1 lb) lean boneless lamb, eg fillet or leg	few allspice berries, crushed
	small bunch of mint

1 Cut the aubergine into 2.5 cm (1 inch) cubes. Put in a colander, sprinkling each layer generously with salt. Stand the colander on a large plate, cover with a small plate and place a weight on top. Leave for about 20 minutes to extract the bitter juices.
2 Meanwhile, trim the meat of all excess fat and cut into 2.5 cm (1 inch) cubes. Rinse the aubergine and pat dry.
3 Heat a large browning dish on HIGH for 5-8 minutes or according to manufacturer's instructions.
4 Put the oil in the browning dish, then quickly add the meat. Microwave on HIGH for 2 minutes.
5 Turn the pieces of meat over and microwave on HIGH for a further 2 minutes.
6 Add the aubergine to the browning dish and microwave on HIGH for 5 minutes, stirring once.
7 Add the tomatoes, breaking them up with a fork, the allspice and pepper to taste. Cover, leaving a gap to let steam escape, and microwave on HIGH for about 15 minutes or until the lamb and aubergine are very tender, stirring occasionally.
8 Coarsely chop the mint and stir into the lamb with salt to taste. Re-cover and microwave on HIGH for 1 minute. Serve hot with brown rice.

COOK'S TIP

It is essential to make this dish using fresh mint, dried does not have such a good flavour. Try serving it with a mixture of plain and wild rice.

LAMB BURGERS

SERVES 4

450 g (1 lb) lean minced lamb	TO SERVE
1 large onion, finely grated	plain or toasted hamburger buns
5 ml (1 tsp) salt	shredded lettuce
1.25 ml (¼ tsp) cayenne pepper	tomato ketchup (optional)
30 ml (2 tbsp) vegetable oil	

1 Mix the lamb and onion together and season with salt and cayenne pepper.
2 Divide the lamb mixture into four and shape each piece into a neat pattie about 2.5 cm (1 inch) thick.
3 Preheat a large browning dish to maximum according to the manufacturer's instructions, adding the oil for the last 30 seconds. (Or put the oil into a large shallow ovenproof dish and microwave on HIGH for 1-2 minutes until the oil is hot.)
4 Without removing the dish from the oven, press 2 lamb burgers flat on to the hot surface and microwave on HIGH for 2-3 minutes. Turn the burgers over and re-position them, then microwave on HIGH for 2-3 minutes until cooked. Repeat with the remaining burgers.
5 Serve the lamb burgers in plain or toasted hamburger buns on a bed of shredded lettuce. Serve with tomato ketchup or other relishes.

CINNAMON LAMB WITH ALMONDS AND APRICOTS

SERVES 2

25 g (1 oz) whole blanched almonds	2.5 ml (½ tsp) ground cumin
50 g (2 oz) dried apricots, halved	salt and pepper
	15 ml (1 tbsp) vegetable oil
350 g (12 oz) lamb fillet	75 ml (3 fl oz) chicken stock
15 ml (1 tbsp) plain flour	1 bay leaf
10 ml (2 tsp) ground cinnamon	30 ml (2 tbsp) natural yogurt

1 Spread the almonds out on a large flat plate and cook on HIGH for 6 minutes or until lightly browned, stirring occasionally. Set aside.

2 Put the apricots into a small bowl with 150 ml (¼ pint) water. Cover and cook on HIGH for 5 minutes. Leave to stand.

3 Heat a browning dish on HIGH for 5-8 minutes or according to manufacturer's instructions.

4 Meanwhile, cut the lamb into 2.5 cm (1 inch) slices and flatten slightly with a meat mallet or a rolling pin. Cut each slice in half.

5 Mix the flour, cinnamon, cumin, salt and pepper together and use to coat the meat.

6 Add the oil to the browning dish, then quickly stir in the meat. Cook on HIGH for 2 minutes, then turn the meat over and cook on HIGH for a further 2 minutes.

7 Stir in the stock and bay leaf and mix well together. Cover and cook on LOW for 10 minutes or until the meat is tender, stirring occasionally.

8 Drain the apricots and stir into the dish. Cook on HIGH for 2-3 minutes or until the apricots are hot. Stir in the yogurt and more seasoning if necessary. Serve hot, sprinkled with the toasted almonds.

LAMB NOISETTES WITH ONION AND SAGE

SERVES 2

15 g (½ oz) butter or margarine	salt and pepper
	45 ml (3 tbsp) soured cream
1 medium onion, finely chopped	4 lamb noisettes, each about 4 cm (1½ inches) thick
75 ml (3 fl oz) chicken stock	15 ml (1 tbsp) plain flour
2.5 ml (½ tsp) chopped sage	15 ml (1 tbsp) vegetable oil
5 ml (1 tsp) lemon juice	sage leaves, to garnish

1 To make the purée, put the butter into a medium bowl and cook on HIGH for 30 seconds or until melted.

2 Stir in the onion, cover and cook on HIGH for 4-6 minutes or until really soft, stirring occasionally.

3 Stir in the stock, sage and lemon juice, re-cover and cook on HIGH for 3 minutes, stirring occasionally. Season to taste with salt and pepper. Leave to cool slightly, then add the soured cream.

4 Heat a browning dish on HIGH for 5-8 minutes or according to manufacturer's instructions.

5 Meanwhile, purée the onion mixture in a blender or food processor, then turn into a clean serving bowl. Set aside.

6 Lightly coat the noisettes with the flour and season with salt and pepper. Add the oil to the browning dish, then quickly add the noisettes, arranging them in a circle in the dish. Cook on HIGH for 2 minutes. Turn over and cook on HIGH for 1-2 minutes or until cooked as desired; they should still be slightly pink in the centre. Arrange on a warmed serving plate and garnish with fresh sage leaves.

7 Cook the onion purée on HIGH for 1-2 minutes or until hot and adjust the seasoning if necessary. Serve immediately with the noisettes.

CALF'S LIVER WITH BACON AND APPLE

SERVES 2

225 g (8 oz) calf's liver	1 red eating apple
15 ml (1 tbsp) plain flour	1 medium onion, thinly sliced
salt and pepper	200 ml (7 fl oz) medium dry cider
paprika	
15 ml (1 tbsp) vegetable oil	30 ml (2 tbsp) soured cream
15 g (½ oz) butter or margarine	5 ml (1 tsp) chopped fresh sage or 2.5 ml (½ tsp) dried
3 streaky bacon rashers, rinded	sage leaves, to garnish

1 Cut the liver into thin strips, trimming away any inedible parts. Coat in the flour and season well with salt, pepper and paprika.

2 Put the oil and butter into a shallow dish and cook on HIGH for 30 seconds or until melted.

3 Meanwhile, cut the bacon into thin strips. Core the apple, cut into rings, then cut each ring in half.

4 Stir the onion and bacon into the fat and cook on HIGH for 5-6 minutes or until the onion is softened, stirring frequently.

5 Stir in the liver and cook on HIGH for 1-2 minutes or until the liver just changes colour. Stir in the apple and 150 ml (¼ pint) cider and cook on HIGH for 2-3 minutes or until the liver is tender, stirring occasionally. Remove the liver, bacon, apple and onion with a slotted spoon and transfer to a warmed serving dish.

6 Stir the remaining cider into the dish with the cream and sage and cook on HIGH for 4-5 minutes or until thickened and reduced.

7 Reheat the liver and apple mixture on HIGH for 1 minute, if necessary, then pour over the sauce. Garnish with sage leaves and serve immediately.

SPICY MINI MEATBALLS WITH TOMATO SAUCE

SERVES 2

1 small onion, quartered	30 ml (2 tbsp) chopped fresh coriander
1 garlic clove, crushed	
2.5 cm (1 inch) piece fresh root ginger, peeled and crushed	salt and pepper
	1 egg, size 6, beaten
350 g (12 oz) lean minced beef	226 g (8 oz) can tomatoes
	15 ml (1 tbsp) chicken stock
15 ml (1 tbsp) mango chutney	10 ml (2 tsp) tomato purée
	5 ml (1 tsp) granulated sugar
2.5 ml (½ tsp) ground cumin	fresh coriander sprigs, to garnish
2. 5 ml (½ tsp) ground coriander	

1 Put the onion, garlic and ginger in a blender or food processor and blend until very finely chopped.

2 Add the beef, chutney, cumin, ground coriander and half the fresh chopped coriander. Season with salt and pepper. Pour in sufficient egg to bind the mixture. Shape into 16 small balls.

3 Arrange in a single layer in a shallow dish. Microwave on HIGH for 5-6 minutes or until cooked, rearranging once during cooking. Leave to stand, covered, while making the sauce.

4 To make the sauce, put the tomatoes and their juice into a large bowl. Stir in the chicken stock, tomato purée, sugar, salt and pepper.

5 Microwave on HIGH for 5 minutes, stirring occasionally, then stir in the remaining fresh coriander and microwave on HIGH for 2-3 minutes or until reduced and thickened.

6 Microwave the meatballs on HIGH for 1-2 minutes, or until reheated.

7 Serve the meatballs with the tomato sauce, garnished with coriander sprigs.

BEEF WITH GINGER AND GARLIC

SERVES 2

350 g (12 oz) fillet steak	30 ml (2 tbsp) soy sauce
2.5 cm (1 inch) piece fresh root ginger, peeled and finely grated	2 medium carrots
	15 ml (1 tbsp) vegetable oil
1 garlic clove, crushed	30 ml (2 tbsp) cornflour
150 ml (¼ pint) dry sherry	2.5 ml (½ tsp) soft light brown sugar

1 Cut the steak across the grain into 1 cm (½ inch) strips and put into a bowl. Mix the ginger with the garlic, sherry and soy sauce, then pour over the steak, making sure that all the meat is coated. Cover and leave to marinate for at least 1 hour.

2 Using a potato peeler, cut the carrots into fine slices lengthways.

3 Put the oil into a large bowl and cook on HIGH for 1 minute or until hot.

4 Using a slotted spoon, remove the steak from the marinade and stir into the oil. Cook on HIGH for 1-2 minutes or until the steak is just cooked, stirring once.

5 Meanwhile, blend the cornflour and the sugar with a little of the marinade to make a smooth paste, then gradually blend in all the marinade.

6 Add the carrots to the steak. Cook on HIGH for 1-2 minutes, then stir in the marinade mixture. Cook on HIGH for 2-3 minutes or until thickened, stirring frequently.

PORK WITH FRESH PLUM SAUCE

SERVES 2

350 g (12 oz) pork fillet	15 ml (1 tbsp) soft dark brown sugar
50 ml (2 fl oz) chicken stock	
50 ml (2 fl oz) fruity white wine	5 ml (1 tsp) lemon juice
	salt and pepper
225 g (8 oz) fresh ripe red or purple plums, halved and stoned	15 ml (1 tbsp) vegetable oil
	coriander sprigs, to garnish

1 Cut the pork into 1 cm (½ inch) slices. Place between sheets of greaseproof paper and flatten, using a meat mallet or a rolling pin, to a thickness of 5 mm (¼ inch). Set aside.

2 To make the sauce, put the stock and wine into a medium bowl and cook on HIGH for 5 minutes or until boiling and slightly reduced.

3 Reserve two plum halves for the garnish, finely chop the remainder and stir into the hot liquid with the sugar and lemon juice. Cover and cook on HIGH for 3-4 minutes or until the plums are tender. Season to taste with salt and pepper.

4 Allow to cool a little, then purée the sauce in a blender or food processor until smooth. Pour back into the bowl and cook on HIGH for 5-7 minutes or until thickened and reduced.

5 Put the oil into a shallow dish and cook on HIGH for 1-2 minutes or until hot. Stir in the pork and cook on HIGH for 4-5 minutes or until tender, turning once during cooking. Season to taste with salt and pepper.

6 Reheat the sauce on HIGH for 1-2 minutes or until hot, then spoon on to two warmed plates. Arrange the pork slices on the sauce, garnish with the plum halves and coriander, and serve immediately.

TOFU AND BEAN BURGERS

MAKES 6

283 g (10 oz) silken tofu	25 g (1 oz) wholemeal breadcrumbs
397 g (14 oz) can red kidney beans, drained and rinsed	few drops of chilli sauce
2.5 ml (½ tsp) yeast extract	1 egg, beaten
5 ml (1 tsp) dried mixed herbs	15 ml (1 tbsp) lemon juice
1 medium onion, grated	grated rind of 1 small lemon
2 courgettes, grated	pepper

1 Put the tofu and drained kidney beans into a bowl and mash together using a potato masher or a fork. Dissolve the yeast extract in 30 ml (2 tbsp) hot water and stir in to the tofu mixture with the remaining ingredients. Beat well together.

2 Shape the mixture into six burgers, about 2 cm (¾ inch) thick.

3 Arrange the burgers in a circle around the edge of a large flat plate. Cook on HIGH for 8 minutes. Carefully turn the burgers over and cook on HIGH for a further 8 minutes. Serve hot, with a salad or in wholemeal rolls.

BEAN GOULASH

SERVES 4-6

100 g (4 oz) black-eye beans, soaked overnight	15 ml (1 tbsp) paprika
100 g (4 oz) aduki beans, soaked overnight	397 g (14 oz) can chopped tomatoes
15 ml (1 tbsp) sunflower oil	175 g (6 oz) mushrooms, thickly sliced
1 garlic clove, crushed	60 ml (4 tbsp) natural yogurt
1 yellow pepper, seeded and roughly chopped	salt and pepper
10 ml (2 tsp) caraway seeds, lightly crushed	chopped parsley, to garnish

1 Drain the beans and put into a large bowl. Pour over enough boiling water to cover and come about 2.5 cm (1 inch) above the beans. Cover, leaving a gap to let steam escape, and microwave on HIGH for 25-30 minutes until tender. Leave to stand, covered. Do not drain.

2 Meanwhile, put the oil, garlic, yellow pepper, caraway seeds and paprika in a large ovenproof serving bowl. Cover, leaving a gap to let steam escape, and microwave on HIGH for 2 minutes, stirring once.

3 Drain the beans, rinse with boiling water and add to the pepper with the tomatoes and mushrooms. Re-cover and microwave on HIGH for 8-10 minutes, stirring once. Stir in 30 ml (2 tbsp) of the yogurt and season with salt and pepper to taste. Drizzle the remaining yogurt on top and sprinkle with the parsley. Serve hot with brown rice.

COOK'S TIP

To save time, you can substitute both kinds of beans with canned varieties. Use three 397 g (14 oz) cans of the beans of your choice and proceed from step 2.

LENTIL, AUBERGINE AND POTATO PIE

SERVES 4

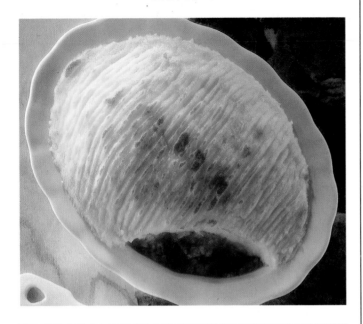

3 medium potatoes, each about 225 g (8 oz), scrubbed	1 small aubergine, roughly chopped
100 g (4 oz) split red lentils	450 ml (¾ pint) boiling vegetable stock
1 medium onion, finely chopped	100 g (4 oz) French beans, trimmed and cut into 2.5 cm (1 inch) lengths
1 bay leaf	60 ml (4 tbsp) milk
5 ml (1 tsp) dried thyme	salt and pepper
15 ml (1 tbsp) tomato purée	25 g (1 oz) Parmesan cheese, freshly grated

1 Prick the potatoes all over with a fork and arrange in a circle on a sheet of absorbent kitchen paper. Cook on HIGH for 10-15 minutes or until soft, turning over halfway through cooking. Set aside to cool slightly.

2 Meanwhile put the lentils, onion, bay leaf, thyme, tomato purée, aubergine and vegetable stock into a large bowl and mix well together. Cover and cook on HIGH for 20-25 minutes or until the lentils and aubergine are tender and most of the liquid is absorbed. Add the beans and cook on HIGH for 2 minutes.

3 Meanwhile, cut the potatoes in half and scoop out the flesh into a bowl. Mash with the milk and season to taste with salt and pepper.

4 Spoon the lentil and aubergine mixture into a flameproof serving dish. Spoon over the mashed potato and sprinkle with the cheese. Cook on HIGH for 1-2 minutes or until heated through, then brown under a hot grill, if liked.

VEGETABLE AND CHICK PEA CASSEROLE

SERVES 6

4 courgettes, trimmed and cut into 1 cm (½ inch) lengths	100 g (4 oz) no-soak dried apricots, cut into quarters
1 red pepper, seeded and chopped	2 garlic cloves, crushed
1 green pepper, seeded and chopped	425 g (15 oz) can chick peas, drained
2 medium onions, roughly chopped	25 g (1 oz) almonds, blanched
2 carrots, thinly sliced	5 ml (1 tsp) turmeric
225 g (8 oz) turnips, thinly sliced	10 ml (2 tsp) paprika
1 small cauliflower, cut into florets	2.5 ml (½ tsp) ground coriander
4 large tomatoes, skinned, seeded and chopped	salt and pepper
	600 ml (1 pint) boiling vegetable stock
	chopped coriander or parsley, to garnish

1 Place all the prepared vegetables, the apricots, garlic, chick peas and almonds in a large bowl and stir in the spices, salt, pepper and stock. Cover and cook on HIGH for 8-10 minutes or until the vegetables come to the boil.

2 Continue cooking on HIGH for a further 30-40 minutes or until the vegetables are well cooked, stirring two or three times during cooking. Serve garnished with chopped coriander or parsley.

BEAN AND RICE BURGERS WITH MANGO CHUTNEY

SERVES 4

100 g (4 oz) brown rice	1 small egg
425 g (14 oz) can red kidney beans, drained and rinsed	50 g (2 oz) medium oatmeal
1-2 garlic cloves, crushed	FOR THE MANGO CHUTNEY
2.5 ml (1 tsp) curry paste	1 ripe mango
10 ml (2 tsp) tomato purée	30 ml (2 tbsp) shredded coconut
1 cm (½ inch) piece fresh root ginger, peeled and grated	finely grated rind and juice of 1 lime
salt and pepper	

1 Put the rice in a medium bowl and pour over enough boiling water to cover by about 5 cm (2 inches). Cover and cook on HIGH for 20-25 minutes or until tender.

2 Meanwhile, make the mango chutney. Peel the mango and discard the stone. Cut the flesh into small pieces and mix with the remaining ingredients. Leave to stand while making the burgers.

3 Drian the cooked rice and cool slightly. Put the beans into a bowl and mash thoroughly with a potato masher or a fork. Add the garlic, curry paste, tomato purée, ginger and the rice. Season to taste and beat thoroughly until the mixture just begins to cling together.

4 Add enough egg to bind the mixture together, then shape into 8 burgers. Spread the oatmeal out on a plate and press the burgers into it to coat lightly.

5 Arrange in a circle on a baking sheet or the turntable and cook on HIGH for 2 minutes. Turn over and cook on HIGH for a further 2 minutes or until firm to the touch.

6 Serve hot, with the mango chutney and a mixed salad or put into pitta bread or wholemeal rolls.

COOK'S TIP

These tasty vegetarian burgers can be made in advance and reheated before serving. Make sure that you mash the beans thoroughly in step 3 or the mixture will not hold together.

SPICY NUT BURGERS WITH CORIANDER RAITA

SERVES 2

45 ml (3 tbsp) vegetable oil	25 g (1 oz) Cheddar cheese, finely grated
1 small onion, chopped	50 g (2 oz) brown breadcrumbs
1 medium carrot, finely grated	salt and pepper
1 garlic clove, crushed	1 egg, size 6, beaten
1 cm (½ inch) piece fresh root ginger, peeled and chopped	30 ml (2 tbsp) chopped coriander
2.5 ml (½ tsp) coriander seeds, finely crushed	150 ml (¼ pint) natural yogurt
2.5 ml (½ tsp) cumin seeds	lemon wedges and fresh coriander, to garnish
100 g (4 oz) mixed nuts, finely chopped	

1 Put 15 ml (1 tbsp) of the oil, the onion, carrot, garlic and ginger in a medium bowl. Cover and microwave on HIGH for 5-7 minutes or until the vegetables have softened, stirring occasionally.

2 Stir in the coriander and cumin seeds and microwave on HIGH for 1 minute, stirring occasionally.

3 Stir in the nuts and microwave on HIGH for 2 minutes, stirring once.

4 Stir in the cheese and breadcrumbs and season with salt and pepper. Mix thoroughly and bind together with the egg. Heat a browning dish for 8-10 minutes.

5 Meanwhile, divide the mixture into six and shape into burgers. When the browning dish is hot, add the remaining oil and microwave on HIGH for 30 seconds.

6 Quickly put the burgers in the dish and microwave on HIGH for 1½ minutes, then turn over and microwave on HIGH for a further minute or until browned. Leave to stand for 1 minute.

7 Meanwhile, make the raita. Mix the coriander into the yogurt and season with salt and pepper.

8 Garnish the burgers with lemon wedges and coriander and serve hot with the coriander raita.

MUSHROOM, COURGETTE AND BEAN STEW

SERVES 4

25 g (1 oz) butter or margarine	two 425 g (15 oz) cans flageolet, borlotti or black-eye beans, drained and rinsed
1 medium onion, chopped	
25 g (1 oz) wholemeal flour	225 g (8 oz) mushrooms, halved if large
450 ml (¾ pint) vegetable stock	450 g (1 lb) courgettes
15 ml (1 tbsp) mild wholegrain mustard	45 ml (3 tbsp) chopped mixed herbs
	salt and pepper

1 Put the butter and the onion into a large bowl. Cover and cook on HIGH for 2-3 minutes or until slightly softened. Stir in the flour and cook on HIGH for 1 minute, then gradually stir in the stock.

2 Cook on HIGH for 4-5 minutes or until boiling and thickened, stirring frequently.

3 Add the mustard, beans and the mushrooms and cook on HIGH for 2-3 minutes.

4 Meanwhile, cut the courgettes into 1 cm (½ inch) slices. Stir the courgettes and half the herbs into the stew. Cover and cook on HIGH for 5-6 minutes or until the courgettes are just cooked. Season to taste with salt and pepper and stir in the remaining herbs. Serve with hot herb bread.

VEGETABLE GOULASH

SERVES 2

30 ml (2 tbsp) vegetable oil	2 medium carrots, cut into 5 mm (¼ inch) slices
1 medium onion, chopped	
1 green pepper, seeded and chopped	2 medium courgettes, cut into 2.5 cm (1 inch) slices
15 ml (1 tbsp) sweet paprika	100 g (4 oz) button mushrooms
2.5 ml (½ tsp) caraway seeds	freshly grated nutmeg
45 ml (3 tbsp) medium oatmeal	salt and pepper
450 ml (¾ pint) tomato juice	30 ml (2 tbsp) soured cream or natural yogurt
	parsley sprigs, to garnish

1 Put the oil, onion and pepper into a large bowl. Cover and cook on HIGH for 5-7 minutes or until softened, stirring occasionally.

2 Stir in the paprika and caraway seeds and cook on HIGH for 1 minute. Stir in the oatmeal and gradually stir in the tomato juice.

3 Stir the carrots, courgettes and mushrooms into the paprika mixture and mix well. Season to taste with nutmeg and salt and pepper.

4 Re-cover and cook on HIGH for 15-20 minutes or until the vegetables are tender. Serve with the soured cream or yogurt spooned on top, garnished with parsley sprigs.

VEGETABLE CHILLI

SERVES 4-6

SMOKY STUFFED PAWPAW

SERVES 4

1 green chilli, seeded and chopped	150 ml (¼ pint) boiling vegetable stock
1 medium onion, thinly sliced	1 green pepper, seeded and chopped
1 garlic clove, crushed	100 g (4 oz) button mushrooms
3 celery sticks, sliced	225 g (8 oz) cauliflower florets
4 ripe tomatoes, roughly chopped	3 courgettes, sliced
10 ml (2 tsp) tomato purée	425 g (15 oz) can red kidney beans, drained and rinsed
2.5-5 ml (½ -1 tsp) chilli powder	30 ml (2 tbsp) chopped coriander (optional)
5 cm (2 inch) cinnamon stick	salt and pepper
5 ml (1 tsp) ground cumin	1 avocado
5 ml (1 tsp) dried oregano	grated cheese, to garnish

1 Put the chilli, onion, garlic, celery, tomatoes, tomato purée, chilli powder, cinnamon stick, cumin, oregano and stock into a large serving dish. Mix well together. Cover and cook on HIGH for 8-10 minutes or until the tomatoes are very mushy, stirring occasionally.

2 Sir in the remaining ingredients and season to taste with salt and pepper. Re-cover and cook on HIGH for 15-20 minutes or until the vegetables are tender, stirring occasionally.

3 For the garnish, peel, halve and stone the avocado, then chop the flesh. Top each serving of chilli with a generous sprinkling of cheese and avocado cubes. Serve hot, with brown rice or cornbread.

2 green pawpaws	100 g (4 oz) smoked cheese
1 yellow pepper	salt and pepper
100 g (4 oz) firm tofu	fresh chives, to garnish
30 ml (2 tbsp) mayonnaise	

1 Prick the pawpaws all over with the point of a sharp knife or a skewer. Cut the pepper in half lengthways and remove and discard the seeds.

2 Put the pepper cut side down on a double sheet of absorbent kitchen paper and put into the cooker with the pawpaws. Cook on HIGH for 8 minutes or until the pepper is tender. Continue to cook the pawpaws on HIGH for 2-3 minutes or until just tender.

3 While the pawpaws are finishing cooking, put the pepper, half the tofu and the mayonnaise into a blender or food processor and purée until smooth. Pour into a bowl. Cut the remaining tofu into cubes and mix carefully into the sauce.

4 Cut the pawpaws in half lengthways and remove and discard the seeds. Scoop out the flesh with a teaspoon and roughly chop. Reserve the skins.

5 Add the chopped pawpaw to the pepper sauce and cook on HIGH for 2 minutes or until hot. Cut the cheese into cubes and stir into the sauce. Season to taste with salt and pepper.

6 Arrange the pawpaw shells on a large plate and spoon in the filling. Cook on HIGH for 1 minute or until just hot; do not overcook or the cheese will melt. Cut the chives into 7.5 cm (3 inch) lengths and scatter generously over the pawpaws. Serve immediately, with a rice pilaff.

DESSERTS

An irresistible collection of mouth-watering desserts, from refreshing fruit salads and compotes, through creamy fools and mousses, to warming crumbles and baked puddings. Some of the recipes take a little while to set or bake, but they are all quick and easy to prepare.

FRUDITES

SERVES 6

2 crisp eating apples	FOR THE DIP
2 bananas	150 ml (¼ pint) double cream
225 g (8 oz) apricots, stoned	150 ml (¼ pint) soured cream
175 g (6 oz) black or green grapes, seeded	30 ml (2 tbsp) icing sugar, sifted
225 g (8 oz) strawberries	
juice of 1 lemon	

1 To make the dip, whip the two creams and icing sugar together in a bowl until standing in soft peaks. Pipe or spoon into six individual dishes.
2 Quarter and core the apples, but do not peel them. Peel the bananas and cut into 4 cm (1½ inch) chunks.
3 Arrange the fruit on individual serving plates and sprinkle immediately with lemon juice to prevent discoloration.
4 Place the dishes of cream dip next to the fruit and serve immediately. Use fingers or small fondue forks to dunk the fruit into the cream dip.

MULLED SUMMER FRUITS

SERVES 4

450 g (1 lb) summer fruits, eg strawberries, cherries, raspberries, redcurrants, blueberries	finely pared rind of ½ lemon
	2 cloves
	1 cinnamon stick
300 ml (½ pint) apple juice	pinch of mixed spice
25 g (1 oz) caster sugar	mint sprigs, to decorate

1 Carefully pick over the fruit, hull and prepare as necessary. Place in a large bowl.
2 Put the apple juice and sugar in a heavy-based pan and heat gently until the sugar dissolves. Add the lemon rind and spices, and bring to the boil, stirring.
3 Remove from the heat and leave to stand for 2 minutes, then strain over the fruit.
4 Decorate with mint sprigs and serve immediately, with double cream flavoured with chopped mint.

COOK'S TIP

This dish is just as good served cold. Cool, then chill the syrup before straining it over the fruit.

157

ORANGES IN CARAMEL

SERVES 8

8 medium juicy oranges	30 ml (2 tbsp) Grand Marnier or other orange-flavoured liqueur
225 g (8 oz) caster sugar	

1 Thinly pare the rind from half the oranges and cut into very thin julienne strips. Place in a small saucepan and cover with water. Cover the pan and cook for 5 minutes until tender. Drain and rinse under cold water.
2 Cut away the pith from the oranges and both rind and pith from the four remaining oranges, reserving any juice.
3 Place the oranges in a serving dish.
4 Place the sugar and 300 ml (½ pint) water in a saucepan and heat gently until the sugar has dissolved. Bring to the boil and boil until the syrup is caramel coloured.
5 Remove the pan from the heat, carefully add 45 ml (3 tbsp) water and return it to a low heat to dissolve the caramel. Add the reserved orange juice, orange rind julienne and the liqueur.
6 Leave the caramel syrup to cool for 10 minutes, then pour over the oranges. Chill in the refrigerator for 2-3 hours, turning the oranges occasionally.

SOFT FRUITS IN RASPBERRY COULIS

SERVES 6

	FOR THE SAUCE
6 ripe figs, quartered	100 g (4 oz) granulated sugar
350 g (12 oz) mixed soft fruits, eg raspberries, blueberries, blackberries	450 g (1 lb) ripe raspberries
	squeeze of lemon juice
	15 ml (1 tbsp) kirsch (optional)

1 To make the sauce, put the sugar in a heavy-based saucepan with 300 ml (½ pint) water. Heat gently, without stirring, until the sugar dissolves, then bring to the boil and boil steadily for 2 minutes. Allow to cool.
2 Meanwhile, purée the raspberries for the sauce in a blender or food processor. Add the lemon juice and enough of the cooled sugar syrup to sweeten to taste. Press through a fine nylon sieve to remove seeds, then stir in the kirsch, if using.
3 To serve, pour the raspberry coulis on to individual serving plates and arrange the prepared fruits on top. Serve with cream or yogurt.

STUFFED FIGS

SERVES 8

225 g (8 oz) ricotta cheese, at room temperature	few drops of almond extract or rose water
150 ml (¼ pint) double or whipping cream	16 ripe fresh figs
	fig or vine leaves and rose petals, to serve (optional)

1 Beat the ricotta cheese in a bowl until softened. Whip the cream in another bowl until just standing in soft peaks, then fold into the ricotta, with almond extract or rose water according to taste.
2 With a sharp knife, cut a cross in each fig at the top (stem end). Continue cutting down almost to the base of the fig, but keeping the fruit whole. With your fingers, gently prise the four 'petals' of each fig apart, to allow room for the filling.
3 Spoon the ricotta mixture into a piping bag fitted with a large rosette nozzle and pipe into the centre of each fig. Chill in the refrigerator until serving time.
4 To serve, place the figs on individual serving plates. Alternatively arrange fig or vine leaves decoratively over a flat serving platter, place the stuffed figs on top and scatter rose petals around. Serve chilled.

COOK'S TIP

Ricotta, a soft Italian cheese, can be bought in tubs or loose by the kg (lb) at large supermarkets and Italian delicatessens. Made from the whey of sheep's or cow's milk, depending on the region where it is produced, it is mild in flavour, yet delightfully rich and creamy. If you are unable to obtain it, curd cheese is the best alternative.

PEARS IN RED WINE

SERVES 4

4 large firm Comice pears	50 g (2 oz) caster sugar
25 g (1 oz) blanched almonds, split in half	300 ml (½ pint) red wine
	2 cloves

1 Peel the pears, leaving the stalks on. Spike the pears with the almond halves.
2 Put the sugar, wine and cloves in a saucepan just large enough to hold the pears and heat gently until the sugar has dissolved. Add the pears, standing them upright in the pan. Cover and simmer gently for about 15 minutes until the pears are just tender. Baste them from time to time with the liquid. (Alternatively, put the sugar, wine and cloves in a bowl and microwave on HIGH for 3-4 minutes until boiling, stirring occasionally. Add the pears, cover and microwave on HIGH for 8-10 minutes until the pears are tender.)
3 Using a slotted spoon, transfer the pears to a serving dish. Boil the syrup in the pan until the liquid is reduced by half. (If cooking in the microwave, uncover and cook on HIGH for 10 minutes or until reduced by half.)
4 Pour the wine syrup over the pears. Serve hot or cold with thick natural yogurt or clotted cream.

VARIATION

Use medium dry cider in place of the red wine.

GINGER
FRUIT SALAD

SERVES 4

2 apricots	50 g (2 oz) green grapes
2 dessert apples	2 bananas
1 orange	30 ml (2 tbsp) lemon juice
241 ml (8½ fl oz) bottle ginger ale	

1 Prepare the fruits to be macerated. Plunge the apricots into a bowl of boiling water for 30 seconds. Drain and peel off the skin with your fingers.
2 Halve the apricots, remove the stones and dice the flesh. Core and dice the apples, but do not peel them. Peel the orange and divide into segments, discarding all white pith.
3 Put the prepared fruits in a serving bowl with the ginger ale. Stir lightly, then cover and leave to macerate for 1 hour.
4 Cut the grapes in half, then remove the seeds by flicking them out with the point of a knife.
5 Peel and slice the bananas and mix them with the lemon juice to prevent discoloration.
6 Add the grapes and bananas to the macerated fruits. Serve in individual glasses, topped with a spoonful of natural yogurt, if desired.

THREE
FRUIT SALAD

SERVES 8

50 g (2 oz) granulated sugar	1 pineapple, weighing about 1.1 kg (2½ lb)
15 ml (1 tbsp) lemon juice	225 g (8 oz) black grapes
15 ml (1 tbsp) kirsch	4 kiwi fruit

1 Put the sugar in a heavy-based saucepan with 150 ml (¼ pint) water. Heat gently until the sugar has dissolved, then bring to the boil and bubble for 2 minutes. Remove from the heat, stir in the lemon juice and kirsch, then set aside to cool.
2 Prepare the pineapple. With a sharp knife, cut off the leafy top and discard. Cut the pineapple into 1 cm (½ inch) pieces. Cut off the skin and dig out the 'eyes' with the tip of the knife. Cut out the core from each slice with an apple corer or small biscuit cutter. Cut the flesh into chunks.
3 Wash and dry the grapes, then halve. Remove the pips by flicking them out with the point of a sharp knife.
4 Peel the kiwi fruit using a potato peeler or sharp knife, then slice the flesh thinly.
5 Stir the prepared fruits into the syrup, cover and chill well in the refrigerator before serving.

INDIAN FRUIT SALAD

SERVES 6-8

3 ripe peaches	5 ml (1 tsp) cumin seeds, dry fried
2 ripe guavas	30 ml (2 tbsp) lemon or lime juice
2 ripe bananas	pinch of cayenne
45 ml (3 tbsp) caster sugar	mint sprigs, to decorate

1 To skin the peaches, plunge them into a bowl of boiling water, leave for 30 seconds, then remove the skins.
2 Cut the skinned peaches in half and remove the stones. Slice the peach flesh thinly and place in a serving bowl.
3 Cut the guavas in half, scoop out the seeds and discard them. Peel the halved guavas, then slice them neatly and add to the peaches in the bowl.
4 Peel the bananas, cut into chunks, then mix carefully with the peaches, guavas and remaining ingredients. Serve immediately, decorated with sprigs of mint.

COOK'S TIP

Fresh guavas are available at specialist greengrocers, Indian stores and larger supermarkets. Guavas are a tropical fruit, originally from South America, with a pretty cream-pink skin. The flesh has a delicately scented aroma and a most delicious flavour. The seeds in the centre are not edible and should be removed before serving the fruit.

AUTUMN COMPOTE

SERVES 6-8

225 g (8 oz) granulated sugar	450 g (1 lb) dessert apples, such as Cox or Russet
juice of 1 lemon	450 g (1 lb) Victoria plums, skinned and stoned
450 g (1 lb) small ripe, but firm pears	

1 To make the sugar syrup, put the sugar, lemon juice and 300 ml (½ pint) cold water in a saucepan. Heat very gently until the sugar has completely dissolved. Bring to the boil and boil the syrup for 1 minute.
2 Thinly peel the pears, cut into half and remove the centre core (if only large pears are available, cut the pears into quarters). Add the pears to the syrup and cook very gently for about 10-15 minutes until barely tender.
3 Meanwhile core the apples. Cut the apples into halves, then cut into slices across the halves. Add the apple slices to the pan and cook for about 5 minutes until the apple slices are just tender. Add the plums and cook for a further 5 minutes.
4 Carefully transfer the fruits and syrup to a serving bowl, taking care not to break up the fruit. Serve hot or cold, with yogurt or cream if desired.

COOK'S TIP

Select very small pears for this compote. Lemon juice added to the syrup prevents the pears and apples discolouring, and adds a tangy flavour.

STRAWBERRIES WITH RASPBERRY SAUCE

SERVES 6

900 g (2 lb) small strawberries	450 g (1 lb) raspberries
	50 g (2 oz) icing sugar

1 Hull the strawberries and place them in individual serving dishes.
2 Purée the raspberries in a blender or food processor until just smooth, then work through a nylon sieve into a bowl to remove the pips.
3 Sift the icing sugar over the bowl of raspberry purée, then whisk in until evenly incorporated. Pour over the strawberries. Chill in the refrigerator for at least 30 minutes before serving.

COOK'S TIP

Freshly picked raspberries freeze successfully (unlike strawberries which tend to lose texture and shape due to their high water content). If you have raspberries which are slightly overripe or misshapen, the best way to freeze them is as a purée; this takes up less space in the freezer and is immensely useful for making quick desserts and sauces at the last minute. For this recipe, for example, you can freeze the purée up to 12 months in advance, then it will only take minutes to assemble the dessert after thawing the purée.

RØDGRØD

SERVES 4-6

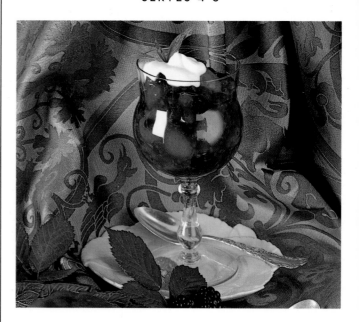

450 g (1 lb) redcurrants or blackcurrants, stalks removed	100-175 g (4-6 oz) caster sugar
450 g (1 lb) raspberries or strawberries, hulled, or cherries, stoned	TO DECORATE
	whipped cream
30 ml (2 tbsp) arrowroot	mint sprigs

1 Place the currants and 60 ml (4 tbsp) water in a saucepan. Cover and simmer gently for about 20 minutes or until really soft. Leave to cool.
2 Meanwhile, purée half of the berries in a blender or food processor until smooth, then press through a nylon sieve.
3 Blend a little of the purée with the arrowroot. Put the rest into a pan and bring slowly to the boil. Stir into the blended mixture, then return it all to the pan. Bring to the boil again, cook for 4-5 minutes and sweeten to taste. Leave to cool for 10 minutes. Stir in the cooked currants and the remaining raspberries, strawberries or cherries.
4 Pour the Rødgrød into individual glasses and chill for 30 minutes. Top with whipped cream and mint sprigs just before serving.

COOK'S TIP

Rødgrød is a Danish dessert which essentially is a thick fruit soup. It is always made with fresh soft summer fruit, depending on what is available. An important point to remember is to mix at least two fruits together to provide good flavour and colour. In Russia, it is known as Kisel.

BOOZY BANANA

SERVES 1

15 g (½ oz) butter or margarine	30 ml (2 tbsp) sherry
15 ml (1 tbsp) soft brown sugar	1.25 ml (¼ tsp) ground cinnamon
30 ml (2 tbsp) freshly squeezed orange juice	1 banana
	orange twist, to decorate (optional)

1 Melt the butter in a heavy-based frying pan. Add the remaining ingredients, except the banana. Heat gently, stirring, until the sugar has dissolved.

2 Peel the banana, then cut in half lengthways. Place in the pan and cook over gentle heat for about 10 minutes until tender. Baste the banana frequently with the sauce and turn the pieces over once during cooking. Serve hot, decorated with an orange twist, if liked.

SERVING SUGGESTION

Serve with chilled cream or vanilla ice cream. Alternatively, if you prefer the combination of sweet and tart flavours, serve with Greek yogurt, Quark or fromage frais.

PLUM CROUTE

SERVES 1

1 large slice of white bread	25 g (1 oz) demerara sugar
15 g (½ oz) butter or margarine, melted	1.25 ml (¼ tsp) ground cinnamon
2 ripe red plums, eg Victoria	

1 Cut the crusts off the slice of bread and discard. Brush both sides of the bread with the melted butter, making sure the bread is coated right to the edges.

2 Place the bread in an individual Yorkshire pudding tin, pressing it down well, but leaving the corners protruding over the edge.

3 Bake the croûte in the oven at 200°C (400°F) mark 6 for 15-20 minutes until crisp and golden brown.

4 Meanwhile, halve and stone the plums, then place in a pan with the sugar and cinnamon. Sprinkle in 5-10 ml (1-2 tsp) water, then cook gently for about 5 minutes until the plums are tender and juicy but still retaining their shape.

5 When the croûte is cooked, transfer to a serving plate. Spoon the plums in the centre and serve immediately, with chilled cream or thick Greek yogurt.

SPICED
FRUIT WAFERS

SERVES 8

FOR THE WAFERS	pared rind and juice of 1 orange
75 g (3 oz) butter, softened	6 fresh peaches, stoned and sliced
75 g (3 oz) caster sugar	
few drops of vanilla flavouring	225 g (8 oz) redcurrants
pinch of grated nutmeg	225 g (8 oz) strawberries
2 egg whites	300 ml (½ pint) double cream, whipped
75 g (3 oz) plain flour	
FOR THE FILLING	150 ml (5 fl oz) Greek-style yogurt
175 g (6 oz) caster sugar	
1 cinnamon stick	icing sugar, for dusting

1   To make the wafers, cream together the butter and sugar until very soft and light. Add the vanilla flavouring and nutmeg. Gradually beat in the lightly whisked egg whites. Fold in the flour.

2   Drop heaped teaspoons of the mixture onto greased baking sheets allowing space to spread. Bake at 200°C (400°F) mark 6 for 6-7 minutes or until set and pale golden around the edges. Remove from the baking sheet and cool on a wire rack.

3   To make the filling, place the caster sugar, cinnamon and orange rind in a saucepan with 300 ml (½ pint) water over a low heat until the sugar has dissolved. Bring to the boil, bubble for 2 minutes then add the peaches and redcurrants. Simmer for 2-3 minutes or until just tender. With a slotted spoon, transfer the fruit to a bowl and add the strawberries.

4   Return the liquid to the heat, bring to the boil and bubble for 4-5 minutes or until reduced and syrupy. Add the strained orange juice and cool.

5   Mix the cream with the yogurt. Layer up the wafers with the cream and spiced fruits. Dust the top with icing sugar to serve.

PINEAPPLE AND
BANANA FLAMBE

SERVES 6-8

1 medium pineapple	125 g (4 oz) demerara sugar
900 g (2 lb) firm bananas	45 ml (3 tbsp) lemon juice
125 g (4 oz) dried figs	2.5 ml (½ tsp) ground mixed spice
50 g (2 oz) butter or margarine	
	60 ml (4 tbsp) dark rum

1   Slice the pineapple into 1 cm (½ inch) pieces. Snip off the skin and cut the flesh into chunks, discarding the core.

2   Peel and thickly slice the bananas into the bottom of a shallow ovenproof dish; spoon the pineapple on top.

3   Cut the figs into coarse shreds and scatter over the fruit. Then put the butter, sugar, strained lemon juice and spice together in a saucepan and heat until well blended; pour over the prepared fruit.

4   Cover tightly and bake in the oven at 200°C (400°F) mark 6 for 25 minutes until the fruit is tender.

5   Heat the rum gently in a small saucepan, remove from the heat and ignite with a match. Pour immediately over the fruit and bring the dish to the table while still flaming.

SERVING SUGGESTION

For a special occasion, you can serve this dessert in the pineapple shells. Any mixture which will not fit into the pineapple shells can be served separately in a fruit bowl.

To make two pineapple shells from one pineapple: with a large sharp knife, slice the pineapple in half lengthways, cutting right through the crown and base. Insert the blade of a long, serrated knife into the flesh of one pineapple half, about 5 mm (¼ inch) in from the edge of the shell, and cut all around the inside. Cut through the flesh in parallel lines, first lengthways and then crossways to produce squares of flesh (take care not to cut through the skin at the base). Scoop out the flesh with a sharp-edged teaspoon. Repeat with the second pineapple half, then turn both shells upside-down and leave to drain before filling.

SPICY MIXED FRUIT FLAMBE

SERVES 4

45 ml (3 tbsp) lime marmalade	227 g (8 oz) can pineapple slices in natural juice, drained and quartered
grated rind and juice of 1 small orange	425 g (15 oz) can mango slices in syrup, drained and sliced
grated rind and juice of 1 small lemon	
2.5 ml (½ tsp) ground cinnamon	2 large bananas, thickly sliced
25 g (1 oz) light soft brown sugar	60 ml (4 tbsp) dark rum
25 g (1 oz) unsalted butter	toasted coconut flakes, to decorate (optional)

1 Place the marmalade, orange and lemon rind and juice, cinnamon, sugar and butter in a large sauté pan. Heat gently until all the sugar has dissolved and the butter has melted.
2 Add the pineapple slices, mango and bananas to the pan. Simmer gently for about 5 minutes.
3 In a small pan, warm the rum, then set alight and, while still flaming, pour over the fruits. Serve immediately, decorated with coconut flakes and accompanied with ice cream, if wished.

PEARS WITH BUTTERSCOTCH SAUCE

SERVES 4

4 ripe pears, peeled, halved and cored, or two 400 g (14 oz) cans pear halves in natural juice, drained	30 ml (2 tbsp) syrup taken from a jar of stem ginger
	300 ml (10 fl oz) Greek-style natural yogurt
125 g (4 oz) light soft brown sugar	pistachio nuts, to decorate (optional)

1 Divide the pear halves between 4 serving dishes.
2 Place the sugar and ginger syrup in a small heavy-based pan, with 30 ml (2 tbsp) water. Heat gently until the sugar has dissolved, then boil for 1 minute. Remove from the heat and stir in the yogurt.
3 Immediately spoon the sauce over the pears, or chill until thick and fudge-like before spooning over. Sprinkle with the pistachios to serve. Accompany with vanilla or chocolate chip ice cream if desired.

COOK'S TIP

If you don't have stem ginger, use 1.25 ml (¼ tsp) ground ginger with an additional 30 ml (2 tbsp) water.

HONEY MOUSSE

SERVES 6

3 eggs, separated	300 ml (10 fl oz) whipping cream
100 g (4 oz) caster sugar	30 ml (2 tbsp) clear honey
finely grated rind of 2 lemons	pistachio nuts or coarsely grated chocolate, to decorate
90 ml (6 tbsp) lemon juice	
10 ml (2 tsp) powdered gelatine	

1 Whisk together the egg yolks, sugar and lemon rind until thick. Add 45 ml (3 tbsp) lemon juice and place over a pan of simmering water until thick and mousse-like. Remove from the heat and whisk occasionally until cold.
2 Soak the gelatine in the remaining lemon juice in a small bowl. Place the bowl over a pan of hot water and stir until dissolved.
3 Whip the cream until softly stiff. Whisk the egg whites until stiff. Fold half the cream into the mousse with the gelatine, honey and whisked egg whites. Turn into a 1.1 litre (2 pint) glass bowl.
4 Decorate with the remaining whipped cream and chopped pistachio nuts.

CAPPUCCINO CREAMS

SERVES 8

550 g (1¼ lb) fromage frais	175 g (6 oz) dark or bitter chocolate
15-30 ml (1-2 tbsp) finely ground espresso coffee	chocolate curls, to decorate
15-30 ml (1-2 tbsp) icing sugar (optional)	

1 Mix the fromage frais with the coffee and icing sugar, if liked.
2 Pulverise the chocolate in an electric blender or liquidiser until very fine. Alternatively grate finely.
3 Spoon half the fromage frais into eight individual ramekins or glass dishes. Sprinkle over most of the chocolate mixture. Top with the remaining fromage frais and sprinkle with the remaining chocolate mixture. Decorate with chocolate curls.

COOK'S TIP

These little desserts are light but creamy and can be made with low-fat fromage frais if preferred. Use a good dark chocolate – the flavour is so much better.

CALEDONIAN CREAMS

SERVES 6

90 ml (6 tbsp) thin shred marmalade	juice of 1 lemon
25 g (1 oz) caster sugar	300 ml (10 fl oz) double or whipping cream
60 ml (4 tbsp) whisky liqueur	

1 Mix together the marmalade, sugar, liqueur and lemon juice.
2 Whip the cream until softly stiff. Gently whisk in the marmalade mixture until the cream stands in soft peaks; take care not to overwhip. Serve in small glasses.

COOK'S TIP

Properly whipped cream is essential when a smooth, airy texture is required. Choose double or whipping cream for whipping. To achieve more volume, add 15 ml (1 tbsp) milk to each 150 ml (¼ pint) cream before starting. Chill the cream and all the utensils thoroughly beforehand. Whip quickly at first, using a balloon whisk or hand-held electric whisk, until the cream begins to look matt on the surface. Continue whipping, a little more slowly until it stands in soft peaks and does not fall off the upturned whisk. Extra care is needed if using an electric whisk.

If overwhipped, the cream will look granular and the flavour will be affected. It is impossible to rescue if this happens. Overwhipped cream will not fold smoothly into mousses, bavarois and other creamy desserts.

RASPBERRY YOGURT FOOL

SERVES 4

385 g (13½ oz) can raspberries in syrup	450 ml (¾ pint) Greek-style natural yogurt
15 ml (1 tbsp) arrowroot	mint sprigs, to decorate
30 ml (2 tbsp) clear honey	

1 Drain the raspberries in a nylon sieve over a bowl and reserve the syrup.
2 Blend the arrowroot with 15 ml (1 tbsp) syrup, to a smooth paste, then stir into the rest of the syrup. Transfer to a saucepan and bring to the boil, stirring. Cook for 1 minute. Add the raspberries and allow to cool.
3 Mix the honey with the yogurt. Spoon alternate layers of the cold raspberries and yogurt into 4 serving dishes. Swirl together, using a skewer.

COOK'S TIP

For a quick refreshing pudding, this is a great combination. If you're counting calories, use canned fruit in natural juice instead of syrup.

GOOSEBERRY MACAROON CRUNCH

SERVES 6

450 g (1 lb) gooseberries, topped and tailed	100 g (4 oz) almond macaroons or ratafias, crumbled
30 ml (2 tbsp) water	150 ml (¼ pint) whipping cream
100 g (4 oz) caster sugar	
30 ml (2 tbsp) kirsch	3 macaroons or 6 ratafias, to decorate

1 Cook the gooseberries with the water and sugar for 10-15 minutes until the fruit is soft and well reduced, then sieve it. Stir in the kirsch. Chill for 30 minutes.

2 Arrange the macaroon crumbs and gooseberry purée in alternate layers in 6 tall glasses. Chill in the refrigerator for several hours for the flavours to mellow.

3 Whip the cream until it barely holds its shape. Spoon some of the soft cream over each portion and top each with a halved macaroon or whole ratafias. Serve immediately.

VARIATIONS

According to seasonal availability, you can use different fruit from the gooseberries and an alternative liqueur to the kirsch. For example, cherries and kirsch would go well together; strawberries or raspberries and an orange-flavoured liqueur (in which case you can use the fruit raw); stewed apples and calvados or brandy; banana with rum; peaches or apricots go well with the Italian almond-flavoured liqueur Amaretto, which would also complement the flavour of the almond macaroons. For a less rich (and less fattening) dessert, natural yogurt can be used instead of the whipping cream.

ZABAGLIONE

SERVES 6

4 egg yolks	100 ml (4 fl oz) Marsala
65 g (2½ oz) caster sugar	

1 Beat the egg yolks and sugar together in a large bowl. Add the Marsala and beat until mixed.

2 Place the bowl over a saucepan of simmering water and heat gently, whisking the mixture until it is very thick and creamy.

3 To serve, pour the zabaglione into six glasses and serve immediately, with sponge fingers.

COOK'S TIP

A classic, rich Italian dessert to serve after a light main course. It should be served as soon as it is made so that it remains light, fluffy and slightly warm. Serve with sponge fingers or crisp dessert biscuits.

BANANA WHIPS

SERVES 4

2 egg whites	60 ml (4 tbsp) soft brown sugar
300 ml (½ pint) natural set yogurt	2 medium bananas
finely grated rind and juice of ½ orange	50 g (2 oz) crunchy breakfast cereal

1 Whisk the egg whites until standing in stiff peaks. Put the yogurt in a bowl and stir until smooth. Fold in the egg whites until evenly incorporated.
2 In a separate bowl, mix together the orange rind and juice and the sugar. Peel the bananas and slice thinly into the juice mixture. Fold gently to mix.
3 Put a layer of the yogurt mixture in the bottom of 4 individual glasses. Cover with a layer of cereal, then with a layer of the banana mixture. Repeat these 3 layers once more. Serve immediately.

COOK'S TIP

A quickly made dessert that appeals particularly to children of all ages.

DAMSON AND APPLE TANSY

SERVES 4

2 large Cox's apples, peeled, cored and thinly sliced	40 g (1½ oz) sugar
	pinch of ground cloves
225 g (8 oz) damsons, halved, stoned and quartered	pinch of ground cinnamon
	4 eggs, separated
15 g (½ oz) butter	45 ml (3 tbsp) soured cream

1 Put the apples, damsons, butter and half of the sugar in a large frying pan. Cook over a gentle heat until the fruit is softened, stirring continuously. Stir in the cloves and cinnamon, then remove from the heat.
2 Beat the egg yolks and cream together and stir into the fruit. Whisk the egg whites until stiff, then fold in.
3 Cook over a low heat until the mixture has set. Sprinkle the top with the remaining sugar, then brown under a hot grill. Serve immediately, straight from the pan, with soured cream.

COOK'S TIP

Tansies originally always included the bitter-sweet herb called tansy, which still lends its name to many custard and omelette-type puddings. This sweet/tart combination with Cox's apples traditionally used the Witherslack damsons which grow south of Lake Windermere.

RUM SOUFFLE OMELETTE

SERVES 1

2 eggs, separated	15 g (½ oz) butter
5 ml (1 tsp) caster sugar	5 ml (1 tbsp) apricot jam, warmed
15 ml (1 tbsp) dark rum	30 ml (2 tbsp) icing sugar

1 Mix the egg yolks, caster sugar and rum together in a bowl.

2 Whisk the egg whites until stiff and standing in peaks.

3 Melt the butter in a heavy-based omelette pan until foaming. Fold the egg whites quickly into the egg yolk mixture, then pour into the foaming butter.

4 Cook over moderate heat for 2-3 minutes until the underside of the omelette is golden brown. Place the pan under a preheated hot grill and cook for a few minutes more until the top is golden brown.

5 Slide the omelette on to a sheet of foil placed on a warmed serving plate. Spread with the warmed jam, then tip the foil to fold over the omelette.

6 Sift the icing sugar thickly over the top of the omelette, then mark in a criss-cross pattern with hot metal skewers, if liked. Carefully remove the foil and serve immediately.

VARIATIONS

Fruit Soufflé Omelette
Replace the apricot jam with sliced fresh fruit or berries, such as raspberries or strawberries.

Chocolate Soufflé Omelette
Omit the jam and drizzle the omelette with 40 g (1½ oz) melted chocolate (in step 5). Add a few chopped nuts. Sprinkle the soufflé omelette with a mixture of icing sugar and ground cinnamon.

BLUEBERRY OAT CRUMBLE

SERVES 6-8

FOR THE FILLING	FOR THE CRUMBLE TOPPING
900 g (2 lb) blueberries	100 g (4 oz) butter
45 ml (3 tbsp) light soft brown sugar	100 g (4 oz) plain flour
30 ml (2 tbsp) plain flour	100 g (4 oz) light soft brown sugar
15 ml (1 tbsp) lemon juice	75 g (3 oz) rolled oats
	50 g (2 oz) pecan or walnut halves, chopped and toasted
	grated nutmeg (optional)

1 To make the filling, mix the blueberries with the sugar, flour and lemon juice in a 1.4 litre (2½ pint) pie dish.

2 To make the crumble topping, rub the butter into the flour in a bowl. Stir in the sugar, oats and nuts. Flavour with grated nutmeg, if liked. Spoon the crumble mixture on top of the berries and lightly press down.

3 Bake in the oven at 190°C (375°F) mark 5 for about 30-35 minutes or until golden brown. Serve warm or cold with custard or cream.

APRICOT ORANGE CRISP

SERVES 4

two 397 g (14 oz) cans apricot halves in natural juice, drained	75 g (3 oz) butter or margarine
grated rind and juice of ½ small orange	175 g (6 oz) plain white flour
	50 g (2 oz) chopped blanched almonds
	50 g (2 oz) demerara sugar

1 Place the apricots in a saucepan and add the orange rind and juice. Warm through gently over a low heat.
2 Meanwhile, rub the fat into the flour until the mixture resembles breadcrumbs. Stir in the almonds and sugar.
3 Spoon the warmed apricots and juice into a 1.1 litre (2 pint) ovenproof dish and sprinkle with the almond mixture. Place under a preheated moderate grill until lightly browned.
4 Serve warm, accompanied by single cream, yogurt or custard.

COOK'S TIP

If you've more time, place the cold fruit in the dish. Top with the crumble mixture and bake in the oven at 180°C (350°F) mark 4 until golden. Make up custard to accompany with a mixture of half milk and half apricot juice. Canned fruits in natural juices have less sugar and so fewer calories than those in syrup.

HOT PEAR AND COCONUT CAKE

SERVES 4

3-4 pears, total weight 450 g (1 lb)	50 g (2 oz) soft tub margarine
grated rind and juice of 1 lemon	1 egg
75 g (3 oz) light soft brown sugar	25 g (1 oz) desiccated coconut
50 g (2 oz) plain white flour	30 ml (2 tbsp) apricot jam, warmed
3.75 ml (¾ tsp) baking powder	toasted desiccated coconut, to decorate

1 Peel, quarter, core and slice the pears. Immediately mix with the lemon juice and 30 ml (2 tbsp) brown sugar.
2 Place the lemon rind and remaining sugar in a large bowl with the flour, baking powder, margarine, egg and coconut. Whisk, using an electric beater, until smooth.
3 Spoon into a 21.5 cm (8½ inch) deep-sided fluted flan dish. Place the pears on top and spoon over any juices.
4 Cook in the oven at 200°C (400°F) mark 6 for about 30 minutes or until just set.
5 Brush with warm apricot jam to glaze, and decorate with toasted desiccated coconut. Serve warm, with custard or Greek yogurt.

COOK'S TIP

Leftovers are delicious served cold with whipped cream.

BAKEWELL PUDDING

SERVES 4

212 g (7½ oz) packet frozen puff pastry, thawed	100 g (4 oz) butter or margarine, melted
FOR THE FILLING	100 g (4 oz) caster sugar
2 eggs	50 g (2 oz) ground almonds
2 egg yolks	30 ml (2 tbsp) raspberry jam

1   Roll out the pastry on a floured surface and use to line an 18 cm (7 inch) pie plate or loose-based flan tin.
2   Beat the eggs and extra yolks together, add the butter, sugar and ground almonds and mix well.
3   Spread the bottom of the pastry case with the jam and pour on the egg mixture.
4   Bake in the oven at 200°C (400°F) mark 6 for 30 minutes, until the filling is firm to the touch. Serve warm or cold, with cream or custard.

WALNUT AND ORANGE PUDDING

SERVES 6

125 g (4 oz) soft tub margarine	5 ml (1 tsp) vanilla essence
50 g (2 oz) walnut pieces, chopped	75 g (3 oz) self-raising flour
75 g (3 oz) caster sugar	5 ml (1 tsp) baking powder
15 ml (1 tbsp) golden syrup	grated rind of 1 orange
2 eggs	60 ml (4 tbsp) fresh orange juice

1   Grease six ovenproof ramekins.
2   Place all the ingredients together in a large bowl and beat thoroughly until smooth.
3   Two-thirds fill the ramekins with the mixture. Place on a baking tray and bake in the oven at 180°C (350°F) mark 4 for 20-25 minutes or until firm to the touch.
4   Turn out or leave in the ramekins if preferred, and serve warm with custard.

BLACKBERRY AND APPLE PANCAKES

SERVES 4

350 g (12 oz) jar or can unsweetened chunky apple	knob of butter
225 g (8 oz) blackberries	lemon juice, for sprinkling
2.5 ml (½ tsp) ground mixed spice	icing sugar, for dusting
4 large or 8 small ready-made pancakes	25 g (1 oz) toasted flaked almonds

1 Mix together the apple, blackberries and mixed spice in a bowl.

2 Halve the large pancakes; if using small ones, leave whole. Roll into cornet shapes and fill with the blackberry and apple mixture. Place cornets seam-side down in a lightly buttered ovenproof dish.

3 Dot the pancakes with butter and sprinkle with lemon juice. Cover loosely with foil.

4 Bake in the oven at 200°C (400°F) mark 6 for 10 minutes. Dust generously with icing sugar and scatter the almonds on top. Serve with soured cream, if wished.

COOK'S TIP

Readymade pancakes can be found in many supermarkets – they are a great timesaver. Keep some on hand in the freezer – they can be stored for up to 2 months.

CINNAMON APPLE SLICES

SERVES 4

50-75 g (2-3 oz) butter	45 ml (3 tbsp) demerara sugar
4 small currant buns, split in half	1.25 ml (¼ tsp) ground cinnamon
2 eating apples, peeled, cored and cut into rings	icing sugar, for dusting

1 Butter the buns thickly on both sides and place on a baking tray. Top each half with 3 halved apple rings and sprinkle with the demerara sugar and cinnamon.

2 Bake in the oven at 200°C (400°F) mark 6 for 15 minutes or until the apples are golden brown and cooked through.

3 Dust with icing sugar and serve with Greek-style natural yogurt.

VARIATION

Alternatively, try using pears. Peel, core and slice 2 pears and use them in place of the apples.

INDEX